CORMAC BURKE
Authority and Freedom in the Church

Monsignor Cormac Burke was born in Sligo, Ireland, in 1927. A civil lawyer who is also a specialist in modern languages, he was ordained a priest of the Opus Dei Prelature in 1955, after taking a doctorate in canon law in Rome.

His more than thirty years of pastoral work have been spent mainly in the United States and England, with nine years in Africa. He has held teaching positions at the Catholic University of America, Washington, D.C., the University of Dublin, and Maynooth College. More recently he was Professor of Moral Theology and Church Law at St Thomas Aquinas Seminary, Nairobi, Kenya. He has authored many publications, mainly in the fields of moral and pastoral theology and ecclesiology.

In 1986 Pope John Paul II appointed him to be an auditor or judge of the Church's High Court, the Roman Rota. He is now resident in Rome, where he also teaches at the Roman Academic Centre of the University of Navarre.

Authority and Freedom in the Church

CORMAC BURKE

IGNATIUS PRESS   SAN FRANCISCO

The typesetting for this book
in 11 on 12 Plantin
was input by Gilbert Gough Typesetting, Dublin
and output by Computer Graphics Ltd, Dublin
for Four Courts Press Ltd, Kill Lane, Blackrock, Co. Dublin.

© Monsignor Cormac Burke 1988

Nihil obstat: Stephen J. Greene, *censor deputatus.*
Imprimi potest: J. Carroll, Diocesan Administrator
14 October 1987. (The Nihil obstat and Imprimi potest
are a declaration that a book or publication is considered to be
free from doctrinal or moral error. This declaration does
not imply approval of, or agreement with, the contents,
opinions or statements expressed.)

Cover by Roxanne Mei Lum

ISBN 0-89870-210-0
Library of Congress catalague number 88-80786

Ignatius Press, San Francisco
Printed in the United States of America

"The mystery is Christ among you" (Col 1:27).

To the students of St Thomas Aquinas Regional Seminary, Nairobi, who have been my intellectual sparring-partners over the past three years and without whose help I doubt that this book would ever have taken final shape: may they and all the coming generations of priests everywhere — and the present generation too — be good and faithful servants of God's People, always seeing and helping others to see the presence of Christ in his Church.

Nairobi, 1 November 1986

Contents

		page
ABBREVIATIONS		8
1	The Lawless People of God?	9
2	Lawlessness and Society	13
3	Individualism and the Church	23
4	Freedom	40
5	Conscience	51
6	Dissent	59
7	Dissent and the Rights of the Faithful	67
8	Law as a Gift	78
9	Law and the Holy Spirit	87
10	The Church: Juridical or Charismatic?	96
11	Authority, Power, Service	109
12	Roles in the Church; Roles in the World	121
13	Authority and Evangelization	136
14	Authority and Truth	149
15	Truth and Definition	167
16	Truth and Communion	181
17	Communion, Unity, Diversity	197
APPENDIX I	Legal Positivism	212
APPENDIX II	Natural Law	215
APPENDIX III	Abuse of Authority	225

Abbreviations

Documents of the Second Vatican Council:
- AA   Decree of the Apostolate of Lay People
- AG   Decree on the Church's Missionary Activity
- CD   Decree on the Pastoral Office of Bishops
- DH   Declaration on Religious Liberty
- DV   Constitution on Divine Revelation
- GE   Declaration on Christian Education
- GS   Constitution on the Church in the Modern World
- LG   Dogmatic Constitution on the Church
- OT   Decree on the Training of Priests
- PO   Decree on the Ministry and Life of Priests
- SC   Constitution on the Sacred Liturgy
- UR   Decree on Ecumenism

c. (= canon) refers to one of the canons or laws of the revised Code of Canon Law promulgated in 1983.

1

The Lawless People of God?

"The People of God": this description of the Church has become so familiar to us that we easily forget how new it sounded to most Catholics twenty five years ago when it began to come into common use. The term, of course, has deep biblical roots and its usage has long been canonised in theological writing. But it only became popular when the Second Vatican Council chose it — in preference to other biblical and traditional terms — as the one most fitted to evoke the conciliar vision of the Church and to encapsulate in some way a whole programme of renewal into a single suggestive phrase.

The Council has come down to us as the work of the Holy Spirit. The task of renewal, however, remains in the hands of men. Evidently if it is to be successful, it must faithfully follow the spirit of the Council and needs, in the first place, to be based on a thorough understanding of conciliar ecclesiology. In this context it is important to remember that "People of God" is not the ultimate root or heart of the ecclesiology of Vatican II. The key concept in conciliar thinking about the Church is rather that of "communio": communion.

The opening paragraph of *Lumen gentium* says that "the Church, in Christ, is in the nature of sacrament — a sign and instrument, that is, of communion with God and of unity among all men" (LG 1). "Communio", therefore, means being one with God in Christ, and being one with other men in Christ; the Church is the sign of this communion and at the same time its instrument.

"Communio" could be described as the most condensed theological expression of the mystery of the Church. It could also of course be regarded as the most abstract. It is not surprising, therefore, if the Council goes on to opt for a descriptive term which, with "communio" as its background, expresses the nature and mission of the Church in a more concrete way. So we see that as the Council develops its ecclesiological reflection, it resolves the Mystery of the Church (Chapter One of *Lumen gentium*) into the People of God (Chapter Two).

"People of God", therefore, is to be understood as a more graphic way of expressing the deeper reality of "communio"; as is true, of course, of any of the other traditional terms for describing the

Church, especially that of "Body of Christ", to which *Lumen gentium* devotes the whole of its seventh section.[1]

This is not meant to imply that the choice of the term "People of God" is not significant, or that it does not convey any more concrete message to us than does the broader term "communio". On the contrary, if the Council deliberately chose this term it is because it is laden with particular significance, and opens up broad and definite horizons for ecclesial renewal.

"The People of God" emphasizes the pilgrim vocation of this new chosen people, their eschatological destiny as they make their way through human history travelling towards the Promised Land. It suggests the particular joy that should be theirs at being summoned and gathered together by God, and belonging to God, with special claims on his love and guidance and mercy. It stresses the calling addressed to each Christian to share in a common endeavour, the radical equality of Christian dignity, and the rights as well as the distinctive graces of each one. These post-conciliar years have been years of exploration and discovery of the rich content of this particular description of Christ's Church. We are still engaged in this process.

This book will endeavour to show that there are particular aspects to ecclesial and Christian life which, since they necessarily emerge from a consideration of the term "People of God", cannot be ignored by any serious work of renewal. Yet they have been largely overlooked in these last decades.

* * *

"The Lawless People of God": where is this expression to be found? Nowhere in the conciliar documents, that is sure. Nevertheless, as a concept and even as an ideal, it is to all intents and purposes being advocated by many post-conciliar theorists.

Much of the post-conciliar theorizing has been based on the thesis that law and authority are oppressive forces, restricting human freedom, violating human dignity and blocking human progress.

---

1 It has sometimes been suggested that the ecclesiology of Vatican II no longer countenances the term "Body of Christ" as applied to the Church. This is quite untrue. Such a rich term, so deeply rooted in Pauline thinking and in tradition, does not pass out of fashion. The whole of *Lumen gentium* 7 is devoted to an exposition of its richness. The term "Body of Christ" or "Mystical Body of Christ" appears in numerous other passages in documents of the Council: e.g. SC 7; LG 23, 50; CD 12, 16, 33; PO 1, 2, 5, 8; AA 2, 3; AG 7, 9, 16, 19, 38, 39, etc.

This view ultimately means that freedom is lawless, and that, in order to be free, man needs to be liberated from law.

It is claimed that this thesis finds support in the teachings of Vatican II. The Council, so it is suggested, by canonising an ecclesiology of the People of God, sanctioned and in fact called for a model of a freer Church — one less ruled by law and authority. The thesis can be seen operating on two levels:

1) On the level of the individual it is suggested that the conciliar emphasis on personal freedom and rights somehow exempts people from subjection to law. Further, it is claimed that man's rights and freedom are not dependent on any objective order but rather derive from the order that he chooses or creates. Objective morality subjugates; subjective morality liberates. Each one must free himself from the yoke of an imposed objective moral law which he himself has not created or chosen. Similarly, in matters of faith and doctrine, of scriptural interpretation, etc., each one should be free to construct his own system of belief, taking what he wishes, omitting what he wishes, and still calling his beliefs Catholic.

According to this view, each man is to be a law to himself. But, as we will see in the next chapter, a people made up of individuals each of whom is a law to himself, is a lawless people.

2) On the more institutional or structural level, it is claimed that where authority (or power) exists, it is in the wrong hands. It is in the hands of the exploitative few — the hierarchy — and must be restored to the hands of the many: the people. The people must be freed from the yoke of a hierarchy that they have not chosen.

The second claim, exemplified in certain liberation theologies, is a more recent development. But it has a logical connection with the moral and dogmatic subjectivism which preceded and accompanies it.

The simple reflection that to be a Christian has always meant to be someone who is subject to the law of Christ — who freely subjects himself to the law of Christ — already suggests that an anti-law mentality fits poorly in Christian life and Christian society. One becomes, or lives as, a Christian not to be freed from law but to be freed by law: Christ's Law.

Anti-nomianism — the anti-law attitude — is in fact something totally unnatural to a Christian. Insofar as it is present in the Church today, it is a foreign importation brought into it from the surrounding secular culture,[2] where its corrosive effects on

---

[2] The Vatican II Declaration on Religious Liberty says that in the modern world, "there are many who, under the pretext of freedom, seem inclined to reject all submission to authority" (DH 8).

individuals and society are evident. Further — and this is our main contention — it is an absolute block to any true renewal of the Church.

In our efforts to rebuild ecclesial society we count on God's grace but also on human intelligence which should include the ability to learn from mistakes: our own and those of others. The anti-law, anti-authority spirit is one of the great mistakes of contemporary secular man which is evidently wasting his personal life and undermining civil society. Must it waste Christian lives and undermine church society too? Or are we Christians capable of renewing our understanding of law and authority, *thence* renewing the Church, and *thence* renewing the world?

★ ★ ★

The reflections of the next chapter will be concerned with the rule of law and authority in human society in general. We will particularly try to show how they guarantee and defend human rights. Chapter Three will work towards a conclusion that the ecclesiology of the Second Vatican Council calls emphatically for a renewal in our understanding of law and in our love for law within the Church, as an essential condition for any real and lasting work of renewal.

2
Lawlessness and Society

There is a growing mood of lawlessness in modern secular society. It has many expressions, some violent, some simply corrupt. The spectacular increase in criminality, corruption and bribery as accepted things, the "rip-offs", the black markets, the sense of arbitrariness in conduct, the one-sided use of force, the ineffectiveness of international organisms devoted to peace and justice, the incidence of terrorism, the pervading aimlessness, the hooliganism, the dislike of the police ... all suggest a contempt and at times a downright hatred for law and order, and for authority, that can have few parallels in history.

Modern secular man has gone a stage beyond Mr Bumble, Dickens' parish beadle whose considered opinion was that "the law is an ass". Contemporary opinion of the law is even worse. The law is not just an ass, a beast of burden. It is a burdensome beast, and a dangerous one at that. It is an enemy: an enemy of freedom and an instrument of oppression.

Authority — which used to be understood as the moral force behind law — is not looked on any better. Today authority is mostly equated with political or physical force (cf. Chapter 11). As such it may be feared. It is not looked up to or revered. It may well be hated. It is generally despised.

This anti-law, anti-authority outlook pervades modern society. That past or present abuses of the law are part cause of it can be readily admitted. It is also no doubt a reaction to the tendency of the modern state to clamp controls on almost every area of its citizens' lives, and the citizens' consequent sense of being straitjacketed in red-tape and legislation. Despite the permissiveness of modern laws in the area of sexual behaviour, many people feel that their lives are being caught in a growing mesh of legal restrictions.

This mentality is often linked to a pining after "democracy", understood not as a mere electoral system but rather as suggesting a society in which people are felt to matter instead of just being objects organized by soulless bureaucracies; a society based less on structures and more on person-to-person relationships, where there is less law and authority or, at least, where authority is exercised in a more human manner.

Some people go further. The more impersonal and oppressive they feel governments and systems to be, the more they dream of an "ideal" society where — they suppose — freedom will exist without laws and will in fact be the consequence of there being no laws. In the democracy of their dreams — which will truly be a "people's" society — the yoke of authority will somehow completely disappear. And, as they turn over in their dreams, they sigh, "If only we were free from laws!"

These are dreams, no more. In fact, a society without laws would not be a dream; it would be a nightmare. Law, as we will try to show, is absolutely necessary for any society where people are held to matter. So is respect for law.

No moral or voluntary body can survive a generalised loss of respect for law on the part of its members. If the members of, say, a football club lose respect for the laws of the club, they leave the club; and the club either acquires new law-abiding members, or else it dissolves. A geographical political society can survive a loss of respect for law and authority on the part of its citizens — by becoming a police state. If the members of a physical society are not ruled by consent, yet cannot leave the society, they will be ruled by force.

This anti-law movement is still on the upsurge. Its social and political consequences are only beginning to make themselves felt. It is already evident however that modern secular society is not in a healthy condition. It may have suffered or may be suffering from unjust laws or unjust exercise of authority. But its anti-authority, anti-law attitude is a more fatal disease still. Bad laws are bad. No laws, the rejection of all law, is worse. Anarchy — the absence of all law and government — means the collapse of society.

Pro-rights, anti-law?

To help the modern mind emerge from this tangled web of anti-law prejudice and to come to understand the positive nature of law, an acceptable starting-point must be found, some stance or position which the modern spirit itself finds little difficulty in sharing. It can be found, I think, in the human rights movement.

Most people today like to proclaim themselves pro-human rights. It is a good position. But it simply cannnot be combined with an anti-law mentality. A pro-rights person must be against bad laws, but must equally be in favour of good laws. A generalised anti-law mentality makes no sense in a pro-rights person for the simple reason that human rights, which are prior to human law, nevertheless require the recognition and the protection of human law.

The human rights philosophy necessarily rejects the thesis that man possesses only those rights which the State grants him. No, says the human rights philosopher; man's rights do not derive from the State, they derive from his human nature.[1] It is as man, and not just as citizen, that he possesses his basic human rights. And he possesses these rights whether the civil law of a particular country recognizes them or not. It is precisely when the civil law does not recognize them that one gets legalised violation of human rights.

Bad laws are a violation of human rights. Good laws are their necessary protection. Three points in particular show this:

1) if rights are to be protected, they must be *defined*. It is part of the work of law to define rights;

2) further, if someone's right is violated, he needs an effective *remedy*, a process that others must respect. And that again is a matter of law: of courts and judges and law enforcement;

3) thirdly, rights imply *obligations*. If I have a right to property, then others have an obligation to respect my right to my property. And I have an obligation to respect their rights to their property. And these obligations — to respect the rights of others — also need to be set out in law.

The human rights campaign, after all, is a campaign to have bad laws abolished and good laws put in their place. It is a campaign to have people's proper human rights recognized and upheld by the civil law. If rights are not upheld by law, people are inevitably going to be exploited.

The third point mentioned above merits special consideration. No philosophy of rights (and for that matter no juridical protection of rights) can exclude the acknowledgement of obligations. If I assert my right to free speech, for example, yet use this right systematically to censor or silence others, then I am a philosopher not of *men's* rights, but of *my* "rights". I accept no obligation to respect the rights of others — undoubtedly because the restrictions involved in doing so inconvenience me.

It is true that law always involves some restrictions and that restrictions are a nuisance — at least at first sight. But only a

---

[1] A coherent human rights philosophy necessarily involves belief in a common law of human nature, i.e. in the Natural Law. Cf. Appendix II.

superficial and selfish approach sees no more than the restrictions involved in law. A deeper and more mature outlook sees law in terms of *reciprocal rights and obligations*; and restrictions then appear as the necessary consequence of the interplay between just rights and just obligations.[2] My just rights restrict other people in the sense that they are justly obliged to respect my rights. And their just rights restrict me, in the sense that I am justly obliged to respect their rights.

The defence of the rights of all is bound to place restrictions on the freedom of some: now mine, now yours. Now I am obliged to yield at a road crossing, now you. If neither of us is prepared to yield, the result is collision and anarchy.

Restrictions, then, may be bothersome. Yet they are essential — to defend both my freedom and that of others. If it is true that someone is always inconvenienced by a law, it is also true that if the law in question is just, the inconvenience is a good thing. It reflects the demands placed on the individual by regard for others or for the common good. Most people, if they reflect on this point, are capable of appreciating it. Then their response to the law need not be one of mere submission or reluctant obedience. It can and ought to be a welcoming response to what is seen as an admirable disposition of justice.

Therefore, the suggestion that emphasis on individual rights signifies a de-emphasis on law is quite false. Emphasis on rights means emphasis on duties, and therefore emphasis on law as the means by which rights are protected and duties enforced.

Declarations of Rights have been frequent and popular in history. Declarations of Obligations are far less frequent, might not be so popular, and yet are equally necessary. Widespread voluntary acceptance of obligations is a real test of social health, an infallible sign of the respect of each member of a community for his fellows.[3]

If we are sincerely pro-human rights, we will love and defend our own rights, but we will love and fulfil our obligation no less — for that is to love the rights of others. That is the test of the true lover of rights. If I love only my rights, then I may easily

---

[2] "In exercising their rights, individual men and social groups are bound by the moral law to have regard for the rights of others, their own duties to others and the common good of all" (DH 7).

[3] The Code of Canon Law lists in detail the Obligations and Rights of Christians: of Christ's Faithful in general (cc. 208-223), of Lay People (224-231), of Clerics (273-289). It is interesting to note, as the title to each section shows, that obligations are specified not only as well as, but *before* rights.

come to love other people's wrongs, i.e. the wrongs that, in my self-assertion, I am almost certain to do them.

The effective presence of justice in a society always depends on people's awareness of their obligations and their readiness to fulfil them. This is true as between individuals. It is also true as between classes, rich or poor. The class that is conscious only of its rights and not also of its obligations will easily defend its rights by doing wrong.

Self-interest or common good?

Here we can see how great is the difference between a society whose members have a genuine participatory spirit, and a society whose members are imbued with individualism.

A society can truly be called "participatory" when a majority of its members share that concern for the common good, are prepared to place its demands above individual self-interest, take pride in the principle of justice for all, and feel a common responsibility to maintain the laws which apply this principle to social life.

A society where individualism is on the upsurge shows the opposite tendencies: the notion of the common good is obscured or forgotten; self-interest becomes paramount; rights are emphasized but duties are not; justice is good if it means "justice for me", and not so good if it means "justice for you"; permissiveness instead of justice becomes the guiding principle of law (the fact that permissive laws, even if welcomed and used, are never *admired*, shows how people sense that such laws are devoid of real justice).

Permissive laws often simply permit people to violate their obligations towards the rights of others. A married person exercising the "right" to divorce violates their partner's right to fidelity (which more often than not is something the partner wants), and especially violates their children's right to an unbroken home, which is something the children always want.

The theory of permissiveness is that each man is entitled to be a law to himself, at least in his personal and private life. But public life is built on the lives and values of individuals; and so the permissive mentality breeds a spirit of lawlessness in public and social life as well — a process which is accelerating all around us today.

The permissive philosopher may suggest that law is an enemy

of life, that the removal of law favours true growth and healthy spontaneity. This is not so. Organic life, the bodily or intellectual life of an individual, and very particularly the social life of a community, develop soundly only if they follow certain laws of health and growth. Failure to follow these laws results in stagnation at best and destruction at worst. A body can grow only because cells and tissues observe their proper laws of growth and their proper relationship to one another. A "lawless" cell is a cancer; and its spontaneous growth can bring death to the whole body. This applies to the social body too.

An individualist society is a flawed structure. Lacking the internal spiritual forces that can hold it together — community spirit, sense of justice, love for the common good — it tends to lawlessness and disintegration.

The strength of the law

To be anti-law is to be anti-social, anti-others. It is, in the truest sense, to be anti-democratic. The anti-law mentality does not favour or defend the freedom of the people. It favours the freedom of the few (the powerful, the clever, the unscrupulous) to exploit the people, who find that as the anti-law mentality grows the strength of the law to protect their rights is gradually eroded.

Society needs the strength of the law. Here we should note that the law cannot truly be said to be strong just because it is feared and obeyed out of fear. If that is simply due to the fact that it is backed by coercive power then it is not the law that is strong but the power behind it. Law needs to be strong in itself, and this only occurs in virtue of its justice.

Both governments and citizens need to realize that the ultimate authority of the law does not derive from its being an expression of the will of party or people. Its binding force does not come from popular consent (nor is it removed by popular dissent). It comes from justice. A law does not have more authority because it is approved by many or less because it is enacted by few, or even by only one. A just measure ought to be obeyed — i.e. it carries authority — even if it is a minority decision; and an unjust measure ought to be resisted — it lacks authority — even if it is backed by a landslide majority. A just law binds as much in a democracy as in a totalitarian state; an unjust law binds in neither.

An excess of legal enactments is undoubtedly one of the plagues of twentieth-century life. Most modern societies could indeed do with far fewer laws. But no society can do with less justice or with less respect for justice. A "democracy" where people feel free not to respect the law is no people's society, nor will the freedom of the people survive long in it.

The positivist or voluntarist concept of law — that the force of law simply derives from man's will in legislating (cf. Appendix I) — can never bring about harmony in society (why, after all, should the minority have to respect the will of the majority?).

Bowing before authority?

Anarchists reject all law, on principle. Most people, even if imbued with the anti-law mentality, do not go so far; they accept some laws as a necessary evil. Yet these same people often retain an unyielding hostility towards any form of authority, for in it they see an unwarranted privilege claimed by some persons over others. They are not, they say, prepared to bow before authority; this seems degrading to them as suggesting that some men hold themselves to be, and are thereby acknowledged as, superior to others....

In a certain sense, unless great pride is present, we should be prepared to bow before anyone because we see the image of God in him or her. For our present purpose, however, we can pass over that point and simply say that what is implied in showing respect for authority is not so much looking up to the persons as looking up to the *relationship between persons*; it is sensing the sacred quality of justice — the will to give each person his due — and therefore being prepared to revere justice, to bow indeed before it, as the basic value of human society.

To be "agin the government" is a common expression of the anti-authority attitude. Many people currently tend to be excessively suspicious of all government. Even when it is not an instrument of actual oppression, government implies *rulers* and *subjects*, and therefore seems to suggest superiority and inferiority. Is there not something degrading in being "under" authority?

Authority indeed implies a relationship between those wielding it and those subject to it. But this is not essentially a relationship of power; nor should it be based on force nor on the ability to bring others into subjection. In a healthy society it is a relationship of free wills, properly ordered towards justice and the common good. So, of its nature, it implies reason and freedom in both those exercising and those accepting authority. Serene reflection tells us that where authority is properly exercised in the application of just laws, it is not opposed to personal freedom but fosters and serves it.

To the thinking man, then, legitimate authority is seen as a positive good. The principle of authority has a certain sacredness to it, because it evidences the presence of justice in society. Acceptance of authority is a reasonable act. Obedience to authority becomes an act of freedom and a sign of maturity. Behind legitimate authority lies the will of God (cf. Rom 13:1); that is the ultimate reason for its sacredness. Acceptance of authority is therefore a truly religious act, just as is the wielding of authority. The one exercising authority realizes that the moral power he is endowed with comes from above (cf. Jn 19:11) and that he will have to answer for any failure to exercise authority in the spirit of God's justice.

These considerations should also help us to understand how false is the suggestion that the "democratization" of a society somehow means that laws are less binding and authority is to be respected less. If anything, precisely the opposite is true.

If by democratization one means that the people are more involved in concern for the affairs of the community, then clearly they — each one — should be more aware of the common good, of the rights of others and of the binding force of the law and the respect due to authority. Their free response to these values shows their "democratic" sense and their maturity.

In a truly participatory society each citizen shares the overall concern for the common good. A society of individualists can never be truly a democratic or participatory society. In fact a society or a community of individualists is a contradiction in terms. A people of individualists is simply not a people.

Each society needs a governing authority. Only anarchists deny this. A society can suffer from the unjust use of authority. But it will also suffer if just authority is not respected. A society is healthy and strong in the measure in which laws are just, authority is exercised — firmly and without partiality, in accordance with the law — and the members of the society obey those laws and look up to that authority.

The human rights movement is urgently calling modern man back to a true philosophy of law. Positivist or voluntarist philosophies — which are the root cause why the acceptance of law has come to suggest servilism to so many — need to be abandoned. A juridical philosophy based on the natural law must be re-established.

No society is possible if each man is a law to himself. The lawless man places himself above or outside the law. He becomes an outlaw; an enemy of society, a threat to the rights of others, to the common endeavour, to the common good.

A society therefore needs a common law, i.e. a law applicable in equal justice to all, binding on all and accepted in general by all. This common law, as between all men, is the natural law. To deny the existence of a natural law is to deny the existence of a shared human nature, a common humanity linking all men. It makes any philosophy of human rights meaningless, and dissolves human society (cf. Appendix II).

Over and above the natural law, Christians have their common law in the Law of Christ. This Law links them, guides them, regulates their mutual rights and duties, and is the basis for their Christian life and freedom, in communion with Christ and with one another.

Enforcement of law

The law is not meant to be a theory or an abstraction. It is meant to serve as a practical norm of action. If the law simply declares or defines rights but does no more, this is admirable but also useless. It must protect those rights against violation, and it must afford a remedy if they are in fact violated.

What happens if a violator of rights is aware of the law but unwilling or reluctant to fulfil his obligations? How is the law to be enforced and the balance of justice restored in such a situation?

Law enforcement in a political state is normally the role of a police force armed with the physical means to compel compliance with a legal decision. In such cases the actual achievement of justice depends on the strength and also on the integrity of the law-enforcement agency. If the police are lax or weak and especially if they are corrupt (e.g. if they can be bribed by an interested party), then a person may find that a court judgment upholding his rights remains a dead letter: he just cannot get compensation for damage done to him, or re-enter the house of which he has been wrongly dispossessed.

In a moral and voluntary body, such as the Church, there is no police force; there is no way of physically compelling a person to obey the law and to fulfil his voluntarily-assumed obligations.

Then the upholding of rights and the enforcement of law has to follow a different path — a moral process where the very solidarity of the society itself is put to the test. In this situation free and responsible agents must be conscious of their proper parts and play them, if justice is to be done.

The part of the holder of authority — once due process has established that someone is violating particular rights or the common good — is to address a moral requirement to that person: "respect this law; accept this decision; obey". For his part, the person so required is morally challenged to a free response: "Alright, I will respect the law; I will obey it; I will do what I am called to do".

It is a moral challenge in the special sense that it challenges him to be loyal to the commitments which he freely undertook in choosing to belong to that voluntary body. A major one of these commitments is readiness to accept the decisions of the legitimate ruling authority of the community.

One truly belongs to a "people" when one wants not just one's own good —despite the cost to the people — but the good of the people, despite the cost to oneself. This loyalty to the common good stimulates responsibility in the individual member of a community — to obey the just exercises of authority without complaint or self-pity — and stimulates responsibility equally in those ruling the community, to exercise authority justly without fear or weakness.

The football player who refuses to accept a yellow card, justly given, is as irresponsible and as unfit for football as the referee who fails to give the yellow card when the rules of the game — the *good* of the game — call for it.

There would be evident childishness in wanting to belong to a voluntary body yet refusing to accept any authority within it. It would be as childish as the attitude of someone who wants to play a game, but only on condition that he does not have to obey the referee or that he can play it according to the "rules" that he himself makes up at any given moment.

3

Individualism and the Church

Even if it does not express itself in hijackings and hooliganism, the anti-law syndrome is present and widespread in the Church. It is not only that church laws are often ignored or that church authority is frequently decried, resisted and disobeyed. The very anti-law attitude is defended in the name of Christian freedom and spontaneity. Furthermore, the suggestion is repeatedly made that all of this is in keeping with, and indeed a product of, the spirit of Vatican II.... The very opposite is true. This anti-law individualism goes badly with the community-consciousness that Vatican II sponsored; that should be clear. But, even more clearly still, it is totally incompatible with the concept of the People of God.

Lumen gentium is quite explicit that individualism is not God's plan for salvation; connection with others is. In the opening passage of its second chapter, it says that God "willed to make men holy and save them, not as individuals without any bond or link between them, but rather to make them into a people ..." (LG 9).

Therefore, the Council continues, God "established a covenant" — a legal contract or agreement — with the chosen race of Israel which was "a preparation and figure of that new and perfect covenant which was to be ratified in Christ" (ibid).

Lumen gentium immediately goes on to quote the great biblical passage from Jeremiah about the People of God, where we are told that it is precisely *the possession and sharing of the law which sets a people apart as the God's People*: "Behold the days are coming, says the Lord, when I will make a new covenant with the house of Israel and the house of Judah.... I will put my law within them, and I will write it upon their hearts, and they shall be my people" (Jer 31:31-34).

A people without law is not a people; it is no more than a horde or a mob. It is the possession and observance of a *common* law that turns a group of individuals into a people, with shared ideals, customs and destiny, who treat one another with justice and respect under an authority that they look up to as the guardian of the common good and the protector of popular rights.

The concept of a "lawless People of God", therefore, is an absurdity. The anti-authority spirit is anomalous in a Christian, however much we may find it among individual Christians today. If it were to become widespread, it would be a total block to the renewal envisaged by the Second Vatican Council.

This becomes more evident still if we reflect that, in most people's expectations, a renewed Church means (among other things) a Church where there is more respect for people's rights. But, as we saw in the last chapter, rights will not be respected unless law is there to protect them, and unless law itself is respected.

The Council, especially in the Pastoral Constitution on the Church in the Modern World, "proclaims the rights of man" (GS 41). It insists that these rights must be acknowledged and defended in civil society (GS 26, 73; cf. AA 11). Particular stress is laid on the right to worship (DH 6), the right to marry and have children (GS 52) and the right to education (GE 1).

But the Council was concerned to stress personal rights — and therefore the corresponding personal obligations — also within ecclesial society. Having established the shared dignity of all Christ's faithful, based on the common grace of their baptism (LG 9, 18, 32), it takes special care to list rights of the laity in particular — the right, for instance, to receive from the spiritual goods of the Church (LG 37), to have their own spirituality (AA 4), to do apostolate (AA 3), to express their opinion on matters affecting the good of the Church (LG 37) — without omitting their obligations: e.g. to collaborate with their pastors (LG 33), to follow the authentic teaching of the bishops (LG 32, 35, 37), etc.

This stress on rights and obligations gives added point to the choice of the term "People of God". An ecclesiology of the Body of Christ, for example, only remotely suggests questions of the rights and obligations of the faithful. But such questions enter naturally and necessarily into an ecclesiology of the People of God, with its emphasis on inter-personal and societal relations, on equality of dignity and diversity of function within a shared enterprise, on a communal purpose and an ultimate destiny.

These reflections build up into a major conclusion: that the Council, in making a deliberate choice of the term "People of God" to describe the Church, is directly inviting us to give new importance to law in the life of the Church. It is in fact emphatically suggesting that we will never discover the true path of renewal unless we approach it also from the juridical perspective.

Clerical service and people's rights

Not everyone in a community has the same role to play. People follow different professions or callings, each of which has its own distinctive rights and obligations. However, rights and obligations are not equally emphasized in all ways of life. *Service* callings — that of a doctor, a nurse, a teacher, etc. — are more strongly characterized by obligations than by rights. The very service nature of these vocations calls on those who follow them to voluntarily renounce certain rights in the service of their fellows. When they pursue their calling in a spirit of generosity and self-forgetfulness, they encourage and uplift the people they serve and act as a leaven of renewal in society as a whole.

Vatican II chose to place very major emphasis on the whole concept of clerical "diakonia" or service.[1] In the internal life of the Church, the clergy are not a privileged class; they are "ministers", i.e. *servants*, of the rest of the people (cf. Chapter 11). In imitation of Christ the Servant, they are ordained and dedicated to ministering his grace and truth to their brothers. In freely answering their particular calling, clerics too have chosen a service-vocation which, as we have said, is a way of life characterized by obligations more than by rights. Their duty of celibacy (c. 277) makes them freer for service; their duty of obedience (c. 273) means that they can be sent on this or that service-mission as the good of the people requires; their obligation of residence (c. 283) is meant to make them available to the people; their obligation of clerical dress (c. 284) is meant to make them identifiable in public so that the people can more easily call on their services, etc.

The conciliar stress on clerical "diakonia" offers a whole key to renewal, but this key must be grasped properly. In stressing the obligation of the clergy to serve, the Council necessarily stresses the *right* of the rest of the faithful to that service. The clergy are meant to be wise and faithful servants, and the rest of the faithful have a strict ecclesial right to that faithful service.

Here we could pause and ask: Do the clergy show renewed awareness of their duty to serve? Have they a renewed awareness of the particular rights of the faithful? Are these rights taken as a main standpoint from which to view efforts at renewal? Are they

---

1 References to the serving mission of the clergy permeate the documents of Vatican II. Cf. for instance: LG 21, 24, 27, 28, 32; CD 5, 9, 16, 28; PO 3, 16, 13; GS 3, 40, 42, 76, 89, 93; AA 3, 8, 10, etc.

taken as main guidelines for policy decisions? Are they upheld and defended in practice? Are the people themselves aware of their rights?

The fundamental right of each Christian is to enter into a growing communion with Christ, and with others in Christ, by drawing on the spiritual riches of truth and grace that Christ himself has left to his Church. This main right is summed up by canon 213 in these words: "Christ's faithful have the right to be assisted by their pastors from the spiritual riches of the Church, especially by the Word of God and the Sacraments".

Many other canons relate more in particular to this fundamental disposition of the Code and are simply aimed at protecting people's access to these riches. For instance, the main church laws regarding the Sacraments are designed to ensure that these seven extraordinary means of grace will always remain what their divine institution has meant them to be — actions of Christ[2] —, and that the people will not be cheated by finding less than an encounter with Christ in each Sacrament. Hence the important laws determining what is necessary for the valid administration or reception of the Sacraments (if a Sacrament is administered or received invalidly, there is an external ceremony but there is no life-giving sacramental encounter with Christ).

Much the same holds good for the people's right to have the riches of God's Word communicated to them. Canon 762 insists that the People of God "are fully entitled to seek this Word from their priests". To this right of the people corresponds the obligation of preachers to exercise a "ministry of the Word which must be founded upon Sacred Scripture, Tradition, Liturgy and the Magisterium and life of the Church" (c. 760). If preaching were to offer — as a message that saves — a word *not* founded on Scripture, Tradition or the Magisterium, it would not be the genuine salvific Word of God, and the people would be cheated in their expectations and rights.

Now it is possible that these last paragraphs, with their insistence that law is needed to regulate worship or the administration of the Sacraments or the preaching of the Word of God, may spark a negative reaction in some readers, especially priests, who feel that such an approach is equivalent to stifling the Holy Spirit or choking rightful personal spontaneity. In Chapter 9 we try to show that a major way in which the Holy Spirit speaks to us is precisely through law, and a main way in which we show our responsiveness

---

2 Cf. c. 840; SC 7.

to the Holy Spirit is precisely through obedience to the law. With regard to spontaneity we should say that, while the right to spontaneity is nowhere defined in church law, it certainly can be legitimately defended. There is indeed plenty of room for spontaneity — *within* the law. Spontaneity outside the law is almost always a sign of individualistic self-assertion and shows a lack of respect for the legitimate rights, tastes and interests of others which the law seeks to protect. Priests, it is worth repeating, are servants of the people, volunteer servants, who have *spontaneously* offered themselves for service. If they sincerely see themselves as servants of the people, they will have little difficulty in seeing themselves as servants also of the law that protects the rights of the people. Excessive and self-assertive insistence on spontaneity and personal approaches shows a weakened sense of "communio" and a lack of the spirit of service, even though the person in question may not be aware of this, especially if he is adept at the use of community rhetoric.

The complementarity of rights and obligations can never be forgotten. It is certainly easier and more pleasant to claim and exercise rights rather than to acknowledge and fulfil obligations. Nevertheless, a true "rights-lover" will also strive to be a whole-hearted "obligations-lover". Self-centredness, self-concern, is the main reason why people tend to see opposition rather than complementarity between rights and duties. Other-centredness overcomes this opposition. It is clear that a sense of respect for others is a basic condition if one is to readily accept one's obligations towards them — precisely as an expression of respect for their rights.

This is true for everyone. But the Christian should go beyond this. If he is imitating Christ, his attitude towards others will be not just one of respect but one of service. To serve others, in imitation of Christ (Mt 20:28), is not only an obligation; it is a right and a privilege — also because he sees Christ in them (Mt 25:40).

All Christians can and should have such a fully integrated view of the relationship between rights and duties. The priest should have it in a special way because of his particular call to ministry. Many complaints about "violations" or "denials" of rights evaporate when Christian life — and particularly the priesthood — is understood and lived in this way; i.e. when rights and obligations are seen in the light of service. Take, for instance, the issue of the ordination of women. It is hard not to wonder whether those women who complain about denial of their rights regard the priesthood as an opportunity for service or as a means to "power-sharing". If the latter, then they have the priesthood all wrong (cf. Chapter 11). If the former, if they really want to serve the Church, would their complaints be so bitter just because one particular way of service — the ministerial priesthood — is not open to them? Those who want to serve do not dictate their conditions of service; they are happy with the particular service God calls them to. Mary, the greatest of human persons, was content to describe herself as "ancilla", servant, slave, of the Lord.

As a genuine spirit of service grows, law and authority come to be not only tolerated and obeyed, but looked up to and loved.

Whose rights are more threatened?

The real threat within the Church nowadays is not so much that the law will oppress individual rights, but that individual action (or rather individualist action) may violate the rights of the great body of the faithful. The law is there precisely to defend those rights of the ordinary people.

The people have the right to liturgical celebrations which express the true purpose and spirit of the liturgy, and not just the moods and preferences of the celebrant. They have the further right (which is a requirement derived from their Christian dignity) that *they* should not be made objects of experimentation in the liturgy (so as to see their "response", how much they will "stand", etc.).

The priest given to liturgical experiment and innovation may find the law restrictive. The reason is that the law, in such cases, is not on his side but on the side of the people.

Similarly, the parish priest who neglects to administer the Sacraments to his people or who imposes modes or ways for the reception of the Sacraments which are not required by church law, is violating the rights of the people.

The Code of Canon Law says that the governing authority of a Catholic University is to ensure that teachers are "outstanding in their integrity of doctrine", and "are removed from office" if they are not (c. 810). This is to protect the rights of students who go to a Catholic University to receive a Catholic formation there.

Effective concern for the rights of the people is a major test of community sense and of service. Who is showing more concern for the people's rights: the theologian who claims the freedom to present — as *Catholic* doctrine — whatever he likes to the people or the Magisterium which says to the people: this or that part of

Fr X's theology is *not* Catholic teaching, is not compatible with the message of salvation that Christ entrusted to his Church?[3]

Who is showing a greater spirit of "diakonia" or service towards the people? Who is showing an awareness not just of personal rights but also of personal obligations and a readiness to fulfil them? ... The theologian is claiming the right not only to teach what he likes but also to give his teaching greater authority by attaching the tag "Catholic teaching" to it. But what obligation — towards God or towards the people — is he fulfilling? The Magisterium is indeed fulfilling an obligation — laid on it forcefully by Christ and never more burdensome to fulfil than today — to guard the deposit of truth for the sake of the people. Thus it is protecting the people's rights.

The theologian can say to the Magisterium: what is at stake is my right to think what I choose. The Magisterium can reply: you have the right to think what you choose, but not the right to call anything you choose to think Catholic. What is at stake here is not only the Truth of Christ but also the people's right — their freedom — to know that Truth without confusion.

Is the Church a democracy?

The Church is not a human institution. It was founded not by men but by Jesus Christ. Christ gave it its fundamental constitution (cf. Chapter 10), which is not that of a democracy — in the sense of a society ruled by the people through delegates whom the people freely choose and can freely remove from office. The Church is not a democratic society, but is in fact a "hierarchically constituted society" (LG 20), ruled by persons appointed from above.

This is the doctrine of Vatican II confirming the teaching of the centuries. It is noteworthy that Chaper Two of *Lumen gentium*, "The People of God", is followed immediately by a chapter entitled "The Church is Hierarchical". In its opening paragraph this chapter states that "Christ the Lord set up in his Church a variety of offices ... (whose) holders are invested with a sacred power" and continues, even more emphatically: "this sacred synod, following in the steps of the First Vatican Council, teaches and declares with it that Jesus Christ, the eternal pastor, set up the

---

3 Behind this, of course, lies the theological question of who is qualified — by means of a divinely-given charism — to judge and know what is in fact the authentic teaching of Christ: a question that we study in Chapter 14.

holy Church by entrusting the apostles with their mission as He himself has been sent by the Father. He willed that their successors, the bishops, should be the shepherds in his Church until the end of the world. In order that the episcopate itself, however, might be one and undivided He put Peter at the head of the other apostles, and in him He set up a lasting and visible source and foundation of the unity both of faith and of communion" (LG 18).

That the Church is not a democracy may well not appeal to the sentiments of contemporary man. But surely what matters here is not the will of men but the will of God. Debate about the question of whether the Church "ought" to be a democracy makes no sense if its divine Founder thought otherwise; to campaign for a democratization of the constitution of the Church is to campaign for a form of church which would no longer be the Church founded by Jesus Christ.

However, in affirming that there are no grounds in Vatican II for suggesting that the Church is a democracy or should be turned into one, we are not implying that Vatican II did not mark a break with the idea of autocratic exercise of power or did not seek to guard against arbitrariness in government. It did. Further, it emphasized concepts — collegiality, for instance, or co-responsibility, or participation — that certainly bear an affinity to what can be broadly called the "democratic process".

The new Code gives ample proof of how this collegial or participatory process is meant to enter into the work of running the Church. The Synod of Bishops (cc. 334, 342-348) gives particular expression to the collegial spirit on a universal level. Its findings or recommendations clearly carry the greatest weight in shaping overall church policy. It would be hard for the Roman Pontiff to ignore them even if he were so inclined. At the diocesan level, a Council of Priests, which acts as the bishop's senate, is mandated by law (c. 495); a bishop would act unlawfully if he did not provide for the establishment of the Council of Priests or did not consult it in major matters (cf. cc. 461, 515, 536, 1263). A College of Consultors must also exist (c.502); and there are certain cases where the bishop cannot act without the approval of this College (cf. e.g. cc. 272, 485, 1277, 1291, 1292) or of the Diocesan Finance Committee (cc. 1277, 1291, 1292). Further, there should be a Diocesan Pastoral Council (cc. 511-514). Similarly, at parish level, the Code mandates a Finance Committee (c. 537) and recommends a Pastoral Council (c. 536).

However, rather than review the modes in which the collegiate or participatory spirit can be applied to church life, I should like here to direct attention to two ideas that seem to be floating in the minds of those who hanker after a "democratic" Church.

Is the Church a free society?

Some people find it hard to accept the statement that the Church is not a democracy because they take it as implying that the Church is not a free society. But does freedom exist only in a democracy, or is a democracy the only safeguard for freedom?

It is enough to think of the self-styled "people's democracies" of communist countries to realize that invoking the magic word "democracy" does not always reveal a concern for true freedom or promote its existence. It is also true that in many democracies of the West, freedom is endangered or on the decline; there is clearly less of it than fifty years ago. Growing interventionism on the part of governments and bureaucracies, the injustice of many legislative measures, the manipulation of people's opinions by the media, exploitation on the part of firms, individualism on the part of private persons, all tend to violate human rights and erode freedom.

The fact is that the key condition for freedom is not democracy but justice: the effective protection provided to freedom by the existence of just laws and their proper enforcement. This is always true. In no society can there be any true or lasting freedom except under the law.

The Church, then, though not a democracy, *is* a free society not only because one belongs to it freely, but — more importantly — because it is built on the knowledge and possession of the Truth of Christ the acceptance of which makes man free (Jn 8:32). That is why its fundamental laws, derived from that truth, constitute "the perfect law of freedom" (Jas 1:25).

St James, be it noted, does not say "freedom from the law" or "freedom without law", but the law of freedom. In other words, it is within the law of Christ that we find freedom.

Another mistaken notion that keeps clouding our mental atmosphere is the idea that in a participatory or collegial society law is somehow less binding. This is quite false. It is a reflection of the erroneous belief we saw earlier that "popularising" or "democratizing" trends loosen the bonds of authority and exempt people from respect towards it.

It is not correct to think that an emphasis on collegiality means a de-emphasis on authority. Collegiality (just like subsidiarity) refers to modes or processes through which authority may be exercised in a society. It refers especially to the way certain authoritative decisions are arrived at. It does not and cannot mean that there is to be less authority, or that each one is entitled to despise authority, to ignore decisions or laws legitimately given and to do what he or she chooses.

Some priests today and some lay Catholics have assimilated a lot of the modern secular spirit that finds submission to authority particularly irksome. That is undoubtedly a problem; but it should remain *their* problem. When they talk and write and agitate as if the majority of the People of God found the yoke of authority oppressive and wished to be under *no* authority, they are basically extrapolating their own problem and trying to communicate their own restlessness to others. I suppose that all Christians today, as those of any past age, find Christ's law difficult; it has always been difficult. But the vast majority of the faithful are not inclined to resent church authority or to rebel against it. No one, after all, is forcing them to be Catholics or forcing them to try, with their ups and downs, to live as Catholics. They are Catholics because they choose to be. And they choose to look to their pastors for ministry, for guidance, for rulings, for the government of dioceses and parishes, etc.

That some elements outside the Church try to stir up a sense of friction between pastors and people may be lamentable, but is easy enough to understand. It is also understandable that some priests burdened with restlessness find their burden a troublesome cross (if they carry it well — which also means quietly — it can become a cross that saves and sanctifies). What is not so understandable is that some of them read their burden into (and, worse, unload it onto) the minds of the people entrusted to their pastoral care. Pastors are meant to carry burdensome sheep, but not to become themselves burdensome shepherds.

A brief but important consideration suggests itself here. A man who does not respect authority when he is under it, is not fit to wield it. A person who has not obeyed just law is hardly likely to administer it justly. Many possible episcopal appointees are no doubt disqualified on this account.

A brief word, too, on exclusion from the community. One can — perhaps — belong to "oneself" on one's own terms. One cannot belong to a people or a community on one's own terms, but only on *common* terms. Common acceptance of goals and laws and guidance defines a people.

One can belong to a constituted people only on constitutional terms. A people must have a common constitution, written or unwritten. In the case of the Church, the People of God, that common constitution was given by Jesus Christ. Those Christians who hold themselves free to redefine or rewrite that constitution in their own terms are separating themselves from the People by a process of self-chosen marginalization.

A person can be excluded from the community — in other words, he can be excommunicated — by the act of those of the community who are invested with authority. The danger nowadays is rather that a person, by refusing to accept the common law, the common inheritance, the patrimony of the People of God, *excommunicates himself* (cf. Chapter 16).

Vindicating one's rights

We have been emphasizing the obligations of the members of a community to accept the just decisions of those in authority. But, what if those decisions are unjust, or doubtfully just?

Naturally if an interested party feels that a particular decision or action is detrimental to the common good or to the rights of others or to his own rights,[4] then in justice it must be possible for him to make recourse through proper channels of appeal.

Title I of Book Two of the Code of Canon Law, listing the obligations and rights of all Christ's faithful, says that "Christ's faithful may lawfully vindicate and defend the rights they enjoy in the Church, before the competent ecclesiastical forum in accordance with the law" (c. 221, 1); this includes the right to appeal. So every one of the faithful is entitled to have recourse to a higher ecclesiastical authority if he or she feels that justice has not been done at a lower level. Canons 1628ff deal with appeals against ecclesiastical judgments; and canons 1732ff with recourse against acts of administration.

With the new emphasis on rights and obligations it is very important that all Christ's faithful, lay people as well as clerics, be aware of what their proper rights and obligations are, and of the channels through which, when necessary, they can defend their rights against abusive action or omission by others. Diocesan bishops have a particular responsibility to respect people's rights to appeal from diocesan tribunals to metropolitan or higher courts (cc. 1438-1439). Not to do so would be a grave abuse of authority and a violation of justice.

---

4 Hopefully, if he is a priest, he is more sensitive about the rights of other people than about his own.

Currently we have a situation in the Church where the clergy tend to be strongly conscious of their rights but, perhaps, do not have an equally keen consciousness of their obligations. Lay Christians, by contrast, are rather hazy about both their rights and obligations; they know little of the conciliar emphasis on clerical "diakonia" or service, and in consequence are largely unaware of the nature of the service that the clergy are meant to provide to the laity and to which therefore they, the laity, have a right.

The press frequently enough reports complaints by clerics that their rights are not sufficiently respected by bishops or the Holy See, yet very seldom reports similar complaints by lay people directed against their bishop or parish priest. This contrast could be explained in different ways. It could be that priests are more respectful towards the rights of the lay people they serve than are bishops or the Holy See towards priests' rights. Or it could be that priests are more sensitive about their own rights than lay people are about theirs. Or it could also be that lay people are simply not aware of their rights, and therefore not aware of possible violations of those rights, committed by clerics.

Let us consider a simple example to which we made a brief reference earlier. Lay people have the right to the ministry of priests and to be able to identify those who are appointed to serve them. Canon 284 prescribes that "clerics are to wear suitable ecclesiastical dress". Most clerics see an irksome element in this requirement; understandably enough they find casual lay attire more comfortable to wear. Some maintain that wearing lay dress brings them "closer" to lay people, without apparently realizing that many lay people object to the lack of openness they find in this tactic. Others, going further, actively criticise the use of clerical dress as if it implied "status-seeking" or the defence of a dated "caste" system. The fact nowadays, in any event, is that few priests wear any distinctive clerical dress in the street,[5] and that lay people complain that they can seldom identify priests in public. It is hard to see what elements of "renewal" can underly this phenomenon.

May we suggest that this is a matter which priests tend to see from a rather narrow and self-concerned viewpoint — that of their own convenience — and not from the viewpoint of the rights of the faithful? The purpose of the law is indeed that the priest should be set apart and distinguishable (cf. PO 3), not however as a man entitled to or claiming privilege, but as one who is ready at all

---

5 A badge is clearly not a *dress*.

time to serve; its clear purpose is that the people should always be able to identify their ministers and servants.

More deeply disturbing, therefore, than the failure to observe the law would be the failure to understand it: i.e. to understand both that it underpins a particular expression of priestly service and that it also protects an important right of the faithful.

Canon 284 is one more example of how a law directed to servants is likely to remain a dead letter if the spirit of service is insufficiently understood or insufficiently present. A general restoration of priestly and religious garb can only be expected when clerics come to understand and to love the law regarding clerical dress — the sign of their interior readiness to serve. The process can be hastened if lay people who like to see their priests dress as priests (the vast majority of lay people) remind the priests whom they know that there is a law to this effect, and that this law confers on the laity a right and an expectation that priests should not defraud. But in the end it is only a renewed sense of service on the part of priests that will lead to a renewed desire to be available and identifiable at all times for that service.

The new code — a key to renewal

Our considerations so far should point to the unique importance of the new Code of Canon Law promulgated in 1983. The fruit of twenty years of study and consultation between Rome and the bishops and experts of the whole world, it has appropriately been called the "last document of the Second Vatican Council". In effect it seeks to give juridical expression to the ecclesiological insights and the pastoral spirit of the Council, so much so that it can well be termed the Code of Vatican II or "the Law of the People of God".

This is a fundamental law of renewal. *Unless this law is known, observed and loved, no renewal of the People of God is possible.*

I am quite aware that this last affirmation may be greeted with raised eyebrows, or with laughter, in certain quarters. If this occurs, however, it is a sign of how confused some people's ecclesiological thinking and social sense has become. All our efforts at renewal will remain ineffectual and will only end in abuse, discouragement and decline, until we see that love for God and love for God's people necessarily implies love for justice and love for law. Rights will not be respected, obligations will not be fulfilled, remedies for abuses will not be found, ministry will not truly express itself as self-sacrificing service, the People of God will not live in the true harmony of a people, nor will they "serve God in holiness" (LG 9), unless the renewed common law of the People — the Code — is known, respected and put into effect.

The present moment in fact presents a critical paradox inasmuch as we have an optimum instrument for renewal, and little desire to use it. We have acquired a well thought-out law, but retain a poor way of thinking about law.

The new Code, in short, comes at a good moment in the post-Conciliar efforts at renewal. It also comes at a bad moment. It comes at a good moment because we need it. It comes at a bad moment because we are not prepared for it. The advent of the 1983 Code necessarily marks a testing point of the sincerity of approaches to renewal. The renewed Code should have been looked forward to expectantly, above all by those who are particularly called to service. Instead it was largely feared. When it came, it should have been welcomed with joy and eagerly put into effect. In fact it is in danger of being ignored and remaining a dead-letter. If this happens, we Catholics can become an increasingly individualistic and lawless people. And a lawless people is a *non populus meus*, "No-people-of-Mine", in the words of the Lord (cf. Hosea 1:9).

The new Code of Canon Law which expresses the ecclesiology and the spirit of Vatican II in juridical form, can be properly described as the legal instrument for renewal.

But — it may be objected — can one bring about reform or renewal simply by legislation or legal enactment? One clearly cannot, at least in a voluntary society like the Church, unless the members of the society themselves actively back the legislation.

But I would maintain that though legislation cannot bring about reform on its own, it remains an essential condition to reform. No spontaneous reform is likely to last or to be just, unless it can be and is legislated. Here it is worth recalling the obvious. Vatican II, considered as a movement or phenomenon of renewal, was not something spontaneous nor did it begin at the "grass roots" level. It began at "the top", with Pope John XXIII; and its renewing message has been conveyed to us through conciliar and post-conciliar legislation. It is this legislation that needs to be implemented at the grass-roots level. Measures of renewal need legal expression, implementation and protection. Otherwise they will be ineffectual and will not enter into the life of the people, bringing renewed Christian spirit to both clergy and laity.

We have a renewed law. We need a renewed approach to law,

so that we neither put the new law cavalierly to one side nor interpret it subjectively. Subjectivism and individualism rupture fellowship. No community can be fashioned of individuals each of whom is a law to himself. A "common" law subordinate to the subjective interpretation of each member of a community is not a *common* law. When people no longer hold themselves subject to the law but rather subject it to themselves, then law can no longer hold people together as a people. The people become a lawless people, and fragment.

The People of God need a common law

This, then, is the thesis of the first part of our study. If we are to be a People — and not just a series of disconnected groups or individuals — we need a common law; we cannot become a renewed people without it.

Despite many achievements in the past twenty-five years, the whole issue of church renewal remains a big question mark. A main reason is that many of the faithful in general, and of the clergy in particular, having failed to grasp the deeper implications of key conciliar ideas — "communio", "People", "diakonia-service" —, have also failed to see how the prevalent individualism of the secular world is at logger-heads with these key conciliar principles, and how its presence in the Church is an effective block to renewal. An individualistic faith is not compatible with any true participation in the life of a people.

Individualism is opposed to *communio*, opposed to service, opposed to any real sense of belonging to a People or any real concern for the good of the People. Individualism means self-centredness, and is utterly opposed to *diakonia, communio, People of God*, all of which are powerful calls to "other-centredness".

This has been, and continues to be, our problem: thinking that renewal is compatible with an anti-law mentality; trying to combine *communio* and individualism, people-centredness with self-centredness, concern for rights with contempt for authority.

Renewal in the Church has never been the work of individualists: schism and heresy have. Renewal has always been brought about by community-centred persons imbued with a spirit of service and forgetful of their personal rights.

Advanced liturgies, trendy sermons, experimental pastoral approaches, do not necessarily show love for others or a spirit of service towards them. Concern for their rights does. This is the turning point we have to reach. When it becomes habitual for priests to ask: what are the *rights* of the people?, what *service* are they entitled to expect from me?, what do I *owe* them?, then the ministers will be truly community servants and community builders; then we will have embarked on the path of renewal.

The Council, in showing special preference for the term "People of God", opened up juridical perspectives that we have yet to pursue in practice. A renewed ecclesiology will not be possible if it does not go hand in hand with a thorough renewal of legal science where the true vivifying and liberating nature of law and authority are understood.

If we want a more positive concept of law we have it in the fact that law is the defence of freedom, the charter on which human rights are proclaimed and held up for all to see. And if we want a less impersonal concept of authority, we have it in the fact that behind church authority stands Christ with his personal call to find him and to respond to him there: "whoever listens to you, listens to me" (Lk 10, 16).

No doubt the Code of 1983 is improvable in its human elements. But renewal of the Church does not have to wait on our once again renewing the law. It depends on our definitively renewing our attitude towards the law. And this will take both an intellectual effort — to understand the positive value of law as the protector of rights — and a moral effort — to conform to the law and to fulfil our obligations at least as keenly as we exercise our rights.

Serene and deep reflection, and plenty of mental adjustment, will be necessary if we are to understand these various key points and act on them.

The Chosen People of old began to be a People — God's People — once they were given a law. They were renewed and prospered and fulfilled their mission when they observed that law. They went into spiritual decline, social decay and subjugation when they turned from the law. No one would wish for a law quite as detailed as the waywardness of the Jewish people apparently demanded. But we do need a law that is sufficiently specific to ensure that the new People of God have access to the Truth and Grace of Christ, so that both the direction they follow and the dynamism they enjoy and communicate come from him.

Only a renewed People of God will renew the world. The signs of the times should be easy to read. Our individualistic world needs the witness of Christians who have overcome individualism, and love the community bonds and obligations that bind and keep them together. Our selfish world needs the witness of Christians who live the spirit of service, and so love all that promotes the good of others. Our lawless world needs the witness of Christians who freely love the law — the liberating law — and look up to authority as the guardian of individual rights and common liberties.

Only a Church which is truly a united people, one in ideals, one in love for laws, one in respect for rights, one in acceptance of authority, can be "that messianic people which is a most sure seed of unity, hope and salvation for the whole human race" (LG 9).

* * *

We will now conclude these broad introductory considerations and go on to deal with more specific topics concerning freedom and authority within the Church. One further point, however, should be noted. The anti-law attitude in the Church is not just anti-authority, it is anti-institution. It tends to be, or become, hostile to the whole concept of institutional religion or of the institutional Church, which it sees as a block to the freedom of the spirit or the freedom of Christ.

This attitude of mistrust towards the institutional Church which is so widespread today is a consequence not primarily of possible past abuses of church government, but rather of weakened present faith in the way Christ is living and working in the visible Church.

Therefore, while our study has begun with more legal concepts — law, rights, obligations —, we will gradually shift through personalist themes of freedom and conscience to an ecclesiological perspective, trying to achieve an understanding of the Church seen as no mere juridical or authoritarian institution but as the organ or means by which the living Christ continues to come to us with his saving power and truth.

In the end is not the merely institutional aspect of the Church's being that ought to enamour us, but the sacramental aspect: the mystery of the Church as "the sign and instrument of communion with God and of unity among all men" (LG 1).

4

Freedom

I. LAWLESS FREEDOM?

The ideal of many people today is a state or society with unlimited freedom but no laws. In the preceding chapters we have tried to show that a lawless society is an absurdity and cannot work.

This social idea is a reflection of the idea many contemporaries have of individual man himself. Man is free, they insist; man has the right to be perfectly free, and this right should be subject to no restraint or law. Any serene consideration of man shows that this view of him is also false. Man is indeed meant to be free, but not without law.

Man has the right to be free, and this is a natural right. Yet, since rights derive from nature and are dependent on nature, the right to be free can only be exercised in accordance with his nature. If he tries to assert a right to be free *against* his human nature, he may destroy himself. Man's freedom, therefore, is conditioned by laws: the laws of his nature. Man is not free to get in the way of an express train — and survive as man. His nature cannot stand it.

If man does not know his own nature — what sort of being he is — and does not respect it, he may forfeit his human rights: the fundamental right to be human, the even more fundamental right to be alive. The man who thinks he should be free to take unlimited drink or drugs, is wrong; his error may prove fatal.

But the laws that derive from man's nature and so condition his freedom are not just physical and external, or merely corporeal. They are also — and more importantly — internal and spiritual. And it is to that internal area of freedom that particular attention needs to be directed.

We have seen that social freedom rests on law, on the legal recognition and defence of human rights, and on the effective presence of justice in the relations between the various persons and powers that make up society. Only in this way will each one receive his due and at the same time make his contribution to the good of the social whole. There is a certain analogy in how individual freedom also depends on law.

Each individual man is a sort of mini-society. He is a composite being made up of body and spirit. He has different organs, powers, tendencies, passions and instincts. His life and his freedom depend on the proper ordering of these various powers and tendencies. If they are rightly ordered — to one another and to higher values — man can grow in true freedom. If there is lawlessness instead of right order, man's life can be laid desolate.

No one would say that an alcoholic or a drug-addict is a free man. He has lost his freedom because one appetite or craving within him is not subject to a norm or measure of "justice" or rightness; it is taking more than its due and is dominating and exploiting his other powers, enslaving them to its rule and destroying the "common good" of the man as a whole. One simply does not know man if one ignores the fact that he has within himself a series of tendecies that can frustrate or even destroy him unless they are properly ordered: greed, anger, lust, fear, irresponsibility, escapism. . . .

Modern man tends to be acutely conscious of what he sees as threats to his freedom coming from outside, particularly from the injustices of other men. But he is remarkably unconscious of the fact that his freedom is also threatened by interior forces: the undue dominance of any one of his tendencies, its "taking over" the government of his life. Nevertheless, a basic truth about freedom is that the worst threat to it comes from inside. Man's freedom is won or lost *from within*. Even in external conditions of anarchy, exploitation and subjection, a man can be or become interiorly free. Many have become free in concentration camps. It is also true, however, that many have become slaves in the free world. Even if he is living in conditions of justice and peace and prosperity, man can become a slave on the inside. He can permit or create his own interior slavery. Let us try to consider some of the dynamics — the laws — of man's interior freedom or slavery.[1]

---

[1] If we are going to take a look inside man, we need to establish some distinctions about the way he functions interiorly. Some people today question these distinctions. They say that man is one being, one person, and it makes no sense to speak of, say, his mind or his will or his feelings, as if they were really distinct from him. One is not saying that they are distinct from him, in suggesting that they are distinguishable among themselves; and that the complexity of man's interior operations cannot be understood unless they are distinguished.

While it is true that in each one of us there is only one person, one "I" who acts, nevertheless we can and should see that personal activity is expressed in clearly distinguishable modes. To think is not the same as to feel, to know is not the same as to love, to be hungry or tired is not the same as to be angry or selfish. Unless we bear these distinctions in mind we can never understand the process by which man can win, or lose, his interior freedom.

Ruling one's self

There must be law and government within man if his interior life is not to be sheer anarchy. The big question for each of us is, "Who or what is going to rule in my life?" We may quickly answer: "*I*. I am going to govern myself". We answer well; but we have not yet given a full answer.

The fact is that every man is being constantly solicited by a number of internal forces each contending to be *the* force running his life. He must choose which will have authority in the process of shaping his personal existence. In man's internal political system, his "I" is truly the electorate; but he has to cast his vote among the different candidates running for governing office: longing for truth, hunger for goodness . . .; but also vanity, lust, greed, desire for power or popularity or possessions. . . . His bodily passions, in particular, which are meant to be junior ministers in his cabinet, are not content to hold such lower portfolios; they want to be policy makers, prime ministers.

Let us consider some of the possibilities that present themselves here. Suppose that a man chooses to place himself under the rule of greed or lust, so letting some lower part of his being take over the government of his whole life. Is a man free in such a situation? No; rather he has freely chosen a rule of slavery. His higher self, his spirit, is enslaved to his bodily passions: the "law of his members" (cf. Rom 7:23). This is selfishness and senselessness run wild. It is anything but self-government.

Of course a man may acknowledge that this is indeed a rule of slavery, that under such government he is quickly losing his real freedom; and he may react. He may, with an effort, subject his passions to the government of his mind and will. This undoubtedly marks a step upwards. But even this form of rule offers diverse possibilities.

He may bring about this rule in a defective way — when he wants his self (even his "spiritual" self) to be the centre and end of his life, and the measure and source of all his values. Then he is under a worse government still that enslaves him to his pride.

In such a case he may be keenly aware of that lower area (the law of his members) where he has proved himself master. But he resolutely turns his attention away from the higher area (the law of God), where he is not prepared to serve. Since he wants to be a law to himself, since he wants his own self to be supreme, he refuses to look above self. He, just as Adam and Eve, plays at being "like gods" (Gen 3:5). And so he remains: large and independent in his own esteem, but actually dwarfed and imprisoned by his inability to look up to anything higher than himself.

A man can govern his life in a proper way only when he centres his mind and will firmly on God. Then he frees himself from the pride of making his own mind (or prejudices) the measure of the truth of things, and his own will (or preferences) the measure of their goodness.

Once he looks up to truth and goodness as divine attributes, he has discovered the law of his being; and of his freedom and fulfilment. He, alone in visible creation, is made *capax Dei*, capable of the possession of God. Man's fulfilment and freedom do not consist in his being lord and god of creation (what a pitiful god each man would be, and how life would then become a pathetic rivalry between pathetic gods), but in his capacity to know and love and possess the infinite Truth and Goodness of an infinite God.

It is only under the rule of the higher faculties that man can find liberation. But he must remember that his higher faculties are not autonomous; they are not a law to themselves. They do not create their own law; they are under a higher law still. The law of man's mind is truth. The law of his will is goodness.

The mind, then, is meant to be governed by the law of truth; the will, by the law of goodness. If they are, man will be made free. You will know truth and truth will make you free (cf. Jn 8:32). You will love goodness, and goodness will make you free.

Breaking the law of the will and the mind

The recognition of freedom lies with the mind; the grasping of it, with the will. The truth will make me free — if I choose to accept it. But I may know the truth (or be in a position to know it), and choose *not* to accept it. Then I am not made free. I make myself unfree.

The law of willing is that I choose God. But I can break that law; I can choose evil (evil that some "part" of me — greed, ambition, self-esteem — is attracted to as "good").

If I choose what is bad — so breaking the law of the will — I can retain the awareness that I have chosen badly; or I can then further *choose to think* (to try to think) that what is bad is good; i.e. I can choose to think falsehood — so breaking the law of the mind.

Just as one can choose to speak falsely, on the outside, and so deceive others, one can choose to *think* falsely, on the inside, and so deceive one's *self*.

Suppose a man has just collected his monthly wage packet, and is on his way home. He passes by a gambling joint, hesitates — being a bit given to gambling ... — but goes in and loses it all. When he comes out, he can decide to go home and tell his wife the truth — "I had a moment's weakness and I lost it all" — and take the consequences. Or he may choose to "justify" what he has done, with an eye to steamrolling the consequences: "Why shouldn't I do what I like with my money? *She* won't like it? Well, let her learn to mind her own business!"

Willing to "justify" what lacks justification lies at the heart of what we term rationalization — the process by which a person chooses to dwell on one side of a case to the exclusion of the other, seeking out "reasons", however superficial and specious, which lend some colour of support to a particular mode of conduct, while deliberately ignoring the deeper and substantial arguments which tell decisively against it.

If I choose to think falsely, to rationalise, I am violating the law of the mind. The law of the mind is that I think not what I choose to, but what I — independently of all feelings, prejudices and preferences — *see* to be true.

In such cases the freedom of the mind is hampered by the attitude of the will. If a man lets himself be unduly attached to a way of thinking or acting, he may as a result simply *will* that his mind should not dwell on (and therefore should not "see") the reasons why that mode of thought or action is wrong. It is not that the reasons are not there, or are not evident. The man *chooses* not to see them.

For instance, that some people do not see that contraception or abortion is wrong, often has its explanation here. At the start they may simply lack the will — the desire — to see it. In the end, they often will *not* to see it. Their thinking is not free; it is ruled not by the truth but by their will — which in turn is not free, for it is ruled not by the choice of goodness but by the choice of convenience. Such people may otherwise be highly intelligent persons. But in these matters, insofar as it is their will and not the truth that rules their minds, they have lost their freedom to think intelligently. Where intelligent thinking would make unwelcome demands on their pride or their moral conduct, they rationalise but do not think rationally.

No man, then, possesses true freedom of thought if attachments or prejudices prevent his mind from exercising its proper function and drawing conclusions that are evident in themselves. The broadest illustration of this is offered by that phrase of the Psalmist, "The fool says in his heart, there is no God" (Ps 14:1).

Is Scripture being fair to atheists? After all, there are quite a number of atheists around who seem to be rather clever people. Yet the Bible says that the atheist is a fool. Why? Because it is not his mind that leads him to say there is no God. It is his "heart", i.e. his feelings, his preferences, his prejudices.

The human mind that is in good working order and is used properly, will never say there is no God. On the contrary, the mind that is in proper order leads naturally and directly to the conclusion: there *is* a God. That is why those who say "there is no God" are not using their minds properly. In this matter of God's existence, they would seem not to be using it at all. They are "thinking" with their heart which is not a proper organ of thought. That is why atheists, however clever they may be in other areas, are fools in this capital point. They say there is no God, but it is not through thinking that they have come to this "conclusion", but through lack of thought.

II. LAW VERSUS FREEDOM?

Freedom is for choosing

Only fuzzy thinking can regard law and freedom as mutually opposed. Some people claim to see opposition because, they say, law binds whereas freedom leaves one free.... But freedom also binds. If it does not, it is good for nothing and there is no point in having it.

Freedom that is not prepared to bind itself is useless. Freedom is for choosing; and in choosing one thing, I necessarily exclude other things. If I am afraid to bind myself to my choice, it is because I lack sticking power (I am a poor chooser), or because I see nothing worth sticking to (the choices before me are poor). In either case my freedom, my power to choose, is next to worthless.

The better the object of choice, the more it is worth choosing, and the more one's choice is worth sticking to. To choose God and to stick to one's choice is the best possible use of freedom. To bind oneself to God is the freest of acts and the one that most sets a man free.

Even on the human plane this is evident. To choose marriage is to choose a good thing: a great thing, if it is a true marriage that is chosen. But to choose a true marriage is to bind oneself indissolubly for life to one person. To choose a dissolvable marriage is not to choose marriage at all. To be afraid to bind oneself to love, is to be afraid of love, to be afraid one has not found true love, or that one is not capable of true love.

We could illustrate the point in a slightly different way. To be free to marry is to be free to bind oneself. If a person feels incapable of binding himself, then he is not free to marry. He may say "I do" at a marriage ceremony. But if he really means "I do not" — to the idea of accepting a permanent commitment — he is not choosing true marriage or the happiness true marriage chosen can bring. He is choosing no more than a limited short-term sexual liaison; and that can never bring happiness.

A basic law of freedom is: *worthwhile choices should be stuck to*. A person is not free if he lacks sticking power, if he is not master enough of self to keep going when the going, though worthwhile, is difficult. His changing — his going back on his choices — is a proof not so much of freedom as of weakness.

Freedom, law and restraint

For some people, freedom means the absence of restraint, and law the presence of restraint. And so they conclude that law and freedom are in opposition.

To place the essence of freedom in the absence of limitation or restraint is to fall into a false idea of freedom, at least as applied to man in his present condition. Freedom must be seen in function of nature, and man's nature is constitutionally subject to many limitations. To want the freedom not to be subject to these limitations — e.g. the freedom not to be obliged to eat or breathe — is to want the freedom not to be man. On the matter of law and restraint, we can simply repeat what we said in Chapter Two: Yes, in a certain sense law always involves a restraint: the necessary restraint in order precisely to *preserve freedom* for myself and for others.

In relation to myself, law seeks to restrain me from actions that go against my nature, that can frustrate me and take away my freedom to be a man, to follow a truly human way of development.

In relation to others, law seeks to restrain me from actions that imply a violation of their fundamental freedom to develop their human life.

The freedom of each one of us is indeed meant to be conditioned or restrained by the freedom of others. A true freedom-lover sees this, and is prepared — voluntarily prepared — to restrict himself out of regard for others; i.e. to freely limit his own freedom where this is necessary so as to enable others freely and legitimately to exercise theirs. The person who loves his own freedom but not that of others, is not a true lover of freedom; he does not truly love freedom as such.

Freedom is not the freedom to do what one likes; it is the freedom to do good. This statement, which might provoke an instinctive objection on the part of many persons, nevertheless states an evident truth.

Does freedom mean freedom to steal, cheat, exploit, rape, murder — even if this is what one likes to do? Man indeed does well to claim freedom as a right. But the freedom to which he is entitled is the rightful freedom to do good, not the wrongful freedom to do evil.

He has the power, but not the right, to use his freedom to do wrong. He is able, but not *entitled*, to do wrong. "The people of our time often cherish freedom improperly, as if it gave them leave to do anything they like, even when it is evil" (GS 17).

Freedom and rights *and* obligations are inter-connected. A truly free man is not only free to exercise his rights. He is also free to fulfil his obligations. And he fulfils them. Freedom and responsibility, freedom and duty, freedom and fulfilment, are inseparable.

Stopping people from going wrong?

No one has the right to do wrong. Further, no one has the right to *go* wrong — even if it is just internally or unconsciously. He has the power to go wrong, but not the right.

If he has no right to go wrong, does this mean we can stop him? Can we stop a crazed or drunken man from throwing himself out of a fifth-floor window? We can certainly try. Can we then try to stop a man from committing spiritual or moral suicide, for instance through engaging in reading — or thinking — that can undermine and destroy his faith or moral life?

Here the answer has to be more nuanced. It is clear we cannot exercise physical coercion on a person's conscience. We certainly have no right (and in fact we have no way) to physically stop a person going wrong in his personal ideas. Conscience cannot be coerced. But we have every right and duty to try to *morally* stop a person from going wrong; i.e. to try to convince a person of the wrongness of his choices, and to get him to see what is right and persuade him to follow it.

If a person going wrong in his ideas is also wronging others, then we have to take the matter a stage further. Once a man with wrong ideas begins to propagandise them, then he is no longer moving in the purely personal area of conscience (where he is answerable to God alone); he has stepped out into the social area and his actions become subject to the laws regulating the common good of society.

Therefore if a person with wrong ideas and values begins to spread them to others — if, for instance, he begins to push drugs, distribute pornography, preach racial discrimination, advocate class hatred or social violence — then those in authority have a duty to restrain him from spreading those ideas.

A man who gathers together a young audience and preaches to them the attraction and liberation of drug-taking or pornography or promiscuous sex can and should be restrained from such wrong-doing. Wrong-*thinking* remains a power though not a right; it can never be physically impeded from outside. Wrong-*doing* is not a right and should always be physically prevented.

Vatican II in its Declaration on Religious Liberty, teaches that there is a right to immunity from coercion "even in those who do not live up to their obligation of seeking the truth and adhering to it". It continues, "The exercise of this right cannot be interfered with" — but adds the all-important proviso — "as long as the just requirements of public order are observed".[2]

The requirement of public order are of course determined by the Natural Law and, within ecclesial society, by positive church law. If they are not respected, then a person's freedom to disseminate his ideas can and should be restricted.

Obeying freely

Since there is no physical force compelling us to obey the law of Christ or the law of the Church, it is clear that if we do obey, we obey freely. Yet many Christians give the impression of obeying the law reluctantly, with a sense of constraint, with little or no sense of freedom.

Must a law — or the call to obey a law — always take away our

---

2 DH 2; the proviso about the requirements of public order is repeated throughout the subsequent paragraphs of the Declaration.

sense of freedom? Is it possible to obey with a full sense of freedom? Of course it is! One obeys with the fullest sense of freedom if one chooses freely and personally to obey, if one obeys willingly, above all if one obeys out of love.

Love: that is the big motive we need to put behind our obedience. Love is what makes our obedience fully free. For the person who wants to follow Christ, the law is never a burden. It becomes a burden only insofar as one fails to discern the call of Christ in the law, or is not keen to follow the call of Christ. Therefore, if the law some time seems burdensome, it may not be the law so much as our keenness to follow Christ that needs amending.

"If you love Me, you will keep my commandments" (Jn 14:15). That is why I *want* to obey you, and your Church, Lord; not primarily because I see the reasonableness of what is commanded (though that reasonableness is often so evident). No; primarily because I want to love you, and to show my love. And also because I am convinced that your commandments come from love and set me free. "Having sought your precepts, I shall walk in all freedom.... I run the way of your commandments since you have set me free" (Ps 119, 45, 32).

The immaturity of obedience?

Some people maintain that it is unreasonable, or a sign of immaturity and even irresponsibility, to obey if one does not see the reasons behind the indications or commands given.

It would certainly be unreasonable, it would in fact be wrong, to obey a law that one *does see* to be mistaken and clearly contrary to God's will. But suppose this is not the case. Suppose it is a matter not of seeing the law to be wrong, but simply of not seeing it to be right. In such a case — where one does not understand the reasons behind the laws or the superior's commands — can it be reasonable to obey it? If we follow the analysis just given — of how love can inspire obedience — the answer once again is Yes. It is reasonable to obey a law the reasons for which one does not see, provided one has *reason to trust* the judgment or authority of the one giving the law.

It is reasonable for a child to obey the indications of its father, even without understanding the reasons for them; it is a sign of love. It is reasonable for a research student aiding a Nobel Prize physicist to carry out the professor's indications even if he does not see the reasons for them; it is a sign of trust. It is reasonable for a soldier to obey the legitimate orders of his commanding officer without understanding the reasons for them. It is a sign of maturity and responsibility. The child that does not obey because it does not understand, does not love. The soldier that does not obey because he does not understand, is neither mature nor responsible.

So it is reasonable for a Christian to accept Christ's word when He tells us that God is Three in One. We do not understand the Blessed Trinity, but we have reason to trust Christ's word. The reason, ultimately, is love. So again it is reasonable to accept not only the Church's moral or dogmatic teaching, but also her disciplinary laws or the indications of our legitimate superiors, whether we understand the reasons behind them or not. We have reason to believe that Christ is behind them, and we want to show our love for Christ. Our reason for obeying is love. There is nothing wiser than love. Obedience is the free choice of love.

Blind, unthinking obedience — where a person obeys like a robot — would be a sign of immaturity. That is not the obedience asked of people in Christ's Church. Christians are not robots. They are intelligent free beings who use their intelligence to reflect on their faith and conclude that Christ wishes them to see his will behind Church authority; and who exercise their freedom so as to obey that authority out of love for him.

* * *

"Laws are not necessary if we practise love". This is one of those nice-sounding phrases one hears at times. It sounds nice, but it is quite false. One might as well say, "Signposts are not necessary if we love to travel". If we want to get somewhere (and especially if we want to get to Someone), signposts *are* necessary.

What is not necessary if we have love, is *coercion*. But laws are necessary; laws that signpost the way love wants to go. We express it more precisely still if we say: laws are signposts placed there by God's Love, pointing out the way his Love wants us to follow; and the way our love wants to follow so as to come to Him.

5

Conscience

"The Rights of Conscience" is one of the main banners under which war is waged today on law. Most people, Christians included, see law and conscience in inevitable conflict. Moreover, if they are asked which stands higher — law or conscience — their instinct is to side with conscience; perhaps without reflecting that, as happens with law and freedom, one can too quickly see opposition between realities that are naturally meant to be in close harmony.

Nevertheless, the theme does seem to pose troublesome questions. Do many laws not represent an imposition on conscience? Does the administration of law not often violate the rights of personal conscience? Must one obey law, or is one free to follow conscience? . . . With the ideas of the last chapter in mind let us try to throw some light on this theme.

"Conscience leaves a man free" . . . ?

"Law binds; conscience leaves a man free" is a variation — frequently enough heard — on a phrase we considered in the last chapter. The phrase shows a total misunderstanding of the nature of conscience, and equally of its relationship to law. Conscience binds, just as law does. It binds even more intimately, for it binds from within. Conscience does not leave a man free, i.e. free to do "what he likes". Conscience says, *"Do* this; do *not* do that — whether you like it or not". Conscience does not "dialogue" with a man; conscience *dictates*. The very first right of conscience, after all, is the right to be *obeyed*. The man who listens to his conscience is not free to do "what he likes". He is bound — under moral compulsion, from within — to do what conscience tells him. He can ignore that moral command and disobey his conscience, but only at the cost of violating its rights; and at the cost also of abusing his human freedom and debasing his essential human dignity.

Conscience binds, just as law does, for conscience is in fact a form or reflection of law. "Deep within his conscience man discovers a law which he has not laid upon himself but which he must obey. Its voice, ever calling him to love and to do what is good and avoid evil, tells him inwardly at the right moment: do this, shun that. For man has in his heart a law inscribed by God. His dignity lies in observing this law, and by it he will be judged" (GS 16).

Conscience itself, then, is a law, an interior law. It is not, however, a law to itself. It is not man's creation, and is not subordinate to man. It is an echo of God's law: an echo which, as the case may be, interprets God's law clearly and faithfully ..., or obscurely ..., or even deformedly.... But in any case it remains an echo of a law that *it* has not created, an echo of a law that is higher than itself.

If conscience is an inner law, can it not find itself in conflict with some external law, with some law of the Church or the State? It can; but it is not in the nature of things that this should normally happen. After all, both law and conscience are guides to human action — hopefully, to the right course of human action. Each is a signpost. Ideally, as signposts, they should both point in the same direction. If they do not, something is wrong.

If both law and conscience are sound, then one reaffirms the other. A good law gives clear light to a sound conscience; a sound conscience approves and welcomes a good law, and urges its fulfilment.

But there can be opposition between them. If this happens, there is bound to be a defect somewhere. Either the law is bad, or else personal conscience is deformed.

We have said enough about what makes laws good or bad. What principles can we establish about conscience?

Rules about conscience

There are two main rules about conscience to be kept in mind:

1) CONSCIENCE MUST BE FOLLOWED. If my conscience gives a *certain* judgment, *commanding* or *prohibiting* some action, then, according to Catholic teaching, I must obey my conscience. Examining this, we see that if it is to be obligatory to follow one's conscience, a double requirement must be fulfilled:

a) it is when the judgment of conscience is *certain* that it must be allowed. If conscience is in doubt, then there is no obligation to follow it. On the contrary, normally one ought not to act with a doubtful conscience;

b) it is when conscience *commands* or *forbids* that it must be followed. If conscience simply 'permits', then one *may* follow it, but one is under no obligation to do so.

If my conscience tells me, with full certainty, that a law is wrong and not to be obeyed — a racially discriminatory law, for instance, or an abortion law — then it is clear: I disobey, I am morally *bound* to disobey.

This can happen with laws of the State. Unfortunately it is in no way difficult to imagine state laws that are morally wrong, or a state constitution that violates justice and people's rights. Such laws, of course, are not laws in any true sense at all. Such a constitution lacks any inherent authority. A citizen may be compelled to submit to them, but they do not and cannot bind his conscience.

Can something similar happen with church laws? Can conscience find itself in conflict with the laws of the Church to such an extent that it feels bound to resist these laws? Here we should distinguish between (a) merely disciplinary laws (Lenten fast, Sunday Mass-going, etc.) and (b) laws that the Church presents as essential laws of faith or morals (papal primacy, the indissolubility of marriage, etc.).

Let us look first at laws that relate to merely ecclesiastical discipline. Can such laws be "wrong"?

Before answering, it is no harm to point out that we do not always use the word "wrong" in a very precise sense; that we often use it when we would do better to use a different word.

A church law can obviously be *unpopular*. This, when it happens, is easy enough to judge. Laws about fasting, for instance, are generally not very popular. But are we, on that account, going to say that they are wrong?

A church law may indeed by *unwise* or *inopportune*. This too can undoubtedly happen, although the judgment that a particular law is unwise is not always easy to make; and, after all, how is one to know that such a judgment itself is wise? Further, supposing that I do judge that a particular church law is unwise, does this mean that it is wrong? Does this mean that it is wrong enough for me to be entitled in conscience to ignore it or to disobey it? ...

We should allow for such imprecisions of language, but we still have to answer our question: can a merely disciplinary law be wrong? The answer of course is that a merely ecclesiastical law could be wrong *in the strict sense*; i.e. in the sense that to obey it would be sinful and to disobey it becomes a duty in conscience. But, frankly, I cannot think of any existing church law anywhere that falls even remotely into such a category. One can *imagine* such a case, of course, e.g. a bishop going mad and decreeing that all the people in his diocese must sign a declaration acknowledging him to be God, and agreeing to turn over all their personal property to him. But, outside of such imaginings . . . ?

Yet it is a fact that some people today maintain that merely disciplinary laws do not bind in conscience, and they disregard them. And the laws they are disregarding are not outlandishly imaginary laws, but real universal disciplinary laws; e.g. laws relating to worship, to the administration of the sacraments, to priestly celibacy. . . .

Their justification for ignoring these laws is often the fact that they are precisely "only" disciplinary laws, and therefore can change; and "therefore" don't bind. I am sorry; the last conclusion does not follow. They do bind.

Laws that relate to merely ecclesiastical discipline — such as are, for instance, the law of priestly celibacy or the law of fasting — are certainly *reformable* laws in the sense that they could be modified or abolished. But — reformable or not, popular or not, wise and opportune or not — as long as they are in force, they *bind* each Christian; and they bind *in conscience*.

The laws of any society bind its members unless some law in a particular case is clearly shown to be contrary to the norm of justice. St Paul, speaking of rulers and authorities, says we should obey their laws, "also" — he adds — "for the sake of conscience" (cf. Rom 13:5). He is referring to civil laws; church laws call for at least equal *conscientious* obedience. All true laws, civil as well as ecclesiastical, bind in conscience; the virtue of justice — what we owe to God and to others — calls on our conscience to obey them. As we shall see in a moment, church laws have a further warranty, besides justice, behind them.

Levels of conscientious difficulty

But can a Catholic not feel "in conscience" that a particular church disciplinary law *should* be changed? He can *feel* it, in conscience (although conscience should be an area not of feelings, but of reason). He can *advocate* it (provided he avoids scandal). What he cannot do, in conscience, is to disobey. If he does, he sins.

Some persons "exempt" themselves from obedience to a church law because — they say — that law "makes no sense" to them, or seems "unimportant", or "outdated" or "restrictive".[1] But

---

[1] In Chapter 2 we saw that any law, precisely in defending the rights of certain persons, does have a legitimate *restrictive* effect on the rights of others.

such personal feelings or appreciations in no way annul the binding obligation of the law. Otherwise no one would be bound to obey any state or church law that simply did not appeal to him.

It is not enough that a person says he does not see, in conscience, why this or that particular law should bind him. "Not seeing" the point or the justice or the application of a law does not justify disobedience of that law. Disobedience is justified only if one is *certain* of the law's *injustice*, certain, in other words that to obey it would be wrong in the strict sense, i.e. that it would be sinful.

Recalling the principles given on pp 52-53, we can observe that the reasons the person in question alleges for disobeying are not that his conscience *prohibits* obedience or *commands* disobedience, but that it simply *"permits"* him to disobey. But, as we saw, no one has a duty to follow a conscience that simply permits. To this we must add that no one has a right to follow it if this means going against other existing serious obligations (including the obligation not to give scandal).

Only an imperative conscience ("you *have to* disobey") justifies disobedience. A simply acquiescent or permissive conscience does not justify disobedience least of all if such disobedience can in any way harm the common good or the rights of others (cf. 1 Cor 10:24, 28).

When a person disobeys a state law — e.g. on abortion or sterilisation — his conscience tells him he *must* disobey, and that to obey would be a serious sin, would be seriously displeasing to God.

It is not easy to imagine anything even remotely similar occuring in the case of disobedience to a church law; to imagine, for instance, a priest's conscience telling him that he *must* disobey the Church's law requiring celibacy, that God would be *seriously displeased* if he were to obey it.

The point made above is worth repeating: it is not enough for a person to say, "I do not see, in conscience, that this or that church law applies to me". The fact that one "does not see" is not a sufficient level of conscientious difficulty to justify disobedience. Nothing less than what one *does see* as an obligation before God, to disobey, can justify disobedience to the law (cf. Acts 5:29).

Let us turn to a different category of laws, laws that express fundamental points of the Church's dogmatic or moral teaching. The question again arises: could the conscience of a Catholic tell him that laws are wrong, and therefore should be rejected or disobeyed?

No. Clearly no; not at least if his conscience as a Catholic tells him, as it ought, that Christ stands behind such laws and teachings. To suggest that the Church's law is wrong in any such matter is to suggest that Christ is wrong; it is to suggest that he has failed in his promises to his Church: "whatever you bind on earth shall be bound in heaven" (Mt 18:18), "whoever listens to you listens to Me" (Lk 10:16).

It may happen that, in some such matter, my conscience (my mind, really) does not "see" the logic or the human reasons behind the law. But my mind, if it is a Catholic mind, tells me that Christ is behind it. If Christ is behind the law (my mind should go on to conclude), then the law must be right; and it must also be right, it must be Christ's Will, that I obey it. But, of course, if the law is right and if it is right for me to obey it, then my conscience — which "argues" against the law or against its acceptance — must be wrong....

Is conscience infallible?

"My conscience is wrong!" For some people today this seems to be the one possibility that they will not admit — which of course means they are ready to attribute to their own conscience the very quality of infallibility that they deny to the Church's teaching....

Obviously, if conscience could not be wrong, then there would never be any reason to look for outside moral guidance at all. God's Revelation, Scripture, Tradition, the Church — all would be functionless. My personal conscience would infallibly decide everything.

No. My conscience is not infallible. It can be wrong in its judgments. And then of course it becomes a bad guide, pointing away from the truth instead of pointing towards it.

Conscience can be wrong. That is why, to the first major rule we gave about conscience — that conscience must be followed — we need to add a second:

2) CONSCIENCE MUST BE *FORMED*. Conscience can be mistaken in the judgments it gives me about the moral truth. Therefore it needs to conform to a higher law, to be adjusted to a more accurate rule of truth.

A simple comparison helps. Think of a watch. I follow my watch, so as to be punctual. But I don't regard my watch as infallible. It may be telling me the wrong time. Therefore I adjust it by some more accurate timepiece....

Is there a more accurate standard of truth, some higher law, according to which man can adjust his conscience? For a non-Christian, it seems not — unless he knows and accepts the Natural Law.

For a Christian, Christ is that standard: "I am the Truth" (Jn 14, 8). Protestants too hold this. But they hold that the Truth of Christ can be known through the Bible alone. And in applying the principle of private judgment, they make the Truth of Christ *subject* to their own personal conscience. They do not look up to the Truth of Christ; their conscience stands higher. Their conscience reigns supreme. They believe in the infallibility of their own watch.

For Catholics, Christ speaks to us in the Bible ...; and in Tradition ...; and in the Magisterium.... And these three precisely form the one living and harmonious Voice of Christ through which he communicates his Truth to us (cf. DV 10). The same voice of Christ communicates his Will to us, speaking to us not only through the Commandments of Scripture, but also through the laws and discipline of his Church. Both the Truth of Christ and the Will of Christ call for our free response.

We look up to Christ's Truth as the highest and ultimate guide: the objective, audible Truth of Christ as taught in the Bible and believed in by Christ's Church through the ages. And we look up to Christ's Will, as to the greatest good — love for which must be shown in deeds. Christ's will comes to us in and through the law of the Gospel and the laws given by those who, in his Name, rule the Church.[2]

★ ★ ★

Another facile but misleading phrase merits a comment here: "each one has to look up to his own conscience". It is not very properly expressed. You look *in* to your conscience; you don't look "up" to it. It is within you; it is part of you; it is not higher than you.

---

2 It is clear of course that the motives for obeying the two categories of law — (a) fundamental laws of faith and morals, and (b) merely disciplinary laws — are not identical. In the case of fundamental dogmatic or moral laws, the motive for our acceptance is respect for Christ's *Truth*, because in these matters Christ has pledged that his Church will not err, that it will teach with his very Truthfulness. In the case of merely disciplinary laws, the motive of our obedience is not the Truth of Christ — which is not at issue in regard to such laws — but the *Authority* of Christ. We obey these laws because we see Christ's Will behind them. *Both* categories of laws are in fact covered by the crystal clear scriptural texts cited above: Mt 18:18; Lk 10:16.

It is not your conscience that you look up to; it is the truth. For the truth is indeed above you and higher than you.

* * *

Conscience then remains our guide; but subordinate to the law. That is why the textbooks tell us that conscience is the proximate but not the ultimate rule of right and wrong. It is not the wisest guide we have, nor the highest Court of Appeal we can look to. It is not higher than Natural Law; it is not higher than Revelation; it is not higher than God's Law.

And that, finally, is why we cannot say that conscience stands higher than law. It is not higher than any law which one has reason to believe is a true law. It can only stand higher than a false or unjust law — which then is no law. One refuses to obey such a "law" precisely because one feels *obliged to follow a higher law*. It is the higher law which not only authorises but *commands* our conscience to disobey.

Our conclusion, then, remains firm: law, true law, always stands higher than conscience.

6

Dissent

The conclusion of our last chapter was that law, true law, stands higher than conscience. Some readers are already probably protesting: but does this not undercut the rights of conscience, especially the conscientious right to dissent of which our modern world is so aware?

Conscience, we have said, should follow true and just law. But what if it does not? What if it *does not see* the truth or justice of some Church law regarding faith or morals? Surely it then has the right to dissent? Here is a matter that merits thorough consideration.

To begin with, let us clarify one point and recall another. We are not referring to "dissent" about what are in fact *matters of opinion*, within Catholic thought or life. In matters that the Church as not ruled on or taught authoritatively, each Catholic clearly has full right to form his or her own opinion and to dissent from other opinions, whether of bishop, priest or layman.

The point to be recalled concerns dissent in a purely disciplinary matter. As we pointed out in the last chapter, a person may "dissent" from such a law in the sense that he thinks —and is entitled to think — that it is unwise or inopportune. He can express his dissenting opinion and advocate the modification or abolition of the law, provided he does so without causing scandal. But, for as long as the law remains in force, ecclesial order calls on him to accept it and to obey it. Not to obey would be personally wrong, and would easily be a cause of scandal to other members of the ecclesial community.

With these two points in mind, we can put the question about dissent into proper terms. "Does a Catholic have the right to dissent in relation to the Church?" means "Can a Catholic refuse, in conscience, to accept or obey some *major* aspect of church law or teaching *without thereby affecting his position as a Catholic?*"

It is evident that there are dissenting Catholics in the Church today, also among the ranks of the clergy. Two questions arise: 1) do they have the right to dissent? 2) what are the consequences of dissent?

The right to dissent

Again let us be clear what we are talking about. The point at issue is not whether Catholics can lose the faith or leave the Church. They can and they do; history gives sad and constant proof of this.

The point at issue is not that. It is whether a Catholic has the *right* to dissent from some major aspect of church teaching or discipline, and *still call himself a Catholic*.

It is again evident that quite a few Catholics claim this very right nowadays. They dissent from some fundamental aspect of church teaching — regarding papal infallibility, for instance, or the true bodily Resurrection of Jesus, or contraception — and still insist on regarding themselves as faithful Catholics, entitled to share in the ecclesial communion, to participate in the Eucharist, etc.

Do they have the *right* to do this? A proper answer to this question can only be given in the light of the basic principle that *rights derive from nature*.[1]

Man has the rights that enable him to live according to his human nature and fulfil its possibilities. He has the right to life itself, to worship, to nourishment, to education, to human society, to friendship, to marriage, etc. because all these make him more a man, they humanise him. He does not have the right to steal or kill or commit adultery, because that dehumanises and denaturalises him. If a woman has not the right to abortion, this is because — apart from violating the right of the child — abortion defeminises and dehumanises her.

A Catholic, as a human being, has the rights of any other human being. But, *as a Catholic*, he has the rights that derive from the nature of being a Catholic. He does not have rights that go against that nature. He has the right to everything that makes him more a Catholic, but not to what makes him less. To claim rights incompatible with the nature of being a Catholic means to denaturalise oneself as a Catholic; one thereby begins to de-catholicise oneself; to "ex-communicate" oneself in the literal if not in the juridical sense.

This principle is clear enough. But of course we cannot apply it unless we define what the nature of a Catholic is; i.e. what it means to be a Catholic. Some of our contemporaries within the Church baulk at this question. They hedge about the answer. If pressed, their answer would probably amount to: "We cannot say what it is to be a Catholic".

1 Cf. p. 40 and p. 217ff.

Such cases of lost identity occur. But if a person cannot say what is Catholic and what is not, he cannot logically claim to be a Catholic himself. The term, and the reality, are meaningless to him. Neither can he logically engage in any debate about Catholic things, except perhaps as an outsider. He is at most in search of the faith, he has not found it. By his own admission he does not possess it.

If an anthropologist says, "I don't know what man is, I don't even know if I am a man", how can he engage in anthropology?

To the vast majority of Catholics, however, being a Catholic is something definite, with a very precise meaning: a meaning so rich that it can be expressed in many different ways, though all ultimately mean the same thing.

The identity of a Catholic

To be a Catholic means to have access to the life of Christ, the grace of Christ, the truth of Christ. More precisely, to be a Catholic is to *participate in Christ's life through communion in and with Christ's Church*. It is to be a sharer in Christ's life by sharing in the life of the Church in which Christ lives. It is to belong to a Body that lives with the life of Christ and communicates it to those who are its living members (cf. Eph 5:30).

In words taken directly from sections 14 and 31 of *Lumen gentium*, Book II of the Code of Canon Law begins by defining who are Christ's Faithful: "those who, since they are incorporated into Christ through baptism, are constituted the people of God" (c. 204). This description applies to all Christians, Protestants and Orthodox as well as Catholics. The next canon defines who are Catholics: baptised persons who are "in full communion with the catholic Church here on earth (and) are joined with Christ in his visible body, through the bonds of profession of faith, the sacraments and ecclesiastical governance".

The nature or identity of a Catholic, then, is clear. Its essential feature, over and beyond baptism, is full *communion* with the *Catholic Church*, by which we are *joined to Christ* through the *bonds* of the faith, the sacraments, and the discipline of the Church. Each of these ecclesial bonds should be seen in terms of a link with Christ. Each represents a special encounter with Christ, and a special acceptance of Christ coming to meet us. They are not bonds that fetter us and hamper our movements, but bonds that join us to him, and so set us free.

Full communion with Christ, therefore, is effected in the Church through:

faith: because in the Church's teaching we meet the TRUTH of Christ;

the *sacraments*: because in the Church's sacraments we meet the GRACE of Christ;

discipline: because in and behind the Church's laws we see and accept the AUTHORITY of Christ.

Just as each man has the right to breathe pure air, and eat wholesome food, and (more importantly) to think what is true and love what is good, because these are activities proper to man, so the Catholic has the rights which are proper to Catholics: the right to a peculiarly intense communion with Christ — the right to be taught by him, cured by him, fed by him, led by him, united to others in him — in and through the Church.

Catholics have the power to reject that communion with Christ. They do not have the right to reject it. They may do so; but if they do, they do wrong. And, as we shall now see, they suffer in consequence.

Particularly and very directly to our point, they do not have the right to "divide" Christ (cf. 1 Cor 1:13). In other words, they do not have the right to communion with Christ's life in the Church's sacraments, if they are not in communion with him — with his Thought and his Will — in her teaching and in her discipline.

The consequences of dissent

But what if a person sincerely believes that a Church law or teaching on a fundamental matter is mistaken? Is he to steamroll his conscience and abjectly accept a doctrine or a law that he believes to be wrong?

If he believes, in conscience, that the law or teaching is wrong, and that it would be *wrong to obey* it, then, as we saw earlier, he should disobey it; he must disobey it.

But, the matter would not stop there. In following this course of action, he has not solved a problem of conscience. He has rather intensified one that already existed.... To explain this we must clarify a radical misconception that pervades the whole presentation of the dissenting position.

It is inaccurate, it is self-deception, for our Catholic dissenter to speak of a conflict between Church authority and his conscience, as if these were two unconnected elements ranged in mutual opposition; as if the authority of the Church were a foreign element seeking to impose itself on his personal freedom.

Church authority — *belief* in Church authority — is not an element opposed to his conscience. It is not an element outside his conscience. It is *part of his conscience*!

Belief in the trustworthiness of the Church's authority is part of his conscience, because he himself has personally and freely chosen to make it part. The whole point is that the authority of the Church has no power over the mind that does not freely accept it, that does not freely believe that Christ stands behind it (Mt 18:18; Lk 10:16).

If a Catholic does not believe in *any* way in the divine mandate behind the Church's authority, then he has totally lost his faith; he is no longer a Catholic, and there seems no justification for his wanting to call himself one. If he does believe in the Church's authority in *some* way, then he does so because he freely chooses to do so. Belief in the Church's authority is then part of his mental make-up. It is part of the elements in his mind by which he judges issues of right or wrong. In other words, belief in the authority of the Church is part of his conscience.

So we are not talking about a conflict between Church authority and conscience, as if a man were fighting to defend his conscience against an external enforced principle. We are talking about a conflict *inside* conscience itself. Within *himself* a man finds two positions freely chosen and freely held, but (he feels) hard or impossible to reconcile; a personal belief, on the one hand, that Christ stands behind the Church's law or teaching; and a personal opinion, on the other, that an attitude or course of dissent — in regard to that law or teaching — seems licit. It is not conscience against authority; it is conscience against itself.

It is a case, so to speak, of a split conscience; and it is the dissenter himself who has split it, setting up opposition between positions he himself chooses to hold. It is he who has ranged his "dissenting conscience" against *his* "Catholic conscience". Only he can heal that split. If he does not, the resulting tension will keep pulling and straining at his Catholic conscience until it tears it totally apart.

After all, either one believes, or not, in the divine guarantee behind the Church's teaching. If one does not, one has not the Catholic faith. If one does, then to take a stand implying doubt or rejection of that divine guarantee, is to allow into one's mind opinions incompatible with those that are already present there. It is to become a house divided against itself.

A person faced with conflicting beliefs or opinions within himself must choose which is to prevail. He may choose to conclude: since Christ stands behind the Church, in major points of her teaching and authority, then my mind, inclining to a dissenting position, must be mistaken. There is nothing unreasonable, nor should there be anything humiliating, in this conclusion: "It seems that I must be mistaken". The possibility of coming to such a conclusion must always be before the man who acknowledges the fallibility of conscience.[2]

But if he rejects this possibility and says, "No; I am not mistaken", he must necessarily conclude: "then the Church is mistaken". With that, his faith in Christ's presence in the Church begins to collapse.

Because things do not stop there: collapse in one point is bound to be followed by further collapses. To begin to doubt some major point of the Church's teaching is to begin to doubt the Church's authenticity; i.e. it is to begin to doubt that Christ is *effectively* present in the Church. If Christ is not present in one major point of the Church's teaching or discipline, what grounds are there to believe that Christ is present in any of the truths or positions the Church maintains: present in its sacraments (especially in the Eucharist), in its worship, in any aspect of its life?

If a person, faced with what he feels is opposition between church authority and his own conscience, "sides" with conscience in one particular issue, he will soon find the same opposition appearing in all sorts of other issues. If birth control can be licitly practised in certain extraordinary circumstances, why can extraordinary circumstances (and, eventually, even ordinary circumstances) not justify homosexual conduct or extra-marital sex? If a man concludes that Christ does not uphold the Church's teaching on contraception, then he has no reason to put faith in its teaching about divorce or euthanasia or abortion....[3]

---

[2] Naturally he should not let himself stop at this conclusion. He should start a positive process of investigation to see where his mind may have been mistaken. He should especially try to investigate, and to reflect more deeply upon, the positive arguments behind the Church's position.

[3] To choose to dissent, on conscientious grounds, from major church teaching, is to put one's conscience higher than Christ, and so make one's conscience the sole guide to own's actions. The person who does so attributes infallibility to his own conscience, and denies infallibility to Christ. In other words, he attributes to his conscience what is not due to it, at the same time as he denies to Christ what is due to him. He puts his trust not in Christ but in himself.

Conscience v. conscience

These reflections may help those Catholics who feel themselves to be in a painful dilemma. Conscience, they say, tells them one thing; and the Church tells them another. In their dilemma, they follow the Church — but reluctantly, with a sense of coercion.... As I have written elsewhere, this sense of conflict is *self-induced*. "It derives not from a real collision, but from superficial thinking, from a lack of self-awareness, of grasp of one's own values.

"Such Catholics need only to reflect a little on their sense of coercion to realize that whatever force they are aware of *does not come from outside* ...; the force comes from within. They are not being forced by the authority of the Church; they are being forced *by their own belief in the authority of the Church*. The teaching of the Church, after all, gains its force only from personal conviction. It holds sway only over the mind that is convinced of its truth. They are being forced, therefore, by their own free conviction, or whatever remains of their own free conviction, that the Church's teaching is divinely guaranteed. They are in effect being forced *by their own conscience*!

"If there is a conflict of conscience, it is precisely because conscience is divided against itself. *It is not conscience against the Church, but conscience against conscience.* The consequence is clear: if a man wishes to protest about an interior conflict brought about by principles which he has personally and freely accepted, he should really protest to no one but himself."[4]

Such Catholics are not being true to themselves, or consistent with themselves, or analysing themselves properly. Self-analysis — of their own freely-held principles as Catholics — should enable them to resolve the problem that they sense within their own conscience.

May we insist: the problem they are aware of is not a problem created by authority. It is a problem created by themselves: by their attitude towards authority. Only they can solve this problem: by a new understanding of authority: seeing Christ behind it. And by a new reaction to it: accepting it as an expression of Christ's will.

Analysis of what it means to be a Catholic — free adherence to Christ in the Church — highlights the tragedy of the dissenter's position. He is dissenting from his own birth-right. He is dissenting from what he has the right to be. His dissent is a refusal to assent to the fullness of Christ's programme for his Christian development.

4 *Conscience and Freedom* (Sinag-Tala, Manila, 1978), pp. 84 and 87.

We cannot know Christ's mind in everything — more is the pity. But in matters that have a major bearing on our salvation — matters of belief and conduct — there we *can* know the mind of Christ. "Lord, what do you say on this: birth control, euthanasia, abortion ...?" And the Lord answers us in the Church.⁵

Allegations that there is "repression" within the Church of the "freedom to think differently" should be seen in this light. As we pointed out earlier, there is complete freedom to think differently in the many areas which Christ has wished to leave to the free debate of theological opinion. But once Christ has spoken his mind clearly (and only the Magisterium has the charism of the Holy Spirit to communicate to us the clear thinking of Christ), then one indeed remains free to think "differently"; but if one does so, one is no longer free to think in harmony with the mind of Christ.

One is always free to think "on one's own terms". One is not free to be united to Christ on one's own terms. One can only be united to Christ on Christ's terms.

* * *

This, then, is our conclusion. The Catholic has not the right to dissent; not without destroying the heart of his own Catholic faith and losing his Catholic identity. Dissent means to refuse to acknowledge or accept the authority of Christ — of his mind and his will — present in the Church. It means to refuse to commune with Christ.

Further, it means to refuse to commune with others — the great body of the faithful — who remain, as Christ willed, united in the one faith; one in heart and one in mind (cf. Acts 4:32). It is to begin to withdraw from the Christian communion, setting in motion a process of "self-excomnunication" by which one separates oneself from the "community of faith and charity", from the *common* Christian belief and life (cf. Chapters 16 and 17).

Dissent is indeed to think "on one's own". It should be noted that I here use the phrase "thinking on one's own" in the literal sense of thinking *in isolation*. I am not for one moment suggesting that each Catholic should not think *for himself*. Rather, taking thought for oneself is what I would like each Catholic, especially dissenting Catholics, to do, so that they measure the consequences of their thinking; so that their thinking does not rupture the bonds that link their mind to the mind of Christ and the mind of the community of the faith.

5 Cf. ibid. pp 105ff; and below, Chapters 14-15.

7

Dissent and the Rights of the Faithful

In the last chapter we discussed the right to dissent in the light of the principle, "rights derive from nature". The application of this principle to priests is of particular importance. It means that priests have the rights that are consistent with the nature of the Catholic priesthood, not those that go against. And the Catholic priesthood is ministerial in its nature; the Catholic priest is ordained for *service*.

The priest has been chosen, and has chosen, to serve. He has therefore the right to serve, and the right to all those things that enable him to serve God and his people better.

But just as the priest has the right to serve, so he has the obligation to serve. Rights derive from nature; so do obligations.[1] In freely accepting God's call to be a priest, he has also freely accepted the obligations that accompany the priesthood: for instance, the obligation of obedience (c. 273) or that of celibacy (c. 277). As regards the priest's teaching mission, the nature of the Catholic priesthood confers the right to teach, but not the right to teach anything, or to teach whatever one likes. On the contrary this right to teach is conditioned by the freely assumed obligation to teach what the Magisterium presents as authentic Catholic teaching. Under the title of "The Ministry of the Divine Word", Book III of the Code says, "The mystery of Christ is to be faithfully and fully presented in the ministry of the word, which must be founded upon sacred Scripture, Tradition, liturgy and the Magisterium and life of the Church" (c. 760).

Rights and obligations are interconnected. They condition each other mutually, not only in the same person but also as between

---

1 As we saw earlier (p. 25), callings of *service* — the medical profession, the teaching profession, the priesthood, etc. — are more strongly characterised by obligations than by rights.

To approach any such way of life with an awareness that obligations are going to outweigh personal rights, is a sign that one is approaching it *vocationally*, i.e. with a real purpose of service. To approach it with an excessive concern for personal rights and with a tendency to place them before obligations, betrays a lack of true spirit of service. It is a sign that one is approaching that way of life with too much self-concern; a true proper vocation is not present or else is not being answered properly.

different persons. If a priest has a special obligation to serve, this is because other persons — the rest of Christ's Faithful — have a special right to his service (cf. Chapter 3). That is why dissent, in the case of a priest, is never a purely personal matter. Dissent in a priest is bound to have consequences not only on his own personal faith and communion with Christ, but very particularly on the faith and life of the people whom he is called to serve. His dissent may violate *their rights*.

The right to guidance

Not all priests are law-givers. Properly speaking, only Popes and Bishops give laws; and even so their power as legislators is severely limited. They cannot enact laws that go against the natural law or the law constituted by Christ. They are basically custodians and servants of the law of Christ.

Not all priests are law-givers. All priests however are *"law-guiders"*, in the sense that all priests have the mission to guide people in the law, and people have the right to find in each priest a sure and qualified guide in the law of Christ and the Church. This indeed is what they expect of a priest.

It can help if we take a few examples from secular fields. What do people expect from a doctor? Sound medicine. They expect a doctor to know sound medicine and to administer it. They do not expect him to treat them as guinea-pigs testing out on them the latest theories he has heard at some medical congress or read in a physician's journal.

Not only do they expect sound medicine from doctors; they have a right to it. If a patient goes to a hospital and puts himself in the hands of the doctors there, he has a right to sound medical treatment. If he were to be made a subject of medical experimentation without his consent, if his health were to be harmed by unsound medical practice, his rights would have been violated and he would have a claim in law for damages.

It is precisely in order to protect people's rights to sound medicine that medical schools are set up, and that the teaching there is in some way supervised so that they turn out true and well-qualified doctors and not amateurs or quacks.

Professional knowledge

Professional knowledge is highly rated today. People feel the need for qualified and specialised knowledge in areas where their own knowledge is inadequate or non-existent. People go to an architect and expect him to know about the construction of houses. They go to a mechanic and expect him to know about motor engines and how to make them work. They go to a lawyer and expect him to know the laws of the country. The lawyer's client, for instance, may have had an apparently profitable business deal put to him. He is attracted, but he has his doubts about aspects of its legality. Is it within the law? He goes to consult his lawyer and expects his lawyer to know. If his lawyer did not know, he would regard him as incompetent.

People expect to be told definite things by professionals. This house can be built this way or it cannot. This engine can be fixed or not. This is legal, or it is against the law. They expect professional knowledge. They expect professional competence.

"Ask the priests".

If people listen to a priest preaching or go to consult him personally, it is because they expect him too to have specialised knowledge. The priest, after all, is a professional is his own area. It is for this that he has gone through his priestly training: not just to satisfy his personal curiosity or intellectual hunger, not just to know for himself, not even just to come closer himself to God, but to be in a position to *serve* others within the specific area of his professional competence. And, in terms of professional knowledge, his area is the Gospel and the law of Christ and of the Church.

The priest, in his professional knowledge, does not regard everything as certain. But he should know what is certain in matters of belief, and present it as certain; and know what is a matter of opinion and present it as such. In matters of conduct, he should know what is in accordance with the law of Christ and the Church, and what is against it.

People have their questions and problems in matters of faith and morals. They look to the Church and its priests for guidance. They have the right to ask, and they expect to be given an answer.

"Interroga sacerdotes legem", we read in the prophet Haggai (2:12): ask the priests for an answer on points of law; and the priests gave an answer. So, canon 762 affirms that "the people of God are first united through the word of God, and are fully entitled to seek this word from their priests" (cf. c. 213).

People are not favourably impressed, but just the opposite, if a priest says, "I do not know what is right or wrong", in areas where he *should* know, because he should possess the knowledge that Christ revealed and communicates for men's guidance through his living voice in the Church. People expect that priests, like Christ himself (Mt 7:29), will speak authoritatively in matters where the Church speaks with Christ's authority.

Taking decisions for others?

Some priests seem reluctant to give clear guidance on the grounds that this would mean *imposing a view* on people or *taking a decision* for them. An architect does not impose a view on his client when he tells him that it is possible or not to build a ten-storey building on a particular site. A lawyer is not imposing a decision on a client when he tells him that the business deal he is thinking about is against the law. Nor does a mechanic impose a view or take a decision for his client when he tells him that his car brakes are worn and may fail at any moment. In each case it is the client who will make up his mind to accept the professional opinion given or not. It is the client who will take his own decision. But when he freely went to the professional man or the expert in the first place it was precisely in order to get more information — reliable information — so as to be in a better position to come to a mature and well-informed personal decision.

When a traveller, at a road junction, asks an A.A. guide which is the road to a particular town, he does not feel imposed on when the A.A. guide tells him; nor does he think that any decision has been made for him or the responsibility of deciding taken out of his hands. On the contrary, he feels relieved, he feels freer to travel, because he now has information he lacked before. Now he can make up his mind more freely than in his previous state of uncertainty.[2]

If the A.A. man were to reply to the traveller's question, "The way to Camden? Sorry, I haven't the slightest clue", the traveller would probably feel strongly tempted to write a letter to the A.A.

---

2 If he had *preferred* to remain uncertain, he clearly would not have asked the way. The point applies: people who do not want the Church's guidance, do not come seeking it. Those who do come seeking it, are entitled to have it.

complaining about Officer So-and-So's ignorance and asking them to please ensure that their guides can *guide*).

Follow your conscience

Imagine what sort of letter would be written if the reply was, "The way to Camden? Yes, I know. Or at least my Association says it knows. But I wouldn't dream of conditioning your freedom by giving you any directions. After all, you are mature enough to decide for yourself. Just follow your conscience; that's my advice ...".

I do not know if this is an unfair parody of how some priests today fulfil their role as preachers, teachers and guides, in homilies and talks, or in person-to-person counselling in the rectory or the confessional. But I would like to make a few points about the not infrequently given pastoral advice, "Follow your own conscience":

a) when a person is told to follow his conscience he is not being told to do anything he chooses. "Follow your conscience" is not an equivalent to "Do whatever you like". *In no way!* "Follow your conscience" means: "Do what your conscience, listened to in all sincerity, tells you to be right. Avoid what your conscience, listened to in equal sincerity, tells you to be wrong".... And, since the experience of all of us is that what we would like to do is quite often judged by our conscience to be *wrong*, following one's conscience can be a very demanding matter indeed.[3] The person who sincerely follows his conscience will often have the impression of going in a direction that a large part of him does not in the least feel like following.

b) "Follow your conscience" is, in any case, a *non-contribution*, as far as advice goes. It solves nothing, precisely because it says nothing new. The Church has always taught that people should follow their conscience — that they are morally bound to do what they think is right and morally bound to avoid what they think is wrong;

c) and *that* is what people are not sure about; that is precisely *why* they seek advice. Hence their constant questions addressed

---

3 It is peculiar that some people who receive the answer, "You can follow your own conscience", in reply to an enquiry about contraception, seem to conclude, "that means it is OK for me to practise contraception"! I wonder if people who do practise contraception are really *listening* to their conscience. . . . Who knows? What is certain is that if a person is *not* listening to his conscience, he clearly cannot be said to be following it.

to priests: "What is right? What is wrong?", they keep asking. "What pleases God and what displeases him? What leads to heaven and what leads away from it? Does the Church not have anything to say, any guidance to give me on this matter? ... I have come to you because you are a priest, and I suppose you are knowledgeable in this field. Or have your studies taught you nothing?"

If the stock answer of priests consulted about moral problems becomes "Follow your conscience", why should people go to consult them at all? It is an answer not worth having.

"But, Father, how can you tell me to follow my conscience? My conscience brought me to you! What is the use of your clearly telling me to follow my conscience if my conscience does not clearly tell me anything?! My conscience is in doubt; it is perplexed. I am not sure what is right or wrong in this matter, and I came to you because I thought you would know"....

When all is said and done, the non-contribution of "Follow your own conscience" can be a cover-up formula, a handy way of evading one's duty to give people the guidance they have a right to.

"But — a priest is not supposed to make people's minds up for them". True, if by this is meant that a priest has no right to take decisions for others. But, if a person comes to a priest precisely because his mind is *"unmade"*, i.e. because he cannot put the elements present in it together in a way that makes sense and enables him to see the moral issues clearly, then the priest can and should help him distinguish the right and wrong aspects of the matter. Once the person has sorted out his mind and found his moral bearings, then *he* takes his own decision. The priest has taken no decision for him. The priest, in his qualified consultant's capacity, has simply given him the technical information he sought as a prelude to his personal decision.

Quite a number of priests seem to have thought themselves into a tangle on this point. They justify their refusal to give concrete moral guidance with the argument that they want people to be "mature" Christians, unafraid to face up to their personal responsibilities. It is a pseudo-argument. A truer analysis of the matter suggests that it is *the priest* who is not facing up to his personal responsibilities and who seems afraid to exercise the function of a qualified guide that people expect to find in him.

A compassionate ministry

This is not meant to suggest that the Church or its priests should have a ready answer for each and every moral situation. Of course not. There certainly are occasions when a priest can and should decline to give *concrete* advice, and can and should say, "I cannot tell you exactly what is right or wrong in the particular case you have put to me. You will have to judge that for yourself". This occurs frequently enough in finer matters of justice (cf. Lk 12:13f), where the *exact measure* of right or wrong is hard to determine. For instance, an employee has been embezzling money from the company he works for, and now he wants to make restitution. But he is not sure of the exact amount to be restituted since he feels (rightly so, it seems) that his firm has unjustly denied him certain salary increments. The priest does not have to determine the precise amount of restitution. In such a case he can and should tell the person to decide for himself, to follow his own conscience.

But such advice can never be rightly given in major and clear matters of morality. No priest can tell a person "Follow your conscience" if that person is consulting him about committing murder or rape or adultery, for instance. The same holds good when the consultation is about pre-marital sex. And the same, when it is about contraception.

Faithfulness to every aspect of his pastoral ministry demands that a priest be clear with people: "This is wrong. That is a grave sin". Where is compassion in all of this? It is emphatically present precisely in that if people are helped in this way to be truly aware of their sins and to be truly sorry for them, they can be forgiven time and again; time and again. And so, in the Sacrament of Pardon, they continually meet God's unfailing mercy. Compassion in pastoral ministry is perfectly compatible with clarity in doctrine. Jesus gives us the example: for instance, in his compassionate but direct way of dealing with the adulterous woman (Jn 8).

For a priest to silence the objective gravity of a sin is false compassion. It could be compared to that of a doctor who, in order to spare a patient mental distress, does not tell him that he has a serious disease.

The doctor's compassion might be justified if the disease in question were incurable. But his silence would not only be unjustified, it would be irresponsible, if he were not to tell a patient he has a serious disease that *can be cured!*; that can be cured provided precisely that the patient is prepared to undergo the proper treatment.

Sin *can* be forgiven. And gravely sinful habits can be *cured*. But they will not, if people are led to believe that they are not sinful, or that they are not grave. They have to be told clearly: that is a sin; and (if it is so) a big sin. But God's mercy is bigger still. Keep on fighting, keep on trying, keep on struggling to avoid the occasions, keep on confessing, and in the end you will see how God's grace enables you to conquer.

The priest's compassion does not mean pretending to people that the effort and burden of following Christ are not there. It means showing them how trust and docility make the burden lighter, and faith and hope make the effort seem more and more worthwhile.

The priest's professional competence

When a priest passes on the certain knowledge that comes from faith and proper theological study, he is not showing arrogance or self-assurance. He is showing assurance in Christ, and in Christ's Church. And this, I repeat, is what people expect of a priest and are surprised if they do not find. Just as people might be surprised if they ask a person with a watch for the time. "The time? Sorry. I just couldn't tell you.... You see, I trust my own watch so little ...".

Since the priest whose advice in a major matter is, "I can't say. You just follow your conscience", is letting people down and disowning his professional competence, perhaps we should say a few more words about that priestly competence to which people have a right.

The priest's competence is of course a unique thing. It derives in part from his ordination and mission; and in part from his personal formation and training.

Ordination makes a priest competent, i.e. makes him able to consecrate and to forgive sins (cf. PO, 2), and at the same time gives him a special competence to teach and lead people in the way of Christ.

His competence in relation to the sacraments is essentially God-given. For instance, he does not have to learn how to consecrate;[4] it is a power given to him from above.

In order to teach and to lead, however, he *does* have to *learn* the way of Christ, the mind of Christ, the law of Christ. What

---

4 Beyond knowing the words to be said, and the matter to be used.

he has to learn also comes from above. It is also *given*, with an *objective content*, which his mind needs to assimilate, through study based on faith (which is what is meant by theological study). Only if he studies and learns in this way will he be competent to pass on the truth and the law of Christ to others.

Proud and intolerant?

A priest should be aware of his competence. He should be sure of his principles. He should be conscious of the clarity and beauty and power of the way he has to teach.

But, is this not pride? ...

Why should it be pride on a priest's part to present himself as one who knows the teaching of Christ? Do people call a doctor proud because he professes to known medicine? Do they expect him to be so humble that he disclaims all medical knowledge?

In some church circles, nevertheless, there exists an impression that any claim to certainty in matters of faith and morals is a sign of a proud and intolerant spirit, while the attitude that everything is a matter of opinion shows humility and a liberal approach full of respect for others.

The fact of the matter is just the contrary. The act of faith — that Christ stands behind his Church's teaching authority — is an act of humility. It is the humility of the mind that is prepared to look up to a Truth that is greater than itself.

The maximum regard for others and respect for their freedom is shown in setting that Truth before them: not as *my* opinion; as *Christ's*! Each one will then decide whether he or she accepts that teaching as coming from Christ, or not.

I like faith; and common sense. I dislike judging any person; that is something that can be properly done only by God and, hopefully, by the person concerned. With that in mind I would add a comment which is meant to be helpful, not harsh. That attitude of superior open-mindedness with which some members of the clergy turn any and every point of Church teaching or authority into a matter of opinion ...: it makes one wonder whether what parades itself under the guise of liberal spirit and humility is professional ignorance (they did not learn what their profession required), or moral cowardice (they are afraid to say what they believe), or simple loss of faith (they do not believe what they learned).

Wanting to be certain

Each Catholic, then, will and must decide in the end according to his personal conscience. Each one must take his own decisions. But he has the right (and the duty) to make an informed decision. And so he can and should look for guidance to the Church, as teaching and ruling in the name of Christ; and to the Church's priests as competent teachers of the law of Christ and the Church. He is not ignoring or renouncing his conscience in seeking guidance. He is *informing* it so as to be able to come to a mature personal decision based on the maximum available certainty.

The "search for certainty" is of course also under fire today. Disparaging references are often made about it as if to seek certainty denoted a lack of character, and were a sign of psychological or intellectual immaturity; and the suggestion is frequently put forward that each one should be mature enough to face up, on his own, to the uncertainties of life, and to work out his own problems.

Of course each one must work out his or her own problems. But most people do not prefer to solve them "on their own", if they have a source of trustworthy information to hand. They prefer to consult.

Most people do not prefer uncertainty. They prefer certainty — if it can be obtained. If it cannot and one has to move in the dark, one does so. But it is not the situation most of us prefer to be in.

People moving in the dark grope along with their hands outstretched before them, or shuffle hesitatingly forward with their feet. They want to be certain what is there, and yet their eyes do not tell them. They want to be certain there is an open road, not a brick wall or a precipice. Their eyes don't give them information, and so they have to rely on their hands and their feet. If they had someone beside them so familiar with the road that he could walk it in the dark — or could see in the dark — they would probably be happier to rely on him and to be led by the hand. Would it be immaturity to let oneself be led so?

Self-reliance is a virtue — up to a point. Self-reliance to the point of not being prepared to accept *any* outside advice is no longer a virtue; it is a sign of unthinking stubbornness, or of pride: which are of course themselves proofs of immaturity.

Few people push self-reliance to the extent of refusing to consult maps or road-signs when they are travelling along unfamiliar roads. Yet quite a number of people who will readily let themselves be guided by an inanimate road-sign, baulk at consulting or listening to a living source of information; basically, they just don't like "being told" what to do by someone else....

Whether it is reasonable and a sign of maturity to follow someone else's advice depends evidently on the grounds one has for trusting that person. When the "Someone Else" telling us what to do is Christ, then the greatest reasonableness and the greatest maturity are shown in wanting to listen to his Voice and to follow it.

The living Voice of Christ, speaking to us in the Church — in Scripture, in Tradition, in the Magisterium — is our surest guide. People have the right to hear that Voice. Priests have the duty to echo it.

★ ★ ★

In summary, then, the priest's role as guide and teacher binds him:

— firstly, to know and communicate the mind and law of Christ, of the Church, as taught by the Magisterium, without obscuring or casting into doubt what the Magisterium itself presents as clear and certain; and without communicating his own personal difficulties or doubts (just as a doctor seeks not to communicate to his patients any germs of illness he may personally have). "The lips of the priest ought to safeguard knowledge" (Malachi 2:7).

— secondly, to realise himself, and to point out to others when necessary, the consequences of not accepting some important point of Church teaching or discipline; i.e. the rupture of full communion with Christ, the undermining and the danger of eventual collapse of one's whole Catholic faith and life.[5]

If someone says that all of the above reasoning is based on insecurity, on not being sure of oneself, I agree. I am *not* sure of myself, not at least where salvation is concerned. But I am sure of Christ. I am sure that he speaks to us in the Church, and sure too that if we make every effort to follow his voice, we may yet make it to heaven. And that is what matters. Making it to heaven is the one unresolved problem in each of our lives that we simply have to work out correctly. We cannot afford to flunk that one. And we won't work it out on our own.

---

5 Cf pp. 62ff.

8

Law as a Gift

Man could have been created a lawless creature in a lawless world. It would have been a miserable state: a living being without purpose or direction, at the mercy of random external forces and enslaved to conflicting internal desires and passions; a being with no bond or norm — neither of love nor of justice — by which to relate to others; nothing but meaningless strife inside and outside.

God did not make man so. He placed him in a world that has a basic order expressed in physical laws; and he put him there to shape it further. In doing so man was to humanise the world, and to humanise himself, giving created things a moral character and purpose that would be a further reflection of God's wisdom and goodness.

God made man rational and free: capable of discovering the divine plan and potential of creation, of freely shaping creation according to that plan, and so fulfilling himself. God made man for a definite goal. He gave him the gift of freedom to control his actions, and the gift of law to guide his freedom. Freedom needs law. Freedom that does not know what to choose or where to go, is useless; or, worse, self-destructive. Freedom calls for trustworthy directions. It calls for law.

Law is a gift of God to man. It is a gift by which God indicates to man his loving designs. We can distinguish three levels or stages of this gift: the Law of Nature, the Law of Moses, and the Law of Christ.

The Law of Nature

This is the Natural Law which, as the Apostle Paul says, is written on all men's hearts; to which fact, he adds, conscience bears witness (Rom 2:15). Through intelligent reflection and through listening to his conscience, man discovers the law of his nature; the way he should live, the direction he should follow, in order to fulfil his natural human potential.

Conscience is the echo of the Natural Law, its first spokesman. Conscience too is an inestimable gift of God, a divinely designed security system to guide us along the right way, to alert us to the danger of moral harm, to safeguard us against straying into roads of self-fustration and self-destruction.

Conscience is to be respected and obeyed. If one does not obey conscience, if one subordinates conscience to pride or selfishness, (if one does *not* subordinate it to the truth), if one manipulates conscience, one rejects the gift of law, one sins against the light, one commits moral suicide and is left defenceless against self-centredness and the whole process of human frustration.

The Law of Moses

God's purpose, however, was not that man should just live on the level of nature. He had further and higher designs for man: designs that were not, as such, written into human nature. They had to be revealed.

The Revelation began with the Patriarchs. The Law of the first Covenant was given by God to Moses and through Moses to the nation of God's choice. It was the law to guide Israel in its life as the people selected to receive the fullness of God's promises in due time.

By the standards of the Law of Christ, by which it was eventually to be replaced, the Mosaic Law is imperfect. Yet we have much to learn from the Old Testament: not so much from the dispositions of the Law itself as from the dispositions of the Chosen People *towards* the Law.

The Israelites were deeply penetrated with the conviction that the Law, which they had received as a Pilgrim People wandering in the desert on their way to the Promised Land, was a sign and a proof of God's special favour towards them.

Possession of the Law make them privileged among the nations, as Yahweh himself reminded them: "What great nation is there that has laws and customs to match this whole Law that I put before you today?" (Deut 4:8). This law is a gift no other nation has, and its superiority will be a cause of envy among other peoples: "When they come to know of all these laws they will exclaim: No other people is as wise and prudent as this great nation!" (Deut 4:6).

For the Jews, the Books of the Law contained the wisdom of God revealed to men (cf. Sir 24:23-29). Knowledge of the Law was a privilege and an urgent duty. Observance of the Law was a source of blessing, and marked each one's free response to God's Covenant. For the pious Israelite the Law was not a yoke but a divine favour and a privileged gift to be jealously guarded: "This is the book of the commandments of God, the Law that stands for ever; those who keep her live, those who desert her die. Turn back, Jacob, seize her, in her radiance make your way to light: do not yield your glory to another, your privilege to a people not your own. Israel, blessed are we: what pleases God has been revealed to us" (Bar 4:1-4).

The Law of Christ

The Law of Christ is the supreme gift, the final revelation of God's wisdom, goodness and purpose. It points out to man a new way; it makes of him a new being and gives him a new life. The new People of God are a chosen race, a royal priesthood, a consecrated nation, a people set apart, called out of darkness into God's wonderful light (1 Pet 2:9), so as to share the divine nature (2 Pet 1:4), and thus become possessors of the glorious freedom of the children of God (Rom 8:18-21).

The Law of Christ makes us freer — for a far greater destiny. The Law of Christ is a divine gift, like the Law of Moses, though incomparably superior. If the Jews, in their better moments, were grateful for the Law of Moses, we should be far more grateful for the Law of Christ. But our gratitude has to rest precisely on the fact that the Law of Christ *is* a law, telling us what to do and what not to do. The Law of Christ, as any other law, has its objective content and its demands: at times hard demands.

Some people, as we have seen before, seize on St James's phrase describing the Gospel law as "the law of perfect freedom" (Jas 1:25) as if this meant that the Christian had a licence to do whatever he felt like. This of course is totally false. The Christian law of freedom makes demands that are very explicit and far from easy. For instance:

> we must keep our hearts free from all covetousness (Lk 12:15; Mt 6:19-21, etc.)
> we must forgive others and avoid judging them (Mt 6:15; 7:1)
> we must avoid impure looks and desires (Mt 5:28)
> we must respect the indissolubility of marriage (Mt 19:6)
> we must obey Christ speaking to us through those in authority in his Church (Lk 10:16)
> we must receive his Body — but never unworthily (Jn 6:53; 1 Cor 11:27-30)

The Commandments are the way of freedom because they are the way of truth. In John's Gospel we are told that if we know the truth, the truth will make us free (Jn 8:32); but to that must be added the clear rider of John's first letter that the truth is not in the person who does not keep God's Commandments (1 Jn 2:4).

The privileges of Christians

Unless we observe the obligations of the Law of Christ we are not entitled to enjoy its privileges. Great indeed are the privileges of this law, and worth dwelling on — much more than on its obligations.

Christians have the right to all the means of becoming God's children (cf. c. 213). As a result of their personal sanctification, they have the right and mission to exercise their royal priesthood, lifting up the world to God (cf. c. 225).

The gift of law and the need for law appear precisely in the fact that the law expresses and protects our access to Christ. We will look on that law as a gift in the measure in which we want to come to Christ and possess what he has to give us.

God offers himself to man! This is the incredible gift that Christ reveals and that Christ represents. Christ is God offering himself to men, in and through his Church. The Church lives with the life of Christ and communicates his life. Communion with Christ is only properly achieved in and through the Church. The fuller our communion with Christ in all the aspects of the Church's life and worship, the more we enter into the glorious freedom he has won for us.

If we are hungry for God's gift of himself, for communion with Christ, then we will want this gift in all its sources.

We will seek it, wonderingly and gratefully, in his Word in Sacred Scripture.

We will seek it with no less wonder in the sacraments; above all — with the greatest reverence and gratitude — in the Holy Eucharist.

We will seek communion with Christ's Mind, with his Truth, in the teaching of the Church.

And we will seek communion with his Will in the law and discipline of the Church.

If the Israelites of old felt privileged at being possessors and followers of the Law given to God through Moses, how much more privileged should we feel at possessing the law given by Christ, that comes to us through his Church and brings us to Him through his Church.

How is it that this sense of privilege — and even more than privilege: of awe and wonder — seems to be lacking in the Church today?

Should we too not have a sense of amazement at being God's chosen people; and at God's closeness to us: a sense of awe at being able to offer to God something much more than the Paschal Lamb; at being fed by something much more than Manna: awe, especially, at being taught and led by God through those in the Church who teach in his name and exercise authority in his name?

If today we too often see a careless approach to the Eucharist, is this not a sign of weakened faith in Christ's Presence in this sacrament? Many people do not seem to realise that it is Christ whom they touch when they touch the Eucharist; Christ that they are fed by when they eat the Eucharist.

If we too often come across a hesitant or reluctant approach to church authority — to the Magisterium, to church law — is this not also a sign of a weakened faith in Christ's Presence in his Church? That reluctant response to church authority is, in the end, a loss of sense of being led by Christ; or an unwillingness to be led by Him.

Faith enters here; of course it does. Faith enables one to discover the sanctifying presence of Christ. The Eucharist *is* Christ; that is why it is the Holy Sacrament. The Bible is not Christ; yet it too is holy, because Christ — God — speaks to us in it. Only those who regard it with faith see in it the *Holy* Bible. And in a real way — however different the order — the law of the Church is holy; holier than the holy Law of Moses.

The law of the Church is holy. It is not inspired, as Scripture is. It is not infallible, as the Magisterium is. But it is holy, because it speaks to us with the authority of Christ and behind it stands his holy will. "Whoever listens to you, listens to Me...". "Whatever you bind on earth will be considered bound in Heaven"....

The Law of the Cross

But (the objection may come) surely it is not being suggested that Christ stands behind every single church law and every expression of church authority? No, not quite. But, precision is needed if we are to answer this objection adequately.

There may be in the present (there certainly have been in the past) exercises of ecclesiastical authority which are unjust, and which a person *should* oppose in conscience. Joan of Arc's resistance to the church authorities trying her is a case in point that shows how such resistance may even be a sign of holiness.

But I would suggest that such cases are rare, extremely rare; and that, such cases apart, an essential condition of true communion with Christ, which is also a condition of apostolic fruitfulness, is wholehearted and joyful acceptance of authority in his Church.

Christ's Truth stands behind the teaching of his Church, just as Christ's Will stands behind the authority of his Church. Christ's Truth cannot lead men into error; we have that guarantee. But we have no guarantee that Christ's Will may not lead men into trials and hardship: the hardship, among others, of being called on to obey in something that they find unreasonable and perhaps personally repugnant. He himself went that way. He became obedient unto death (Phil 2:8) even though he found it repugnant in the extreme (Mk 14:33-36). Vatican II says that the Church, and therefore all Christians, "must walk the road Christ himself walked, a way of poverty and obedience, of service and self-sacrifice even to death" (AG 5).

Christ learned to obey, and found it hard. We also have to learn obedience. It is not easy, but it is made easier if we contemplate Christ's example and reflect on the great value he attaches to obedience. Contrariwise, it becomes very hard indeed if we see *no* reason for obeying, if obedience remains for us just an imposition or a limitation.

Christ made no promise either that his Church would always be governed with perfect prudence and wisdom, at least to human eyes.

An ecclesiastical law may easily appear — to me — unwise or imprudent. Does that impression of mine give me any grounds for thinking that God is not behind that law, or that he wants me to ignore or disobey it? Or could it be that I have yet to learn that God has foolish ways — foolish to our human eyes — that are wiser than human wisdom (cf. 1 Cor 1:18-25)?

Only the certain and absolute conviction that an ecclesiastical law is *unjust*, and that fulfilment would be displeasing to God because it would cause real injustice (not mere hardship) to others, could legitimise or compel disobedience. Anyone tempted to think he is faced with such a law would do well to reflect and ask himself if the hardship he senses — for himself or for others — may not be the simple Christian burden of the Cross — which Christ wants all men to carry, and which saves. "It is for us to glory in the cross of our Lord Jesus Christ, by which we are saved and set free".[1] The Law of Christ — the law of freedom — is also the Law of the Cross.

The key to so many difficulties lies here. We have no guarantee from Christ (nor should we need any) that every single law in his Church will be timely, wise and prudent. But we do have a guarantee not only that we will not be going wrong in obeying church laws, but that we will be doing something very good and very pleasing to him, by obeying.

"Whoever listens to you, listens to me". Divine words that we might well paraphrase as: "If you have a superior who issues an unreasonable, burdensome, trying, stupid law or order, then have I not given you enough grounds, in the Gospel and in my own example, for you to suppose that that order, with its clear element of the Cross, comes from me, and that I want you to accept it?"

It is always easy for a subordinate (who necessarily has only a partial view of things) to see a lack of judgment in a superior's decision. It is true that if the superior — Pope, Bishop or whoever — is guilty of imprudence or injustice in enacting or applying a law, he will have to answer for it to God. It is also true however, to go once more to that pregnant passage from St Paul, that God uses the foolish things of this world for his own divine purposes.

Perhaps what most often frustrates the divine purpose is not the possible foolishness of the superior so much as the actual lack of faith and love of the subordinate.

Faith and love: these are the first virtues that church discipline should call forth in those subject to it. This is the ultimate reason why church law is a gift: because *it makes it easy for us to prove our faith and love towards our Lord*. It provides us with the opportunity to exercise faith and see his authority behind a human decision; and to answer his will with our love.

"Love means deeds".[2] It means doing the will of the loved one. If we want to prove our love for God, church authority never makes it difficult for us to do so; just the contrary. If we are really keen to love Christ, then obedience to His Church becomes easy. If we find obedience to the Church difficult, it almost always comes down to a lack of keenness to love Christ.

---

1 Entrance Antiphon for Holy Thursday; cf. Gal 6:14.
2 Josemaría Escrivá, *The Way* (Dublin, 1986), 933.

Joy and evangelization

This suggests a point that we will have occasion to enlarge upon later (cf. Chapter 13): reluctant Christians will never evangelise the world. Why should anyone be attracted to a Church whose members appear to be permanently discontent and in constant protest against their own leaders? This is a major obstacle to evangelization: that Christians seem incapable of giving to the world the proof of joy in service, in obedience, in self-denial, as Christ found his joy in serving, obeying and denying himself.

If the Gospel spread like wild-fire in the first centuries, it was also because the early Christians gave the impression of being bearers of Good News: the joyful followers of One who carried the Cross out of love, who learned obedience through suffering (Hebr 5:8), and so saved us.

The early Christians were joyful people in a sad world; and their joy came from their freely following the demanding law of Christ as he had freely followed the demanding will of his Father.

It is in the context of how "God loves a cheerful giver" that Paul praises the Corinthians for their generosity towards those of Jerusalem, by which "you show them what you are, and that makes them give glory to God for the way you obey the Gospel ... and they are drawn to you on account of all the grace that God has given you. Thanks be to God for his inexpressible gift!", the gift of joy in the fulfilment of the Law of Christ (2 Cor 9:7-15).

* * *

The Law of Moses has been superseded. Man is left with the *Lex Naturae*, the Law of Nature, on which is built the *Lex Gratiae*, the Law of Grace or the Law of Christ.

Despite apparent contemporary resistance to the idea of natural law, it is not hazardous to affirm that the moment is here, or will very soon arrive, for a strong reawakening of a desire for a natural law.

As the sense spreads that everything which most matters to man — order, loyalty, respect, honesty, integrity, love, marriage, friendship, community — is tottering, so will men turn to look for a strong common basis on which to rebuild truly human values and a coherent social life (cf. Appendix 2).

Yet it is probably not hazardous either to affirm that the restoration of the natural order, of the *lex naturae*, can only be brought about by those who adhere most firmly to the *lex gratiae*.

It is a truth of always, but one that has special force today, that a fully human life can only be lived with the help of divine grace.

9

Law and the Holy Spirit

A longing for the Spirit would seem to characterise many Christians today. The upsurge of charismatic movements since the Council is but one sign of this. Now, there is no doubt that the thought of the Holy Spirit calls up a sense of freedom, movement, joy, spontaneity, enthusiasm, that seems to fit ill with the idea of law.

Some writers absolutise the contrast, and claim that the life and development of the Church, which have hitherto been subjected to law and legalism, must now be entrusted to freedom and the Holy Spirit. Phrases such as "the Church should be led by the Holy Spirit" are frequently heard; behind them is the implicit suggestion that the Church should be led by something "freer" than law, that the People of God should be led along charismatic ways of joy and freedom rather than along juridical ways of coercion or legal power.

The direct answer to this is that the Church *is* led by the Holy Spirit, but that part of the Spirit's leading is precisely through law. The Spirit does not rely on coercion, but does rely on our capacity to perceive the value of law, and on our free response to it.

Marching orders

Salvation history exemplifies this throughout. The Pilgrim People of old were led by the Holy Spirit (who, we should add, often led them along ways that must have seemed devious and illogical to their human eyes). But the Spirit was practical, and sent them both leaders and laws, as well as the constant exhortation to obey.

A pilgrim people, a people on the move, needs to move in good order, so that no one if possible gets left behind; so that all, especially the weaker, are cared for. A marching people needs marching orders, passed on by leaders who themselves are moving in unity of purpose and direction.

This applied in the Old Testament; and continues to apply in the New. The very spiritual dynamism of the new People of God calls for laws and leaders — to safeguard its life, to protect its members, to foster its unity, to ensure its expansion.

Who gives the marching orders in the Church? Who marks the

rhythm and direction in which the people of God should move? The Holy Spirit? — Agreed.

And who in the Church possesses the Holy Spirit? Through whom does the Holy Spirit speak? These are in fact two quite different questions that require separate and distinct answers.

Who in the Church possesses the Holy Spirit? The obvious answer is: every Christian who has retained the grace of Baptism, or recovered it if it has been lost. The Gospel phrase, "the Spirit breathes where he wills" (Jn 3:8) underlines the fact that only God knows those whom he has chosen and the individual gifts he bestows on each one for his or her personal salvation and sanctification. No one can claim a monopoly of personal graces or charisms; that is clear. It is also clear that if each one responds to the grace given to him personally, he in turn becomes a channel of grace for others.

Looking down the centuries, we see how the Holy Spirit has spoken — and speaks — giving good guidance and inspiration to the faithful, through many individual voices, through the work and words of saints, founders, spiritual authors, theologians....

But what if these voices are in disagreement? This, as we know, has happened and does happen. Then it is clear that not all speak with the voice of the Holy Spirit, for the Spirit of Truth (cf. Jn 15:26) cannot disagree with himself; he cannot leave his people bewildered by contradictory marching orders. Hence arises the great public gift — so essential to the welfare of God's People — of the divine protection of revealed Truth. Where this gift is concerned, the Spirit has willed to breathe in a particular direction and through a definite organ.

So we come to the second question, giving it a very concrete formulation. When it is a matter of clarifying the truth, of resolving a debate or disagreement about the truth, of declaring the truth definitively, who speaks with the voice and authority of the Holy Spirit? The answer is also concrete and clear: the Magisterium. The infallible Magisterium is a peculiar gift of the Holy Spirit to the Church, and it has its specific organs: the Pope, and the College of Bishops in union with the Pope. The Magisterium is given by the Holy Spirit as a *service* to the People of God.

A step back in time could be helpful here. Let us place ourselves in the shoes of the ordinary members of the faithful in, say, sixteenth century Germany or England. People were perplexed; and their perplexity was caused by some theologians and preachers who, with raised voices, were saying that man's nature is intrinsically corrupted, that grace does not make us truly pleasing to God, that Matrimony or Penance are not sacraments, that the Eucharist is merely bread and wine given a religious significance, that the Mass is blasphemy.... These were new voices, new opinions, in clear contradiction to the voices Christians had been hearing for centuries.

In such a situation, where confusion threatens, the thinking Christian asks himself: "But where is the Spirit of Truth, whom Christ promised us, in all of this? What does *he* have to say?" Those who heard the voice of the Spirit in the Magisterium remained in the Church. Those who listened rather to the voices of dissenting theologians and preachers left the Church.

A "second" magisterium?

Some theologians in recent years have attempted to stake a claim to a special and privileged share in the assistance of the Holy Spirit, such as would promote theologians to the level of a sort of "second" magisterium.

The suggestion they put forward is that church leadership — at least in doctrinal matters — is now to be divided between two elements: one, the hierarchy, generally more conservative; and the other, the theologians, more liberal.

The point at issue, however, is not which element or agent is conservative or liberal, but which possesses the Holy Spirit in the strict sense of possessing a divinely-backed mandate to speak and teach and guide the People of God in the name of Jesus Christ.

The Hierarchy possesses that special mandate;[1] the theologians do not. The work of theological research — if it is truly theological — is indeed a great service to the Church. But the claim made by some theologians that their work represents a second or parallel magisterium has no foundation whatever in Scripture or Tradition.

The Apostles were not "theologians" in the sense in which we tend to use the word nowadays. They were by and large unlettered men. Yet, at the Council of Jerusalem, they taught and legislated with full assurance and authority: "It has seemed good to us and the Holy Spirit" (Acts 15:28). They did not call in theological experts. They realised that they, as a body, had a special assistance from the Holy Spirit to give the Christian people true divine guidance. And they gave it.

---

1 See below, pp. 154ff.

Charisms

Everyone in the Church has a peculiar charism or grace, i.e. a special gift of the Holy Spirit, to help him fulfil his peculiar role in the life of the Church (cf. 1 Cor 7:7). It would be presumptuous for any person or category of persons to say that his or their charism is of greater utility to the Church than that of others. The hidden charism exercised by St Teresa of Lisieux, in her own lifetime alone, probably served the Church at least as much as the work of the most renowned catholic thinkers of her time.

What must be said is that possession of a charism carries no guarantee that it will be used well. Whether a gift of the Spirit is used well or badly depends on the dispositions of each one, especially on humility and docility (essential virtues if one is to respond rightly to the working of the Spirit), on an attitude of service and a readiness to subordinate one's own interests or preferences to a higher concern for the good of the community. That is how Paul concludes his remarks on the use of charisms: "Let everything be done with propriety and in order" (1 Cor 14:40).

So the good use of a charism is not something automatic or guaranteed — with one exception, a very important exception, which is in regard to the service or teaching charism of the Magisterium in its mediation of the truth to the faithful. The Church has a constitutional guarantee that the Holy Spirit will not allow that charism to be used to deceive the faithful or lead them into error.

Therefore, if there is a conflict between the Magisterium and a theologian about a point of doctrine, a Catholic should have no hesitation about which view God is calling us to heed. The Holy Spirit's protection covers the message relayed by the Magisterium to the faithful: "This is right; that is wrong. This is in accordance with the message of Christ; that is not".

It is true that the protection of the Holy Spirit does not extend to the prudence or even the justice with which the theologian personally may be treated. We should feel certain about the truth of the doctrinal issue; we can feel as we choose about the handling of the case, the propriety or otherwise of the tone of monitions addressed to the theologian, of sanctions inflicted on him, etc.

If a theologian feels that he — as distinct from his views — has been unfairly handled, without due process, by the church authorities, he may — or may not — have a case. The Holy Spirit does not necessarily guarantee that perfect justice will be done to the theologian or protect his interests. The Spirit protects the truth. He protects the interests of the broad body of the faithful.

An interior law?

There is a fringe area to this theme of Law and the Spirit that is full of vague affirmations; for instance, that the law of the Spirit (or the law of Christ) is "primarily an interior law"; or that the law of the Spirit is the law of freedom "precisely because its demands are not imposed from outside" .... While it is not easy to pin down the precise meaning of such statements, they do suggest a few points worth clarifying.

What exactly is meant, in this context, by the "law of the Spirit"? If it means something more than conscience, if the law of the Spirit is ultimately the law of Christ, then of course its demands *are* imposed from outside.

The law of Christ is something objective, just as Christ himself is Someone "objective". He exists, to begin with, as an "Outsider" to each one of us, though, by his grace and our free response, he wishes to become an Insider in our lives; i.e. to enter into us — if we let him — with his liberating law.

It is true that the law of Christ speaks to the heart, and response to it is meant to come from the heart. But the law of Christ is not an internal law in any sense that *it* comes from the heart.[2] The law of Christ is not "imposed" from outside, but it certainly *comes* from outside. Like the Incarnation, like Revelation (all work of the Spirit), it is something objective, something given, which men accept as it is, or reject; or try to turn into something different.

The Holy Spirit gives the gift. He also ensures that it is preserved in its purity and that men can always find it so, provided they know where to look and provided they are prepared to look for it there. But He will not stop individual men (except one) from making counterfeits of his message. If that happens all he does is to point out clearly — clearly, to those who have faith and humility — where his genuine message is to be found; and leave those whose vision is blurred with the counterfeit they prefer.

The grace of obedience

The fulfilment of the law of Christ is not a matter of enthusiasm, nor is it normally done without effort. The Holy Spirit can indeed facilitate our fulfilment of the law of Christ. The main way he does so however is by speaking clearly, by putting that law to us

---

2 It is the Natural Law which in a certain sense comes from the heart.

in plain and unmistakeable terms, and by communicating to us the inspiration and strength to obey. One of the most typical graces of the Holy Spirit is the grace of obedience. One of the commonest inspirations of the Holy Spirit is the inspiration to obey. These are also the graces and inspirations to which pride offers most resistance.

Here we can trace a clear sequence of gifts and graces. *Law*, as we saw in the last chapter, is a gift of God. *Preservation* of the law, in its purity, and in its sources, is a special action of the Holy Spirit (LG 27). Furthermore, *observance* of the law and, better still, *response* to the law, are particular gifts and graces of the Holy Spirit. Here again there is a gradation. Observance of the law could be no more than mechanical or external: mere servile obedience. The Holy Spirit inspires us to go beyond that: to answer the law with a personal response, not with the servile obedience of a slave but with the filial obedience of a son (cf. Rom 8:15). In this way the Holy Spirit "interiorises" the law within us. Once we recognise God's fatherly will in the law, we are in a position to welcome it lovingly into our hearts; and to respond to it, freely and filially, from our hearts.

"Where the Spirit of the Lord is, there is freedom"(2 Cor 3:17). If we want freedom, therefore, we must look for it where the Spirit is. We have to locate the area of freedom within which the Spirit works. The area of the freedom of the Spirit is the area of grace and truth. Grace and truth have limits set by the Holy Spirit: the limits of the truth he teaches us through his Church, and the limits of the sacraments and the law he administers to us through his Church. In order to be within Spirit-given freedom, we need to walk within these Spirit-set limits of grace and truth.

A second point to comment on — in the area of vague affirmations we have mentioned — is the underlying suggestion that an 'interior' law is somehow obeyed without much difficulty.

Conscience is an interior law by definition. Yet, as we saw in an earlier chapter, the demands of conscience are often peremptory and by no means easily obeyed. On the contrary, the person who takes this interior law seriously, who is determined not to ignore it but to obey it, often finds that he has to maintain a titanic struggle to follow his conscience. It is true that the demands of conscience do not come from outside. But the demands are there; and we have to impose them on ourselves — a difficult course; or ignore them — a suicidal course.

A few words about some concepts with which the Holy Spirit, willy-nilly, is often linked today: creativity, dynamism, dialogue.

Creativity

To be "creative" — to express oneself, to do "one's own" thing or "new" things — is one of the urges of the age. When it is a Christian who is being creative, especially in relation to matters of doctrine or worship, he often attributes this creativity to the Holy Spirit, the *Creator Spiritus*. The attribution is not to be lightly made.

The creativity of a Christian is both an important and a humble thing. It is important because God indeed counts on us to complete his work of creation and re-creation. It is humble because if it is to be effective, it must operate within God-given conditions. If it is not prepared to do so, it is not Christian creativity.

If the Holy Spirit is the Creating Spirit, then our contributions to what he does can be creative only if they retain the character of a *sub*-creation in relation to his work. Once the Holy Spirit has created something, he expects us to respect that creation with the nature and laws he has given it.

To tamper with the Natural Law is not to respect the work of the Spirit, but just the opposite. It is not creative but destructive. This is a criticism which must be made of "creative" approaches to morals nowadays that advocate such anti-natural practices as homosexuality, contraception or abortion.

In the re-creation which is Christianity our creativity must work even more within divinely-given limits.

When we reflect on Scripture and Tradition as works of the Spirit (DV 7-10), our reverence towards these sources of Divine Revelation grows. Then we realise that our creative role in their regard is not independent but essentially subordinate. It consists not in diluting or explaining away the message the Spirit has communicated (that again is destructive not creative), but in understanding, illustrating and passing it on, according to the authoritative interpretation and vivifying guidance of the Magisterium — another major creation of the Holy Spirit.

The Spirit — the demanding Spirit — is also working in and through church law and discipline. There he creates the challenging conditions within which each one of us can be renewed and sanctified so as to become a "new creation" in Christ (cf. 2 Cor 2:17).

A bishop may be a plodding figure, with nothing to him that the news media would today call "charismatic". His office, however, is charismatic; the Holy Spirit works through it. And the members of his diocese — priests and lay people — if they have faith, should find his decisions and indications charismatic: through them the Holy Spirit is reaching out to us, calling on our love and testing our faith. Charism, in such a case, has nothing to do with the bishops' virtue or ability; it has everything to do with our response.

Examples could be multiplied, especially perhaps in the field of liturgy. Let us mention just one. Each Mass is, in itself, a unique charismatic action because the Holy Spirit is at work in it. If a priest tries to turn the Mass into a matter of personal creativity to the detriment of the liturgical laws (given for the protection of the faithful), he is obtruding his personality and his whims on the work of the Spirit. On the altar the priest acts "in the person of Christ" (LG 10). And the sanctifying Spirit wants our attention in the eucharistic celebration to be drawn to the Person and redemptive action of Christ, not to the person and creative action of Father So-and-So.

Dynamism?; dialogue?

"The law of the Spirit is more dynamic". Dynamism means power; and in phrases such as that just quoted, it presumably implies effectiveness. If the law of the Spirit calls people together into unity — and if people come — then it is indeed dynamic. Not if the effect is the contrary.

Marching orders are meant to unite people, to call them to work and travel in unison and in the same direction; then they are dynamic. Marching orders are not more dynamic if they set each person marching off in a different direction.

It is easy to claim to be moved by the Spirit no matter what direction one is moving in; the history of Protestantism exemplifies this. What is worth pondering is whether a thousand contradictory voices, each claiming to speak in the name of Christ, can represent the dynamism of the Spirit . . .; or do they rather suggest the explosive fission of individual opinions run wild?

The Holy Spirit inspires us to act not so much independently as freely, as parts of the one whole, as members of the same Body. He draws scattered hearts, scattered wills, scattered minds into a unity of affection and a unity of purpose; the *cor unum et anima una* of the first Christians (Acts 4:32).

One may question if the Holy Spirit is present where there is unity without diversity; one can be sure he is not present where there is diversity without unity.

I recall the comment of a cleric referring to pastoral directives for the development of his diocese: "We would follow the Holy Spirit better if there were more dialogue between the bishop and each one of his priests. After all, both parties are temples of the Spirit".

There is an element of truth in this that bishops would do well to bear in mind. Members of a diocese, however, would also do well to remember that what makes pastoral work effective is not so much the mutual dialogue of superior and subordinate, as the personal dialogue of each one with God. What is needed is not that the bishop listens to me, but that I listen to God. The more a person is on the wavelength of the Spirit — the demanding Spirit — the more effective he will be, the more flexible, the more docile; and the less concerned to find others on *his* wavelength.

★ ★ ★

No one, we said earlier, has a monopoly of the Holy Spirit. But it is important to have some sure standard by which we can know if, without any monopoly, we at least possess him or not. St Augustine mentions one clear criterion of supreme importance: "In the measure in which we love the Church, we possess the Holy Spirit".[3]

---

3 *In Joann. Ev. Tract.* 32, 8. Cf. OT 9.

10

The Church: Juridical or Charismatic?

Law and Church: in some minds these two realities do not harmonise; they rather seem contradictory.

The "law opposed to Church" idea is often an expression of the "law versus freedom" syndrome that we examined in earlier chapters. Some people, feeling that law is restrictive of freedom, hold that law has no place in the Church since it is an enemy of the freedom that Christians are meant to have as God's children (cf. Rom 8:22). We tried to analyse the faulty thinking behind this, showing that law is necessary for individuals and for societies precisely in order to protect personal freedom, to protect freedom in mutual relations, and to protect rights against the arbitrary use of office or power.

Others, seeking deeper theological ground for their objection, claim that Christ founded an essentially spiritual Church, and that all the institutional and juridical structures present in the Church are a later human introduction out of harmony with the intention of Christ and with the original nature of the Church he founded.

This is scarcely a matter to be settled according to personal preference, i.e according to the type of Church that each of *us* might want or prefer. It is rather to be clarified by trying to see what type of Church *Christ* actually wanted and actually instituted.

Those who defend the thesis that Jesus wished to set up a Church of a purely spiritual, non-institutional, non-juridical nature, immediately run into two major difficulties: a theological difficulty and an historical difficulty.

The theological difficulty

The theological difficulty is that a purely spiritual Church would be completely out of keeping with the pattern of God's plan for our salvation, the plan of the Incarnation.

The Redemption of man was not accomplished in an invisible manner. It could have been. God could have chosen other ways than the Incarnation in order to save mankind. He could have justified each soul by a totally hidden process, communicating grace to each one directly. But in fact God did not choose such a purely spiritual way of saving man. God came to earth to bring about our salvation. And his coming was not invisible. God who is Spirit, chose to manifest himself materially. He chose to vest himself in matter, in order to save us. He chose to become Man, taking on a bodily nature that is tangible, audible, real. . . .

What was the scope of the Redemption he worked? He not only wished to free man from the power of sin and the devil. He also wished to give to man a new destiny: to call him to share in his divine Sonship through saving contact with his sacred Humanity.

He saved us by the merits of each one of his acts as Man-God, from his first baby wail in the manger to his last cry of agony on the Cross. But he also came to reveal himself, and to teach man by his words and example, and to sanctify them by his presence and power.

His self-revelation is already in operation during those thirty years of hidden life; and there is so much, so many lessons, for us to discover there. Nevertheless, his main self-revelation takes place in his public life, in the short space of less than three years. In those thirty months or so, he reveals himself more fully. He reveals himself as Lord of all creation, as Master of all mankind; as Divine Teacher, whose words are Truth and lead to Life; and as Divine Healer and Saviour who cures, feeds, frees, forgives, and calls men from death to Life, with the power of God.

For those thirty months men were enabled to hear the voice of no mere prophet, but the voice of God himself speaking in human language about divine and human things. They were able to question him and listen to his answers. They could be touched, cured, fed, led by him. They had direct immediate physical contact with God made man. . . .

That these immediate benefits could be received only by a few and over a short period of time was the necessary consequence of his having chosen one concrete physical body which, having moved among men, went up to heaven on Ascension Day. When God chose to dwell in the Human Body of Jesus Christ, a historical moment of encounter between man and God was realised. But God did not wish to limit this encounter to just one moment in history or to just a few privileged men. He intended the force and presence of his Incarnation to reach everyone everywhere. And so one sees the divine logic of his choosing to dwell in another Body — still his, but capable of becoming present in all places and all times: a Body that would still speak with his voice, still cure with his mercy, still feed with his flesh, still rule with his authority: the Mystical — though visible — Body of his Church.

The logic of the Church as the Body of Christ[1] is then simply the logic of the Incarnation continued. It is the continued application of a broad and fundamental principle that permeates the whole mode of our salvation — the *sacramental principle*, i.e. God's use of material and natural realities as means of communicating spiritual and supernatural goods and achieving spiritual and supernatural ends.

The Church is in the line of the sacraments, just as both Church and sacraments are in the line of the Incarnation. The principle of the sacraments is the very principle of the Incarnation: visible reality expressing and communicating invisible grace. In a true sense, the Humanity of Christ is a Sacrament, indeed the first sacrament. And in the logic of God's plans, the Church too has the nature of a sacrament.[2] It exists, visibly, tangibly, audibly, actively, so that all men of all times can have personal contact with the saving power of the God-Man.

The sacramentality of the Church is fundamental for understanding its visible or material nature. It is also a help for avoiding any 'scandal' at the defects which may appear in the organs that make up this Body of Christ; specifically in us men who are its members. Given our human nature, human defects are bound to appear. One should pray and work for their removal. It would be ideal if they were not there. Yet their presence does not necessarily render grace ineffectual or prevent its being communicated.

The sign used in a sacrament may not always signify as clearly as one would wish. The water used in Baptism is meant to signify cleansing; and therefore it itself should be clean. But God can use even dirty water as an instrument for bringing about the interior cleansing of souls. So the Church, a sign and an instrument. We see the visible people of the Church, and their defects. We do not see the invisible working of the Holy Spirit.

The incarnational or sacramental principle — spirit working

---

1 Cf. Note 1 to page 10.

2 Cf. the opening paragraph of *Lumen gentium*: "the Church, in Christ, is in the nature of sacrament — a sign and instrument, that is, of communion with God, and of unity among all men". And *Ad gentes* says that Jesus "founded his Church as the sacrament of salvation"(AG 5; cf. also LG 48; GS 42). The spiritual and the institutional aspects of the Church are harmonised, in Vatican II, in a thoroughly christocentric ecclesiology. The dialectical approach — of contrasting and opposing the material and the spiritual, the human and the divine — which characterises much of Protestant thinking, is basically a failure to accept the full implications of the Incarnation.

through matter — carries with it an inherent likelihood of causing scandal, at least to "over-spiritual" persons. God knew that if He chose to work through the Humanity of Jesus Christ, some would take scandal. The likelihood of scandal is immeasurably greater when he chooses to work through *our* humanity.

The historical difficulty

The second difficulty that the proponents of an exclusively spiritual Church run into is the fact of what Jesus actually did. What contrasts, what surprises in our Saviour's way of acting! To our human minds, it is full of mystery and paradox.

The hidden life of Jesus seems to have been characterised by peace and calm. His public life is filled with a pressing sense of urgency. There is an urgency in his actions (Lk 4:42-44; Mk 14:42), just as there is in his preaching and in his parables (Mt 24:42-44; Lk 14:21). He is acutely conscious of time (Mt 26:18; Jn 2:4; Jn 7:6; Jn 7:30; Jn 11:9; Jn 13:1) and resolutely sets himself to make good use of it (Lk 9:51; Jn 9:4; Jn 13:27).

And yet he is Lord of time, as he is Lord of space, as he is Lord of the entire world. As the Church sings on Holy Saturday: "All time belongs to him, and all the ages".

Christ has a lot to do, and yet he gave himself very little time to do it. He had a lot of ground to cover, and yet he did not move beyond one small corner of the Roman Empire.

He could have chosen to spend another thirty years, another sixty years, teaching, working miracles, forming his Apostles, bringing his word and his power to the ends of the earth. He was urgent to use his time; and yet he did not extend his time. He was urgent to go to other towns and places of Israel (Lk 4:43), yet he scarcely preached a word outside Israel.

His urgency is mysterious; and the mystery seems to deepen when we realize that it is an urgency to disappear from the visible scene (Jn 16:7).

How much more logical and effective — to our human way of thinking — if he who died publicly on the Cross before the whole of Jerusalem, had risen with equal publicity. What an impact on the Jewish people, and on the whole world! What a confirmation of our faith! And yet his Resurrection was hidden to all but a chosen few. He could have risen in public triumph. He did not choose to do so.

What did he mean by saying that it is better for us if he goes

(Jn 16:7)? We do not see it as that obvious. Surely it would have been better for us if he had stayed? How much more logical, to our minds, if he had not gone to heaven after a mere forty days, but had remained, with his risen and glorious body, as visible Head of the Church to the end of time. Our faith in him and our following of him would then be so much more concrete and so much easier.

He clearly has not wished our faith in him to be made easier in that way. He has wished it to be concrete indeed: faith in his real presence in his Church. But he has wished this faith to be subject to the particular difficulty that we are to believe in him present in his Church in and through, and even at times despite, those who make up this Church and especially those who rule it.

He left his new-born Church without his visible presence, but not headless and not without him. He, his power, his authority, his gifts, his grace, his worship, all remain in his Church; but remain in and through men.

To ensure the continuance of his work of salvation, Jesus did not choose pure spirits. He could have carried on his work through angels, as he had already used them to announce its initiation (Lk 1:11; 1:26; 2:9). After all, angels — being confirmed in grace — would have been much more reliable. One cannot imagine Gabriel carrying out his mission in a lax fashion, or running away from its responsibility (as did Jonah, for instance, or Demas: cf. 2 Tim 4:10). Yet he did not choose angels. He chose men: unreliable, unconfirmed men. And again he did not choose geniuses. Paul was an exception; and he was to come later. From the start, Jesus chose very ordinary and very weak men. The defects of the Apostles are so visible through the pages of the Gospel. And yet they, those defective, vain, cowardly, fishermen and villagers of Galilee were to be the pillars of his Church and the rulers of his People.

Jesus called disciples to himself, and from among these he chose twelve (Mk 3:13-14) who were to carry on his mission (Jn 15:16). He endowed them with power: with his power and the power of the Holy Spirit:

— to teach his saving truth to all nations (Mt 28:19-20; Acts 1:8);
— to govern in his name (Mt 16:18-19; Mt 18:18; Lk 10:16);
— to cleanse souls and to pardon and nourish them, and to offer the Sacrifice of his Death and Resurrection (Jn 20:22-23; Lk 22:19; 1 Cor 11:23-27).

Therefore, the claim that the Church as an institution, and concretely the Church with its hierarchical structure, was not in the thought and the intention of the historical Jesus, is contradicted by what history in fact tells us about the actions and the expressed purpose and design of Jesus.

The life of the Church from the start has been the experience of the presence and action of Christ — within and despite the limitations and defects or sins of men. There are therefore two ways of contemplating the Church's past history or its present life. With faith, and then we will see or sense Christ's work, and rejoice. Or with human outlook alone, which will limit us to seeing men's work and men's defects; and then we may easily become discouraged or scandalised.

The early Church

Alongside the historical facts of what Christ actually did, we should place the historical evidence of the actions of his first followers immediately after the Ascension and Pentecost.

From the very first moment the Christians appear as an organised community, united not only in faith and baptism (Eph 4:5), but also in government and discipline. The early Church appears from the start as a juridical, hierarchical, structured body. It has its overseers and rulers (Act 20:28; 1 Pet 5:3; 1 Tim 3:2, etc.) and these act with a full sense of authority, conscious of their power to organise (Tit 1:5), to govern and give laws (Acts 15:23ff; 1 Cor 6:1; 1 Cor 7:12ff, etc.), to judge and even to punish (1 Cor 4:18-21; 2 Cor 10:5-6; 2 Cor 13:10, etc.).

It is true that the bulk of positive church law developed after the time of Christ. This was inevitable, given the fact that positive law is meant to develop from life,[3] to correspond to life, to keep abreast of life, to keep life in line with objective right and justice.

It was only as the society of the Church grew that the need for church law also emerged. Ecclesiastical laws appeared in response to concrete situations and needs, and marked out the basic structures and main lines of stress[4] holding the fast expanding community together.

From the very start we see how law and administrative measures acccompany the spread of the Gospel. The Acts of the Apostles

---

3 Though it is not strictly speaking from life but from justice, that it takes its norm.

4 Stress or tension. For law always involves tension: the good tension of holding wayward man to the line and path of justice, and binding him to his fellow-men in the community.

give us examples of relatively minor points as well as of major matters. For instance the very living of the evangelical spirit of generosity soon gives rise to administrative problems. Spontaneous giving creates a fund. But once a fund exists it must be administered; and the administration in favour of the widows and poor becomes an especially time-consuming task. So deacons are appointed; and we get the first church administrators (Acts 6).

Someone has to be assigned to take Judas's place among the Apostles whom Jesus himself had chosen. One might well have expected a direct divine intervention, as happened in the choice of Paul. But no; Peter unhesitatingly involves the community in a human mode of choice. He reminds them how important this choice is. They pray that God will signify his preference; but they do not expect him to do so by any external miraculous sign. They go through an electoral process, and all accept the result as binding and as a sign that the Holy Spirit has chosen through their administrative action (Act 1:15-26).

As the community expands, problems requiring juridical solution keep emerging, especially when the Church, originally composed of Jews with Jewish ways, begins to admit Gentile converts, in fulfilment of its universal mission. This gives rise to the most noteworthy example of positive juridical action in the early Church: the Council of Jerusalem (A.D. 49-50), with its deliberations and its authoritative and binding decision to exempt pagan converts from a main requirement of the Jewish law (Acts 15).

In considering the growth of disciplinary and administrative legislation in the early Church, a main point to note is that the Apostles and elders, in exercising the function of lawgivers, clearly felt not only that they were fulfilling the mission given them by Christ, but that what they legislated came in fact from God as well as from them. It is enough to recall the striking words with which they announce the decisions reached at the Council of Jerusalem: "It has been decided by the Holy Spirit and by ourselves . . .". (And it is worth emphasizing that the decisions may were speaking of were basically *disciplinary* decisions, however great their theological overtones.)

The principle of the Incarnation

History, then, shows us what theology would lead us to expect: that Jesus, in order to perpetuate his saving mission on earth, followed the pattern of the Incarnation by founding a Church:

a divine and human society at one and the same time. A distinctive and unique society, therefore: a society composed of men — and of the Holy Spirit. A society with a supernatural end — men's salvation — but with a visible and tangible structure.

So if one asks whether the Church is meant to be charismatic or juridical, spiritual or hierarchical-institutional, the answer is: *both*.[5] Just as a sacrament is both material and spiritual; and the spiritual, in God's design, must necessarily pass through the material.

> The society structured with hierarchical organs and the mystical body of Christ, the visible society and the spiritual community, the earthly Church and the Church endowed with heavenly riches, are not to be thought of as two realities. On the contrary, they form one complex reality which comes together from a human and a divine element. For this reason the Church is compared, not without significance, to the mystery of the incarnate Word. As the asssumed nature, inseparably united to him, serves the Divine Word, as a living organ of salvation, so, in a somewhat similar way, does the social structure of the Church serve the Spirit of Christ who vivifies it, in the building up of the body (LG 8).

It cannot be over-emphasized that this simply continues the very principle of the Incarnation. Christ is God materialised, in one point of time and space. And the Church is the work and action of Christ materialised, throughout space and time (AG 5). A materialised though spiritual God. And a material though spiritual Church.

Christ reaches us through the Church; and we must reach Christ through the Church. Whoever wants Christ without the Church, wants to take Christ on his own conditions; and only gets — at the most — "part" of Christ, part of his Truth, part of his Grace, part of his Will and Love. Whoever wants to take Christ on Christ's conditions must take Christ "as a Whole" in and through the Church. Then he is in a position to receive *all* that Christ gives.

To "pick and choose" in the Truth of Christ, as mediated in the doctrine of the Church, is the approach of heresy. To pick and choose in the Will of Christ — as meditated in the law and

---

5 To see the 'institutional-juridical" as necessarily opposed to the 'spiritual-charismatic' is another example of that dualist tendency we commented on earlier, which makes some persons see opposition where a truer vision sees complementarity. Institutional and spiritual are no more necessarily opposed than are law and freedom, authority and conscience, common good and individual good.

discipline of the Church — is the schismatic approach. The schismatic, it should be remembered, remains one in faith, and one in worship and sacraments; but not one in discipline. There he breaks communion. He wishes to adhere to Christ's Truth, but is not prepared to adhere to fundamental ecclesial expressions of his Will. He divides Christ.

Making the Church holier?

Christ is God and Man, his Church is divine and human. Jesus willed to have a body, a true human body. And so he willed to be subject to its needs and structures and limitations. He willed to be subject to the laws of the body's growth (Lk 5:22). He willed to have a mouth for speaking, but also for food and drink, legs for walking, hands for working at the carpenter's bench and, in the end, to be crucified.

So, in choosing to found a visible Church — also his Body, but with members that are men — he willed a Body structured in a certain way, a Body designed to spread and grow in a visible world, a Body with material as well as spiritual needs. A Body too with suffering members and disfigured members; and even atrophied and dead members who can still be recalled to life.

The Church is not a human body which we have to perfect. It is a divine body, made up of human members who indeed need perfecting. But the divine elements in the Church remain all holy. And they can make us holy if we maintain a holy attitude towards them.

The Mass is the Holy Mass — even if the celebrant is the greatest and most unrepentant sinner. We cannot make the Eucharist holier. *We* are made holier in offering and receiving it. And we can offer and receive it in a holier *fashion*: with more faith and love.

Just as the action of Christ sanctifying us in and through the sacraments is all holy, so his action of teaching and leading us through the Church's Magisterium is all holy. We cannot make the teaching of the Church holier. We can make our attitude towards it holier; we can listen to it in a holier fashion, in other words with more faith and gratitude, hearing Christ's voice and guidance in it: "Whoever listens to you listens to Me".

Continuing the parallel with the sacraments, we could add that while men cannot make the Eucharist more holy, they can develop liturgical celebrations that make the holiness and sanctifying efficacy of the Eucharist more — or less — evident. Similarly, man cannot make the Word of God, as received in Scripture and Tradition and taught by the living voice of Christ in the Magisterium, more holy; but they can, through sound theological investigation, make its saving efficacy and meaning more apparent, or, through unsound investigation or speculation, obscure its power for salvation.

Just as happens with the sacraments, the real nature of the Church can be discovered only by the eyes of faith; a merely human scrutiny — the eyes of reason alone — will never reveal its true identity.

Christ is present in the Church as he is present in the sacraments, hidden under human forms and actions. Each day at the altar, the priest — acting "in the person of Christ" (LG 10) — pronounces the words "This is my Body" over the host, and shows it to the people. Then those with faith rectify the judgment that what they see is just bread. No; it is Christ. And recognizing him, they adore.

"This is my Body", Christ repeats to us each day as he presents his Church to us. It is also a call to faith; a call to rectify our natural judgment so that, where human eyes see no more than doctrines, rites, decisions and laws — words and actions of men — our faith sees Christ.

Judging humanly

The temptation to judge the Church and each aspect of its life in purely human terms will always be with us. It is perhaps especially with us in an age such as ours when trust in others seems to come hard to men. A great lover of the Church has written that we should not:

> judge the Church in a human manner, without theological faith. We cannot consider only the greater or lesser merits of certain churchmen or of some Christians. To do this would be to limit ourselves to the surface of things. What is most important in the Church is not how we humans react but how God acts. This is what the Church is: Christ present in our midst, God coming towards men in order to save them, calling us with his revelation, sanctifying us with his grace, maintaining us with his constant help in the great and small battles of our daily life.... We might come to mistrust other men, and each one of us should mistrust himself and end each of his days with a *mea culpa*, an act of contrition that is profound and sincere. But we have no right to doubt God. And to doubt the Church, its divine origin and its effectiveness for our salvation through its doctrine and its

sacraments, would be the same as doubting God himself, the same as not fully believing in the reality of the coming of the Holy Spirit.⁶

To oppose the Holy Spirit and the institutional Church, to say that no institution can take the place of the living presence of the Holy Spirit, is to miss the point of the Incarnation principle. The institution *is* the living presence of the Holy Spirit; the audible, visible, tangible presence of the Spirit through whom Christ continues his work among us and in us. The Church is, if not the incarnation, then the materialization of the work of the Holy Spirit.

When we are tempted to judge the Church or to react humanly to church teaching or authority, it is helpful to stop and reflect: if I had lived in Palestine two thousand years ago, how would I have judged Jesus of Nazareth? If I had met Christ in the flesh, speaking blunt and at times uncomfortable truths at me, making uncompromising demands of me, how would I have reacted to him?

Would I have reacted like the crowds of simple folk who, we are told, were attracted to him precisely because of his *authoritative* way of putting things (cf. Mt 7:29)? Or would I have reacted like the scribes and Pharisees, who would not go along with a Jesus who was not prepared to go along with them?

How would I have reacted if I had met Jesus in the flesh? It is not such a hard question to answer because I meet him each day in the Church, telling me to believe his Truth in this, or to do his Will in that. In reacting to the Church, I am reacting to Jesus Christ.

Saul of Tarsus saw an institution which he did not like, which he opposed and wished to destroy; and then he discovered that the institution is Christ: "I am Jesus and you are persecuting me" (Acts 9:5).

Modern dissenters could learn a lot from Saul's experience. The position of Saul, if not exactly that of dissent, was certainly one of violent tension *vis-à-vis* the Church. No doubt he had not sufficiently pondered the question: what is this institution I am in tension with? But he was given an answer to that question: an answer that drove a shaft of light through his mind and heart bright enough to enlighten the theological reflection of the centuries about the essential nature of the Church: I am Jesus and you are persecuting Me. Jesus identifies himself with his Church. He

---

6 Josemaría Escrivá, *Christ is passing by* (Dublin 1986), 131.

speaks the same message to the dissenters of all ages: what you are in tension with is Me.

It is not sound ecclesiology therefore to oppose charismatic and hierarchical gifts. The Hierarchy itself *is* a charismatic gift. Hierarchy, infallibility, Magisterium ... are not opposed to the working of the Spirit, but are tangible and concrete expressions of the Spirit's way of working.

The conciliar decree *Ad Gentes* on the Church's missionary activity has words that are very much to our point. Quoting *Lumen gentium*, it says, "through the ages the Holy Spirit makes the Church 'one in communion and service; and provides her with different hierarchic and charismatic gifts' (LG 4), giving life to ecclesiastical structures, being as it were their soul and inspiring in the hearts of the faithful that same spirit of mission which impelled Christ himself"(AG 4).

Passages truly worth noting. *Lumen gentium* sees hierarchical gifts on the one hand and charismatic gifts on the other, not in opposition to one another but proceeding from the one and same Spirit.[7] *Ad gentes* sees the Holy Spirit precisely giving life to church structures. Therefore these structures are living, are brought alive by the Spirit, and are instruments of the operation of the Holy Spirit who watches over and maintains the work of Jesus Christ. "The Holy Spirit preserves unfailingly that form of government which was set up by Christ the Lord in his Church" (LG 27).

Was Jesus anti-law?

It is clear then that the Church is, by divine will, a visible society. And a visible society is necessarily a juridical society: a visible society necessarily has laws. Christ wished his Church to be truly visible. He wished it to be truly spiritual. What he did not wish is that it be lawless.

It is of course quite false to suggest that Jesus was in any way anti-law. On the contrary, he clearly presents himself in the Gospel as a law-giver and as someone on the side of the law. He explicitly defended the law ("Do not think that I have come to abolish the law": Mt 5:17). He clarified it (Mt 19:3-9). He perfected it (Mt 5:22, 28, 32, 34, etc.). He eventually surpassed the Old Covenant and replaced it with the New. But he ratified all the main

---

7 And in certain cases coinciding in the same person or persons; e.g. the hierarchic and charismatic gift of infallibility.

commandments of the Old Law (cf. Mk 10:19), at the same time as he legislated new laws and commandments (Jn 13:24; 14:15; 14:21).

Naturally when we say that the Church is a juridical society by divine will, we are not saying that Jesus gave the Church all its laws. No. He gave it some of its laws; but what he particularly gave it is its juridical nature. He gave the foundation, and gave the Church the right and duty to organise itself on that foundation; and promised that in organising itself, it would enjoy special divine assistance (Mt 18:18).

In this Body of the Church, then, certain elements of the structure are foundational, i.e. have been put there by the Founder himself, with a specific shape and content, and are therefore permanent and unchanging (sacraments, papal primacy, episcopacy ...). Other elements are accidental; they have been introduced by men, and are left to men, to improve or disimprove, according to the measure of their wisdom and prudence or lack of it. And yet, even there, behind the possible or inevitable mistakes of men, Christ is still present, perhaps with the folly of the Cross, calling us to follow Him.

★ ★ ★

There is another aspect to this question that should be mentioned here, however briefly.

Some Christians today, even some priests, unconsciously "divide" Christ. They sincerely love the historical Christ. But they do not love the Church, failing to see that the Church is also Christ in history.

This is not just deficient ecclesiology; it is also deficient christology. It implies that Christ did not love us sufficiently to remain with us; that he has not been able to bridge the gap of time and place; that he is a remote and dwindling figure, progressively lost with the passage of the centuries.

Such a defective christology has its consequences. Lack of faith in Christ present in the Church leads inevitably to weakened faith in the historical Christ: his virginal conception and birth, his miracles, his Resurrection, his Divinity. . . . It leads to weakened faith in his presence and action in the sacraments; and, of course, to weakened faith not only in Scripture, but also in Christ's presence and action in Tradition and in the Magisterium. . . . One is left loving Christ at an ever-growing distance. His voice becomes harder to hear, his will harder to follow, his presence harder to find. He is no longer with us.

11

Authority, Power, Service

The Church, therefore, is not just a spiritual society; it is also juridical, with its institutions and its laws. Where there is law, there must be authority. We would expect that, in God's Church, authority should show distinctive features. If this is so, what are these distinctive features? In what spirit should church authority be exercised by those holding it? How should it be regarded and accepted by those under it? Does its possession imply privilege and domination over others? Is it, in particular, akin to political power as found in purely human societies? Or is it fundamentally different?

Imprecise or incorrect answers to these questions are bound to lead to confusion. This happens particularly when church power is viewed in terms of political domination. Such a view reflects deep misunderstandings not only about church authority itself, but also about the relationship between clergy and laity, about their respective roles, and even about the whole mission of the Church in the world.

As we set about trying to answer these questions, it is good to recall once more that the age we live in is very suspicious of any kind of authority. Authority to many people simply implies power. And power — they feel — has consistently appeared through history as a means of domination and exploitation. Indeed it could be tempting, after a quick glance at the centuries, to sum up human affairs in just one terse expression: a power-struggle. Men struggling for power, or struggling against power; few ready to relinquish power; few using power except for personal advantage.

The power-pyramid

"Authority means power". In the Church too this concept of authority has been, and still is, widespread. If we start from the principle that all authority comes from God (cf. Rom 13:1; Jn 19:11), it is easy to form a mental picture of how authority and power descend from God through the different ranks of the hierarchy and finally reach the people. This could be depicted graphically in the form of a "structure-pyramid" or a "*power-pyramid*":

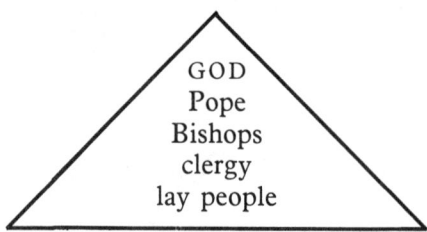

God is at the top of the pyramid. Under him, we are presented with the visible authorities (the "power-structures") of the Church: the hierarchy, the clergy; and under them — in the lowest place, as the ultimate subjects — the Christian laity.

Since most people will probably accept this as reflecting their mental picture of how the Church is organised, we will leave for later the question of whether or not it is an adequate graphic representation of the matter. For the moment let us just develop a few thoughts suggested by this power pyramid.

Everyone agress that the *advancement of the laity* was a main aim of Vatican II. For those who conceive the Church in terms of the pyramid just drawn, advancement of the laity can appear as a straightforward matter, a goal whose pursuit takes an obvious direction. It simply means raising the laity "upwards" into the structural level of the hierarchy, promoting them into the ranks or at least into the functions of the clergy.

For moderate thinkers along these lines, a major step in this promotion of the laity was the post-conciliar establishment of "lay ministries", which may be conferred not only on candidates for the priesthood, but also on persons who intend to remain in the lay state. A further broadening of the concept of this sort of lay ministry is being urged.

The role of the laity, in this view, has been greatly enhanced by the fact that it is now commonplace not only to have lay readers at Mass and lay people acting as distributors of Holy Communion, but to find lay persons active on parish or diocesan pastoral councils or finance committees; according to the new Code of Canon Law, lay people can even be chancellors of diocesan curias.[1]

It is of course quite clear that Vatican II warranted this sharing by the laity in certain roles or functions formerly reserved to the clergy. It is not at all clear, however, that the Council regarded this as sharing in "power"; or that this, in the thinking of Vatican

---

1 c. 482; cf also cc. 228, 230, 231, 492, 537, 910.

II, was meant to be but the first step in a *power-sharing process* that the Council wished to initiate and encourage.

Nevertheless, "power-sharing" has become a sort of slogan in certain ecclesiastical quarters to describe what is considered to be an essential condition for renewal. And Vatican II is still claimed as a warrant for how the power-sharing mentality has developed its own particular logic. Developments in this sense have been rapid. Some of them have been extreme.

Politicising power

Some more recent writers — still obviously thinking in terms of the pyramid we have drawn — have taken the idea of power-sharing farther, very much farther; they have in fact radically *politicised* it.

That the laity should share in certain liturgical functions formerly reserved to the clergy retains scarcely any interest for them. That the laity can have a certain part or say in how parishes or dioceses are run seems peanuts to what is really involved.

A mere *share* in power is no longer seen to be the laity's right. *Power itself* is the goal! Power in the Church is the issue; and here — according to this way of thinking — the laity and the hierarchy are related as exploited to exploiters. The laity must therefore be awakened so as to confront the hierarchy (the most extreme presentation would say: to *overthrow* the hierarchy) and to wrest power from them.

This is the way of thinking that characterizes certain liberation theologies, which could also be called "theologies of power" or "theologies of exploitation". They maintain that power in the Church has for far too long been the exclusive domain of the clergy. The hierarchy, according to them, long ago appropriated power to themselves, i.e. took it unjustifiably from the faithful. They continue to expropriate it from the laity, who are thus exploited and deprived of their rightful share in power and decision-making in the Church. In this view, advancement of the laity means promotion into the power-echelons within the Church, so that the laity can at last recover the power which was wrongfully taken from them. The laity will then be no longer under the domination of the hierarchy. Then the Church will truly be the People's Church.

It is not to my purpose to point out the deficient soteriology of this type of liberation theology; i.e. its failure to understand that the fundamental evil for men is personal sin, and that the radical liberation wrought by Jesus Christ and mediated through the Church is liberation from sin.² Where I would fault it — in the points just mentioned — is for its ecclesiology, for its concept of the Church: concretely for its concept of "power" in the Church; and, just as concretely, for its concept of the roles of both hierarchy and laity, within the Church and in relation to the world. Leaving the question of ecclesial roles for the next chapter, let us try to elucidate the distinctive nature of power and authority in the Catholic Church.

Moral — not political; and sacred

Of course there is authority in the Church, as there must be in every society. But that authority is very far removed from any type of political power. It will help to explain this if we distinguish between the two terms in question — "authority" and "power" — for while they may at times be used indifferently, a look at their etymology or root meaning will show that they suggest distinct things.

Authority comes from the Latin "auctor", i.e. author or source of something. It implies above all a creative and guiding function: that of directing the proper development of the affairs of a society. The holder of authority, if he duly fulfils his office, has a *right* to a response in those he is guiding. Authority speaks in moral terms; it calls for free acceptance. It should be accepted. As we shall see later, it is essential for the well-being of a community that the authority guiding it be exercised effectively. But the effectiveness of its exercises depends on the free and voluntary response of those making up the community.

Power comes from the Latin "posse", to be able. It implies the simple ability to do things. In the case of power over persons, it easily suggests being in a position to exercise physical coercion that cannot be resisted. Power, as such, does not speak in moral terms but in physical terms. It is something that makes itself accepted. It does not call for a free response; it compels its own acceptance.

Now we have just said that in the Church, as in every society, there is authority. It is moral authority to guide us. It is not political power to dominate us, or physical power to coerce us. And, clearly,

---

2 Cf. Instructions of the Congregation for the Doctrine of the Faith, on Liberation Theology, of 6 August 1984 and of 22 March 1986.

those who choose freely to belong to this society of the Church are morally bound to obey church authority.

All authority comes from above. This is uniquely so in the Church since church authority comes directly from Christ himself (Mt 28:18-19).

Christ made his Church hierarchical (cf. LG 18-29). He conferred his authority on the first hierarchy, the Apostles, and through them on their successors, the Popes and the Bishops (and, in a participatory though more limited way, on other clerics).

Hierarchical authority in the Church shows certain features that distinguish it radically from secular authority. The very etymology of the word 'hierarchy" reveals one main distinctive character. The word is made up of a combination of the Greek roots: "ieros" (sacred) and "arkhein" (rule). So hierarchy means sacred rule. Sacredness is the first distinguishing feature of church authority or rule. Because it is sacred it should be given the special respect due to sacred things, without forgetting that its holy or sacred character depends ultimately not on the wisdom or goodness or merits of the men who exercise it, but on the fact that it derives from Christ and is an expression of his saving will for his people.

But the mission that the rulers of the Church have received from our Lord shows another very peculiar feature that *Lumen gentium* brings out in the following phrase from its third chapter (precisely entitled "The Church is Hierarchical"): "That office which the Lord committed to the pastors of his people is, in the strict sense of the term, a service, which is called very expressively in sacred scriptures a 'diakonia' or ministry" (LG 24).

The service-pyramid

So, authority in the Church does not imply privilege, much less domination. It implies mission; it implies service. It is the authority of Christ who came not to be served but to serve (Mt 20:28). He came to serve — to save — all men, to teach them and lead them to salvation. He continues to serve and save and lead the world through his Church: through all those in the Church, lay persons as well as clergy, each in his or her own proper way carrying on the saving work of the servant Christ.

Maybe we can make this clearer if we draw another pyramid, built on the premise: Christ is the servant of all; he serves the Church, ministers and laity, and through them he serves the world, in a serving mission of salvation. On this basis we build not a "power-pyramid" but a *service-pyramid*:

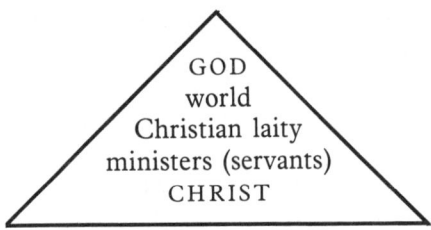

Christ, in order to save the world, became a servant (Phil 2:7). He serves (saves) all men; but he does so in and through his Church. By his guiding and sanctifying presence in the Church he ministers to all his faithful. Through his ministerial priesthood he especially ministers to lay Christians so that they, fulfilling their proper role, carry the sanctifying work of the Church to the world.

Through the clergy, then, Christ works to serve and vivify the laity. Through clergy and laity together he works to serve and save the world, and raise it to God.

Church authority, therefore, is clearly to be seen as service.[3] Jesus taught the lesson explicitly to his Apostles: "You know that among the pagans the rulers lord it over them, and their great men make their authority felt. This is not to happen among you. No; anyone who wants to be great among you must be your servant, and anyone who wants to be first among you must be your slave, just as the Son of Man came not to be served but to serve" (Mt 20:25-28).

The "higher" one is in the church's hierarchy, the more one is obliged to serve. A deep sense of this truth lies behind the traditional title attached to the papal office: "servus servorum Dei"; servant of the servants of God.

The hierarchy serves the people in fulfilling the three-fold office of Christ which he entrusted in fullness to the Apostles and their successors: his priestly, prophetic and kingly office, the ministry of sanctifying, teaching and ruling (cf. LG 19ff).

It is not difficult to see a work of service in the hierarchical ministry of sanctifying; specifically through the priest's role in worship and the sacraments, in particular the Eucharist and Penance.

That the ministry of teaching is similarly a work of service should also be easy to see; although, we might add, this depends on one's readiness or desire to be taught (to be taught by Christ!). Those who don't want to be taught won't see it.

---

3 Cf. page 25 above, note 1.

Where there can be most difficulty in seeing the work of the hierarchy as service is undoubtedly in relation to the office or ministry of ruling. Obviously the same comment applies here: those who do want to be ruled, to be led (again: by Christ!), will see this readily enough; those who do not want to be led, will not. Here in any case there are some finer points that merit further reflection.

Understanding hierarchical authority as service undoubtedly makes authority more appealing. But, we must add, it does not make it less authoritative. We must add this right away, lest our graphic representation be misinterpreted. In our service-pyramid we have placed the whole hierarchy, from Pope down, among the ministers. They appear as "under" the laity; and so, in a true sense, they are, for as ministers they are servants. Nevertheless, though under the laity, they *rule* the laity.

Our pyramid is not intended to suggest that the laity have authority over the clergy. The point is simply that the real ecclesial authority which the clergy have over the laity constitutes a mission of service. This should not seem too strange. One can indeed be in a serving position, and so "under" someone, and yet to be there in that position with the mission — the responsibility and the authority — to rule and to lead.

So, at the Last Supper, Jesus, despite Peter's protests, takes the servant's role and washes his Apostles' feet. But in explaining the lesson to them, he emphasizes that it is precisely *as Master* that he serves them; "Do you understand what I have done to you? You call me Master and Lord, and rightly; so I am. If I, then, the Lord and Master, have washed your feet, you should wash each other's feet. I have given you an example so that you may copy what I have done to you" (Jn 13:13-14).

The imitation of Christ is always filled with challenge and difficulty. Given our human pride there is perhaps no more difficult point, for those endowed with the sacred authority of Christ, than to rule as their Master and to serve as their Master.

"Serving through ruling" may at first sight seem a paradox. It is certainly no easy thing to accomplish in practice. Yet the theoretical difficulties about whether one can truly serve by ruling are more apparent than real. A little thought dispels them.

A desert-guide or a mountain-guide is a servant. He is paid to serve. But his service consists in leading; that is precisely what he is supposed to do. That is what those following him expect.

If he refused to lead ("Now you people do what you like; go where you like"), he would be abandoning his service mission and failing those who are entitled to look to his lead.

The guide's authority is moral. But the people "under" him (his masters!) expect him to exercise that moral authority so as to rule them: to rule their straying tendencies, their laziness about climbing over necessary ridges, their squabbles if not about who should go first (who but the guide!), then about who should go next, their carelessness about unknown dangers, their lack of knowledge of avalanches or precipices or swamps or quicksands, their attraction towards showy but poisonous insects or plants....

They expect their guide to lead and to rule. They expect him to command, they expect him to reprimand, to shout even, if the situation calls for it. That is why he is their servant; a "ruling" servant.

So, the hierarchy truly serve the laity by ruling them: in the spirit of Christ and within the terms and limits of the ruling mission Christ has entrusted to them.

Authority, in our pyramid, flows upwards from Christ. It is an elevating authority. It marks out a direction of ascent. But it must be obeyed.

Community

Service is one key to the understanding of Christian authority, just as it is a key to harmonising Christian authority and Christian obedience. One serves by exercising authority; Christ served by exercising it. And one serves by obeying; Christ served by obeying. All in the Church have to obey the authority of Christ (the Pope more than anyone). And all have to exercise that authority, though each in his own proper way, by bringing that same saving authority to the world; and all do so by obeying, by freely obeying.

These reflections may complement what we tried to show earlier: that there is no necessary conflict, there is rather harmony, between law, authority, freedom, personal responsibility, personal dignity, private conscience.

Service is one key to this harmony. Community is another. It is only in the context of a true sense of community that suspicions of power fade, that respect for authority grows. It is only in the context of a true community that the proper roles of authority, on the one hand, and of personal freedom and conscience, on the other, are easily understood and are seen to be in natural harmony, not in enmity or opposition.

A community is a group of persons united for common and shared ends. It is a voluntary association. It is based on a coincidence of wills.

A community of people realise that they cannot achieve their common goals except under the guidance and coordination of some authority. Authority itself is regarded as a task of service. People look to authority. If it is lacking they set it up. The tendency to accept authority within the community is not the product of a servile or a collectivised mentality. It is precisely the natural tendency of each individual reflective conscience. Each one, because he wants to belong to that particular community with its concrete goals, freely and personally looks to the common authority. His tendency is to accept it. He would only resist authority if he felt it was no longer serving the common good. To resist it simply because it seems to be contrary to his personal interests would show a loss of sense of community; an individualistic and selfish approach that would estrange him from the community, putting what he regards as his own personal good above the common good.

Individualism and a true sense of community are in mutual opposition. Community or communion means union with one another; *and* union with a common or central principle of authority. Individualism — each determined to do his own thing and to give priority to his own way — undermines community.[4]

Ordinary life provides countless examples of this tendency of community to seek authority: from social or sports clubs to trades-unions, to professional associations; down to the spontaneous on the spot organization that emerges once a group of boys comes together for a football game.

The first thing they do is choose captains, and divide into teams. Along with the captains, a referee is chosen, and perhaps linesmen. Both captains and referees are chosen because the boys realise that without someone "in charge" — some authority — there will not be any proper game. They accept that the game has rules, i.e. laws, that it has to be played according to the rules; and that someone — the referee — has to be judge of when the rules apply. If a new boy turns up who wants to play (to take part in that community action), he has to be taught the rules; and he is keen to learn them. And if some player simply will not abide by the rules or if he defies the referee's authority, he is sent off the field. It is by his own action that he separates himself — he "excommunicates" himself

---

4 This of course has its application within the contemporary Church. Can those modern theologians who not only lack union with the Magisterium, but are not even at one among themselves, inspire a new sense of community among Christians? Or do they not rather run the danger of forming a series of splinter-groups disconnected from the mainstream of Catholic thinking?

— from the community. Games — and life; life in society and life in the Church — are like that.

In a true community — where people are one in common goals and ideals — authority is not feared by those under it. It is looked up to. Personal conscience feels no natural suspicion of authority and no instinct to rebel against it, but rather welcomes it and backs it.

In the Christian community — the community Christ set up — the harmony between concepts is clearer still. Authority, which comes from Christ, means service: service and guidance of the common good; and service and guidance also of individual conscience.

Authority seeks the free response of personal conscience (Christ inviting each person to follow him); and individual conscience looks for guidance in trustworthy authority (each person wanting to be led by Christ).

Authority in the Christian community derives from Christ. That is what makes it so trustworthy. And so attractive! I want to be led by Christ!

We have said above that if authority is lacking in a human community, its need is felt and it is set up; normally by the people. Some say this is how it should be in the Church: authority coming from the people. But they miss the point. Authority is not lacking in the Church. It does not have to come from the people. It is already there, coming from Someone whom the people themselves trust much more than they trust themselves. Nevertheless, the idea that "authority comes from underneath" has of course a true application in reference to the Church; not in a democratic sense that authority is conferred by the people, but in the sense suggested by our "service-pyramid": that it comes from Christ, who is "under" us all, supporting us all, raising us all, ruling us all, serving us all.

The Church is a community of free and voluntary persons. It is not a concentration camp or a police state. It has no closed frontiers, although it has moral limits. One is not forced to belong to the community that Jesus Christ set up; but neither can one belong to it on one's own terms, one has to belong on Christ's terms. Just as no one can play soccer according to his own personal rules; he must keep to the set rules of the game. If someone insists on handling the ball, he will be sent off the field. He remains free to go and play rugby, or invent roller-ball. But he can't play soccer.

In the Church there are no geographical borders, no passports, no visas. You move freely — but always within a spiritual domain.

It is your attitude — your way of thinking — not your physical movement, that can take you out of the Church boundaries.

Resistance to authority

If authority means guiding and serving in the spirit of Christ, why is it we still find today such resistance to authority in the Church?

Mainly, I believe, because we have not properly understood and assimilated the thinking of Vatican II about authority, about the ruling-serving mission that pertains to all Christians, and the challenge that this way of thinking puts to each of us.

For pastors, the challenge presents a double aspect:

a) to understand that authority is to be exercised *in a spirit of service* — serving the truth, serving justice, serving others — and that therefore they must avoid serving just themselves, their pride, their comfort, their preferences, their self-assertiveness.

b) to understand that, in exercising authority, they *are* serving; in other words, that their mission of service *requires* precisely that they exercise authority (and therefore they must not be afraid to exercise it) for the sake of truth, of justice, of the common good.

Some pastors today would seem not to understand or to accept the first aspect of the challenge. They see privilege in their authority; and authority seen as privilege can easily become power used as domination. These pastors do not truly reflect Christ's way of exercising authority. They remain overbearing, dictatorial, personalistic, imposing their views on those under their care without respecting people's rights and without any real concern for the common good. This, it may be added, can happen also among those who consider themselves progressive, especially when the basis on which they are determined to progress is their own ideas.

Other pastors (and perhaps there are more of these) seem not to understand the second point: that they are required and expected (by their people as well) to *lead*; that their service *consists in leading*; and that if they do not lead, they are *not* serving. Leading and teaching — serving — in the spirit of Christ, also means guiding authoritatively, just as Christ did (Mt 7:29), with pastoral compassion but without diminishing the demands that the following of Christ so often makes.

It is worth recalling the words of Jesus about the shepherds who do not care enough for the flock to lead and defend them (Jn 10:12ff) whom he declares not to be true pastors but hirelings or mercenaries; i.e. false shepherds whose concern for their flock is subordinated to more self-centred interests (not necessarily just a concern for money; it could equally be a concern for a quiet life, for popularity, a good press or a favourable public image).

Vatican II likewise poses an immense challenge to the Christian laity: not only to obey authority — to follow the lawful lead of their pastors — but also to *exercise* authority. Pastors and laity have to serve, to obey, to rule; each in his own way. On this, moreover, depends the evangelization of the world. But before we go into that, the idea of serving, obeying and ruling, each in his or her proper sphere and way, calls for deeper comment.

12

Roles in the Church; Roles in the World

One day, in a seminar with theology students I sketched out the two pyramids of the last chapter, side by side:

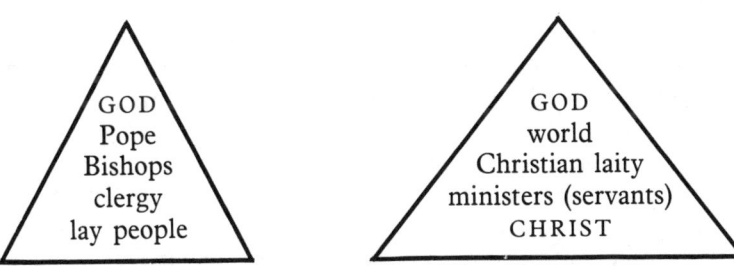

After a few minutes' reflection one of them remarked, "Yes, that makes sense. After all, in the first pyramid, *where is the world?*"

Where indeed is the world? It is a telling comment that suggests further defects — which in fact represent a major gap — in the power-struggle mentality.

The theory that clergy and laity are competing for "power" takes energies — the salt and light and leaven of Christianity — that are meant to be directed towards the world, for its transformation, and turns them inwards, to be consumed in sterile and at times acrimonious debates about church organization and structures and functions.

It is questionable if such an in-turned ecclesiology can renew the Church. It is certain that it cannot renew the world. What sort of church-view do we have if it is not big enough to embrace the world? The Church is not a closed system. It exists not for its own sake, but for the sake of the Gospel, for the sake of the world: to bring the message and work of Christ to the whole world. Of its nature the Church must be open to the world — so as to save the world. A church-view that is not at the same time a world-view is radically defective.

To this the reply might be made that the power-sharing thrust is a necessary process or stage in renewal; that the Church, once renewed in this way — with the laity given their proper status and able to play their proper role — will then be an effective instrument of evangelization. In other words, a renewed — and evangelizing — Church depends on the laity having their proper role opened to them.

This is interesting; it suggests that we should refocus our attention, transferring it from the question of power to that of roles. If we do, I think we can show that a misconception of power or authority is only one side of the coin of the power-pyramid mentality; for there is another side which is a radical misunderstanding of ecclesial and Christian roles: the proper role of the clergy and, especially, the proper role of the laity.

The role of the clergy has been sufficiently considered in the last chapter. It is a ministerial role of service primarily to the People of God. The people need the full-time service of the ordained priest living, acting and ministering among them in a priestly way that is clearly identifiable as such. A priest shows his solidarity with the people by serving them in a priestly way, not by imitating their secular life-style. The imitation by a priest of lay ways is not welcomed by the vast majority of the laity, and in far too many cases it leads to a loss of identity and sense of mission on the part of the priest himself. But we will not expand further on that, as the purpose of this chapter is rather to study the proper role of the laity.

The proper role of the laity

Can anyone be seriously satisfied with the idea that the desired "advancement of the laity" lies along the lines of the *lay ministries* we mentioned in the last chapter? Lay ministries obviously merit our respect as a genuine service to the ecclesial community. Yet these ministries, and all the current projections more or less connected with them, have very little to do with the true role of the laity as presented by Vatican II.

Few people seem to advert to the evident danger of the gradual "clericalization" of those lay people who follow a way of active engagement in roles formerly (and still, of course, mainly) associated with the clergy.[1] Fewer still advert to another point that should also be evident: the enormous majority of lay people simply *cannot go that way.*

---

[1] Attempts at "clericalization of the laity" and "secularization of the clergy" are parallel dangers that Pope John Paul II has drawn attention to (cf. *Insegnamenti di Giovanni Paolo II*, VII, 1 (1984), p. 1784.

A few moments reflection shows this. What percentage of the lay members of a parish can be actively involved in liturgical roles or in pastoral or administrative positions? Two per cent? Five per cent? What then of the other 95 per cent? Have they no proper church role? And, of the 5 per cent who are active, what percentage of their time — i.e. of their normal week — is spent in such church activities? Ten per cent? What then of the remaining 90 per cent of their week spent in their job, family, etc.? Is all of that marginal or unimportant? Is it of no real ecclesial significance? Is it a second-rate activity before God? Has it no apostolic potential or value? Does it not properly fit into their *role* as Christians?

How can advancement of the laity lie along a path that can be followed, in the best of cases, by only a tiny fraction of lay people, but which remains an ecclesial dead end for all the others? If advancement of the laity means this, then it is a way that is blocked to the vast majority (blocked, be it noted, not by ecclesiastical obstructionists, but by the very conditioning factors of the laity's own life).

If the role of the laity is not in the line of lay ministries, where does it lie? Vatican II is totally explicit about the distinctive role of the laity and the field in which it is to be exercised. *The proper field of the laity is the world.* It is in the world that they have to sanctify themselves, each one being an incarnation of the spirit of Jesus Christ in his or her secular activities. And it is in the world, on the basis of that union with Christ, that they are also to be evangelizers, striving to penetrate the whole human order with the saving and vivifying power of Christ.

"By reason of *their special vocation* it belongs to the laity to seek the kingdom of God by *engaging in temporal affairs* and directing them according to God's will" (LG 31).[2] They have "to *animate the world* with the spirit of Christianity" (GS 43); "to *sanctify the world from within*" (LG 10, 31); "to permeate and perfect the *temporal order* with the spirit of the Gospel" (AA 2; cf c. 225). "The laity are given this *special vocation*: to make the Church present and faithful in those places and circumstances where it is *only through them* that she can become the salt of the earth" (LG 33). "The *characteristic* of the lay state being *a life led in the midst of the world* and of secular affairs, laymen are called by God to make of their apostolate, through the vigor of their Christian spirit, a *leaven in the world*" (AA 2).

---

2 Emphasis added in this and the following quotations from the Council documents.

The priestly, prophetic and kingly office of the laity

The proper role of the laity then is not to share in *clerical* power. It is to share in the power and mission of Christ, so as to impregnate their own secular lives, and the world around them, with his spirit.

Following the thought of the Council we can spell out the distinctive way in which the laity participate in the mission of Christ, specifically in his three-fold office (cf. LG 31ff; AA 10).

Their share of the priestly office of Christ implies, of course, a life centred on the Eucharist. But their eucharist participation is not only expressed by their being actively present in Mass, nor is it mainly expressed by particular liturgical roles performed in church. It is by "worshipping *everywhere* and in *everything* by their holy actions (that) the laity consecrate the world itself to God" (LG 34). And so "all their works, prayers and apostolic undertakings, *family* and *married* life, *daily work, relaxation* of mind and body, if they are accomplished in the Spirit — indeed even the hardships of life if patiently borne — all these become spiritual sacrifices acceptable to God through Jesus Christ" (ibid).

So their share in the priestly office of Christ is expressed above all and essentially in their struggle to sanctify their everyday work and secular activity.

What about the share of the laity in the prophetic or teaching office of Christ? The Council insists that Christ "fulfils this prophetic office, not only through the hierarchy who teach in his name and by his power, but also through the laity. He accordingly both establishes them as witnesses and provides them with the appreciation of the faith and the grace of the word so that the power of the Gospel may shine out in *daily family and social life*" (LG 35; cf no. 12).

For a lay person to announce the word of God in church is no doubt an exercise of this prophetic function. That this is now done where it was not done before may well be considered an advance. But if our perspective advances along that road alone, we are, I repeat, looking down a dead end.

Where the specific vocation of the lay person calls him to announce the word of God is not in the church but in the world: in his factory, in his office, in his club, in his family. He has to do this not only by his example but also by directly communicating doctrine — i.e. his knowledge of the faith — ensuring that in his prophetic mission it is truly the word of God that he communicates. It is not in "sermonising" that he will do this (the role of preacher fits the layman poorly) but in the normal exchange of views among colleagues and friends, where the impact of the Christian truth inspiring him will hit home.

His prophetic role also means that he is not afraid to bear witness to the word when it is unpopular, nor is he discouraged or tempted to convey a watered-down version of the word when it appears to be rejected or when he faces persecution (cf. Mt 13:21). The Council insists that the laity must not hide their hope or faith, but rather "express it *through the structure of their secular lives* in continual conversion and in wrestling 'against the world rulers of this darkness, against the spiritual forces of iniquity' (Eph 6:12)" (LG 35).

And the kingly role of the laity? It is on the basis of the grace and truth of Christ that the laity must set about fulfilling, in the world, their Christian ruling mission. It is here that the greatness of the challenge facing them becomes more apparent; it is here too that partial understandings or fundamental misunderstandings can most easily arise.

Christ the Lord and Saviour of all creation wants to serve, save, rule the world, raising it to God. He does so through his Church: through his ministers, but more immediately still through his lay followers.

The first aspect of the lay Christian's kingly role relates to his work in its personal dimension, and is simply enough expressed. He is meant to be king in relation to his personal work, as Christ was King of the everyday work he performed during those thirty hidden years.

This means that the Christian in his kingly role is meant to dominate work, not to be dominated by it. He should realise that his work, to which he freely dedicates himself, is not just a means to money or self-affirmation. It serves a divine plan. And he should rule and direct his work to the fulfilment of this plan.[3]

Ruling the world

But the kingly role of the laity has a more ambitious scope still. Man is placed to rule and shape all creation. Christ empowers his lay followers, most especially, to exercise this rule on his behalf. The Council speaks in noble and solemn terms of the task facing the Christian laity: the task of establishing the kingdom of Christ in the world. "The Lord desires that his kingdom be spread by

3 Cf. Pope John Paul II, Encyclical, *Laborem Exercens*, 25.

the lay faithful also: the kingdom of justice, love and peace. In this kingdom creation itself will be delivered from the slavery of corruption into the freedom of glory of the sons of God (cf. Rom 8:21). Clearly, a great promise, a great commission is given to the disciples: 'all things are yours, you are Christ's, and Christ is God's' (1 Cor). . . . *The laity enjoy a principal role* in the universal fulfilment of this task" (LG 36).

The laity's role is not enhanced when they look for or are given a share in clerical authority or service. They can go in that direction. But not many can go; and it is not their proper direction. Their share in the kingly mission of Christ is not essentially there but in the world. Their "primary and immediate task is not to establish and develop the ecclesial community — this is the specific role of the pastors — but to put to use every Christian and evangelical possibility latent but already present and active in the affairs of the world".[4] They are not meant to be mini-priests or super-sacristans; they are meant to be the light and salt of Christ's presence in the secular world.

In one of the passages from *Lumen gentium* quoted above, the Council says that the distinctive vocation of the laity is not only to engage in temporal affairs but also to "*direct* them according to God's Will" (LG 31). This sends out a powerful call and challenge to the laity. It underlines that their role is to exercise the authority of Christ in the world, not merely by giving moral guidance as the hierarchy especially do, but by actively *guiding and directing* secular affairs — professions, business, politics, trades-unions, culture, education, mass media, entertainment, social and family life — by their forceful presence and courageous leadership. There is where, by ruling, guiding, serving, they exercise the kingly authority of Christ. "The *effort to infuse a Christian spirit into the mentality, customs, laws, and structures of the community* in which a person lives, is so much the *duty and responsibility of the laity* that it *can never be properly performed by others*" (AA 13).

The kingly mission of the laity involves permeating the whole social order with those Christian principles which humanise and elevate it: the dignity and primacy of the human person, social solidarity, the sanctity and inviolability of marriage and the home, the principle of responsible freedom, love for the truth, respect for justice at all levels, the spirit of service, the practice of mutual understanding and fraternal charity....

Why should lay Christians want to run the Church — when

---

4 Cf. Pope Paul VI, Apostolic Exhortation, *Evangelii Nuntiandi*, 70.

they are meant to run the world? The challenge to the laity is not to "overtake" the clergy, it is to "take over" the world.

Here is where misunderstanding might arise. It could be grave and needs to be avoided; although those who are no friends of Christianity, or of evanglization, are not likely to avoid it.

This lay Christian rule or "running" of the world will not imply or involve clerical domination or ecclesiastical penetration of secular society. It will mean the world animated by ordinary citizens who truly understand the world and love it; and so, respecting its distinctive secular nature, can lead it to its proper fulfilment and end.

"Let Christians be proud of the opportunity to carry out their earthly activity in such a way as to integrate human, domestic, professional, scientific and technical enterprises with religious values, under whose supreme direction all things are ordered to the glory of God" (GS 43).

"It pertains to the laity in a special way so to illuminate and order all temporal things with which they are so closely associated that these may be effected and grow according to Christ and may be to the glory of the Creator and Redeemer" (LG 31).

The Christian renewal of the world will mean the world enlightened with the light of Christ (LG 36). And this light will be spread above all by individual Christians acting not as "agents" of the Vatican, not on orders from the hierarchy or from some particular church institutions, but precisely as individual citizens possessing and exercising full personal freedom and full personal responsibility (cf. AA 7).

We are evidently not suggesting that the clergy have no specific mission in the world. Of course they have. The whole Church has (AA 7). The clergy fulfils a sanctifying mission through ways of prayer and worship whose effect goes beyond any human power of appreciation. The effect of the clergy's prophetic mission to the world is more evident. The hierarchy has to preach the Gospel, "welcome or unwelcome" (2 Tim 4:2), declaring to the world, time and again, the eternal principles of the law of God and the plan of Christ.

However, as we know, men frequently do not listen to the clergy. The fact is that, from the world's point of view, the clergy and the hierarchy often appear as "outsiders". They may want to go to the world, to preach the Gospel. But so often the way to the world is blocked to them; physically or morally. Men's doors — factory doors, office doors, assembly doors, neighbourhood doors — are often closed to them. Men's ears too are often closed to them.

Christian lay people in the world are "insiders". They do not have to *go* to the world; they are already there. They are in the world, as ordinary citizens, like the rest of their fellow-men — to whom, in so many cases, they and they alone can be effective evangelizers. "It is a fact", the Council emphasizes, "that many men cannot hear the Gospel and come to acknowledge Christ *except through the laymen they associate with*" (AA 13).

Christian lay people have to exercise their "kingly service"[5] by leading their fellowmen to Christ. How are they going to do this? They are not going to do it by subterfuge, evidently; Christ wants clarity and openness. Nor are they going to do it at the point of a gun; Christ does not want coercion or violence. He is only interested in free followers. I think we can underline two main requirements which Christian lay people (always on the basis of their personal union with our Lord) must meet to carry out their role "to spread the divine plan of salvation to all men of every epoch all over the earth" (LG 33).

Competence and doctrine

The first element necessary if Christian lay people are going to lead and guide human affairs is *competence*: competence in their profession or job. Their right to hold directive positions in secular affairs is something to be won on sheer professional merit, on the quality of their study, training and research, and on the quality of their actual work. In expounding the kingly mission of the laity, the Council insists on this precise point: "by their competence in secular disciplines and by their activity, interiorly raised up by grace, let them work earnestly in order that created goods through human labour, technical skill and civil culture may serve the utiliy of all men according to the plan of the Creator and light of his word" (LG 36).

It should be clear that lay people with a true sense of their Christian vocation have every reason to acquire outstanding professional competence. After all, since sanctity is what they seek in and through their job, love for God is the mainspring impelling them to work. And this motive is higher than the noblest human motive and more powerful than the most self-centred ambition; therefore they work and work a lot.

The other element Christian lay people need if they are going

---

5 Cf. Pope John Paul II, Encyclical, *Redemptor Hominis*, 21.

to lead the world to Christ is *doctrine*. The Council again is very specific on this. Insisting once more that "laymen ought to take on themselves as *their distinctive task* this renewal of the temporal order", the Decree on the Apostolate of Lay People adds that their direct and specific action in this field must be "guided by the light of the Gospel and the mind of the Church, prompted by Christian love" (AA 7). And *Gaudium et spes* adds that it is the task of the laity "to cultivate a properly informed conscience and to impress the divine law on the affairs of the earthly city" (no. 43). When professionally competent lay people have assimilated the message of the Gospel and attuned their minds to the mind of the Church (Christ speaking to us in both), then, under the prompting of Christian love, they are qualified to lead the world.

If faith in Christ and love for him are the real mainsprings of the lay person's competence and doctrine, then he will possess *unity of life*; thus, living in an incarnational way (cf. AA 4), he will avoid that divorce between faith and daily life which the Council describes as "one of the gravest errors of our time" (GS 43).

As we can see, then, the role of the clergy and the role of the laity are complementary but distinct. The role of each Christian, in answer to the universal call to holiness (cf. LG, chap. V), is a role of service and evangelization, modelled on Christ the Servant and the Saviour of all: the clergy serving mainly within the Church; and the laity serving essentially within the world. The priest has to be Christ to the Christian laity, in a priestly way. And the laity have, in a lay way, to be Christ to the world.

In the last chapter we criticised the "power-sharing" mentality, when it presents clergy and laity jostling each other for positions of "influence" within the Church. This, we tried to show, betrays a poor understanding of power or authority within the Church. Nevertheless, the notion of power-sharing can of course be refined and expressed in a proper sense. If authority is understood as service, then "power-sharing" becomes *service*-sharing: each one, by serving in his or her proper way, shares in the power of Christ to save the world.

Each in his or her *proper way*: this is the key to the matter. That is why the nature of ecclesial power cannot be adequately clarified without at the same time clarifying the nature of ecclesial roles. The "power" of each Christian is the power to *serve* in the specific *role* God has given each one. To want a different power is to want not to serve.

Who is going to be boss?

Why is it that more than twenty years after the Council these notions of roles and service are still so imperfectly grasped? The answer, I think, is that the spirit of clericalism is a hardy body; it can assume new forms but it takes a long while to die.

Already before the Council there was a reaction against the centuries-old tradition of regarding the laity as the passive "praying-paying-obeying" members of the Church. Vatican II gave guidelines for a truer concept of their ecclesial role. It is questionable, however, if these guidelines have been properly understood on any broad level or if they inspire much of the post-conciliar debate about means of "promoting" the laity.

The fact is that the clerical mentality which characterised so much thinking about the laity before the Council has (despite appearances) largely continued to dominate thinking on the same subject even after Council. It has changed its tone and presentation, but it reasons from the same defective appreciations.

The caricature of the autocratic pastor of thirty years ago showed him with a sign hanging outside his parish office; "I AM THE BOSS". Whatever the truth in the caricature (and there was undoubtedly some), this is taken today to represent the pre-conciliar clerical mentality: "We are the bosses".

Since the Council there has been a growing number of clerics telling the laity, with apparent generosity, "Come. We will share our power. You can be bosses with us". And there is a number of lay people insisting, "We want a share in that power of yours. We want to be bosses with you (or even without you . . .; or, if necessary, against you!)".

The first comment that comes to mind is that we are not thinking like Christ if we squabble about who is going to be boss (Mt 20:28). In any case, all of this — whether pre- or post-conciliar — betrays the same substantial misconception of power and of roles. In the Church there are no bosses, apart from Christ our Master; we are all servants, with different, Christ-assigned, modes of serving. Some, the clergy, with a special ministerial mission of serving (first of all) their fellow-Christians; and others, the laity, with a specific service mission to the world, so as to lead it to Christ.

The same false ecclesiological evaluation lies behind suggestions that the laity in the past have been too "subservient" to the hierarchy, and are now entitled to be liberated from this tutelage. The laity should indeed obey the hierarchy in those clear but limited areas where the hierarchy speaks with the voice of Christ.

This shows faith in Christ and love for Christ. It does not show subservience. The laity do not have to be subservient to the hierarchy. They do have to serve the world, as the hierarchy has to serve them.

Again it is suggested that the laity, in contrast to pre-conciliar days, are no longer prepared to be the *lunga manus*, the long arm of the hierarchy, which the hierarchy uses to reach out in order to manipulate the world.

The laity are not, and were never meant to be, the "long arm" of the hierarchy. They are not a part or an extension of an official Catholic system. They, or rather each one, in his or her own right and on the basis of his or her piety and competence and doctrine, is meant to be the presence of Christ in secular affairs.

The laity do not depend on the hierarchy for their secular life, nor do they have to render any sort of account to the hierarchy for the civic or professional activities they undertake individually or in association with others. We have to remember that while Christ has a plan for the world, he has allowed for different possible modes of applying this plan. Christian lay people, working within clear though broad moral principles — but seeing things from different angles — are bound to come up with different practical solutions all of which can be regarded as legitimate Christian contributions to the proper development of human affairs (cf. GS 43). This is an expression of Christian pluralism. The hierarchy can give general moral guidelines but has no right to narrow the practical options where Christ has left them open.

"Lay leaders"

Vatican II, then, calls us to an immense broadening and deepening of vision if we are to grasp the true role of the laity. We need to get our minds off the "lay ministries" track. Lay ministries represent a valid and useful contribution, by some lay people, to the work of the clergy and the service of the Christian community. Let us not push their value or potential beyond that. Lay ministries must always, of their nature, remain *non-typical* for the immense majority of lay people. The documents of Vatican II in fact nowhere speak of lay ministries. These ministries — which could more properly be termed "non-ordained ecclesiastical ministries" — were introduced by Pope Paul VI in 1972[6] and, as we have pointed

---

6 Cf. Apostolic Letter *Ministeria Quaedam* of 15 August 1972.

out, they in no way correspond to the Vatican II vision of the distinctive role and mission of the laity. They should be seen for what they were intended to be: a minor post-conciliar disposition with a certain functional or organizational utility for the internal life of the Church. It is illusory to see in them a wedge in a door through which, if forced open a little wider, the laity as a body can eventually pass and so occupy their rightful and allotted place.

This is too narrow a door for the vast majority of lay people, and the quarters on the other side are far too confined for them. The place of the laity is not the other side of that door. It lies in a different direction. Their role is not primarily participation in church organization, nor in semi-ministerial aspects of liturgical worship. It is proper participation in the life of the Church in the world, especially in that overflow of the Church's vitality which we term evangelization.

Leadership of *the world* — "fashioning it anew according to God's design and leading it to fulfilment" (GS 2) — is the mission and challenge that Christ, through his Church, entrusts above all to his lay followers. Lay leadership is misconceived if it is not understood in this sense. It is commonplace, in some circles, to speak of "our lay leaders" as a way of describing those who in fact are doing a (very useful) job of helping the clergy in the organization and administration of church life. We even hear expressions of satisfaction at the "growth of lay leadership", when what is meant is simply that some few lay persons (that disproportionate and wholly unrepresentative 3% or 5%!!) occupy directive positions in Catholic secretariats, are present on steering committees connected with church affairs, or lecture at ecclesiastical faculties. In all of this there is much that is useful; but there is also — in the use of the phrase "lay leaders" — much that represents the old clerical thinking rather than the new conciliar thinking.

The Council nowhere says that the laity are called to vie with the clergy for "leadership" in ecclesiastical affairs. Lay people with a genuine lay spirit have no time or interest for such intra-church competitions, and in fact find the notion comic or repellent.

The true conciliar message — addressed and open to all lay Christians and not just a clerically-inclined few — is: get out into the world; face up to the challenge of your secular calling; do your job with the fullest human competence; sanctify it; know your faith; spread it; and then you will be a true lay leader to lead the world round you to human fulfilment and to Christ.

The proper leadership potential that has to be developed,

especially in young Catholics, is not for ecclesiastical tasks. Our young people are capable of more, and will be attracted by more. Their potential is to lead the world. It is a far greater challenge, and needs to be put to them.

The current rather general use of the term "lay leader" or "lay leadership" only spreads clericalism and a faulty approach to evangelization. It would be better if it were dropped. Some term such as "lay auxiliaries" could be used instead. This would avoid confusion.

"Representative" Catholics

Another phrase of doubtful validity that has come into vogue in recent years is "representative Catholics". It is a description that is commonly applied to those lay people who are involved in parish councils, who work on diocesan or national committees or secretariats, etc.

One in no way questions the value of their work in questioning whether it can be regarded as "representative" of lay Catholicism. If the true spirit of the Christian laity according to the mind of the Second Vatican Council is as outlined in this chapter, then it is clear that the lay people just mentioned represent that spirit far less than other lay Catholics whose love for Christ and zeal to make him known is expressed not within ecclesiastical structures but rather "through the structure of their secular lives" (LG 35); and whose apostolate, based on professional prestige, is expressed in normal moulds of human friendship and social contact; and so, in full dedication to their secular calling, they "sanctify the world from within" (LG 10; 31).

Representative democracy is a grand phrase. Democratic representation is of course easy to speak of and quite hard to achieve in practice. Simple reflection on the sheer number, variety of jobs, personal circumstances, interests and opinions of the Christian laity, would seem to exclude the possibility of their being truly *represented* by any number of individuals, however chosen.

In practice the statements of principle and lines of action adopted by different Catholic lay groups — youth groups, associations of married couples, etc. — tend to represent just the thinking or decisions of a committee or a small nucleus of people. When their way of thinking or acting is in full harmony with true Christian principles, then these people may perhaps be said to "represent" Catholic *ideals* (though it would be truer to say that they *re-echo* them); but that does not make them representatives of other *Catholics*.

In other cases the approach to Christian living which they articulate may simply be one among the many legitimate approaches open to Christians; or, in extreme cases, it may be at total variance with Catholic teaching. In any case, whatever the *views* they represent, such people do not represent other *persons* besides themselves.

Again, we read at times of "representative gatherings" of lay Catholics meeting on a regional or perhaps a national scale. It regularly turns out that the majority attendance at these meetings is made up of people working full-time in Catholic organisms or at least deeply immersed in ecclesiastical affairs. One wonders on what grounds they can be termed "representative" of the ordinary run of lay Catholics. There might be something to be said for calling such lay people "official" Catholics, but they certainly cannot be called "representative".

Some people bandy these concepts of "lay leaders" and "representative lay Catholics" as if they constituted advanced conciliar thinking and pointed the way to significant post-conciliar break-throughs. For me all of this marks a break-through to a dead end. It is not advanced thinking; it is a continuation, in new forms, of pre-conciliar clericalism. It easily degenerates into the sterility of the power-struggle approach. It denotes a fundamental lack of understanding both of priestly "diakonia" and of the real role of the laity in the Church and in the world. It is a brake applied to evangelization.

★ ★ ★

A word of clarification is due before ending these considerations.

The incidental reflections and comments of these last two chapters are mine. The substance of the ideas — on ministry and service, on the role of the priest and, especially, on the role of the laity — I owe totally to the work and thinking of Monsignor Josemaría Escrivá, Founder of Opus Dei.

Mgr Escrivá was a main forerunner of Vatican II. For more than thirty years before the Council he had been preaching (and showing people how to live) the universal call to holiness, the priesthood seen as sacred service, the lay person's call to sanctify himself, his daily work, and the world around him, with a truly lay spirituality, the fundamental equality of all Christians and at the same time the functional diversity of their respective roles....

In these points, as in so many others — ecumenism, the relationship of the Church to the world and of the Gospel to culture, the dynamism of theology, the nature of evangelization — Mgr Escrivá was and remains a man ahead of the times. His work and writings are an inexhaustible source of ideas and practical inspiration for all who believe that Our Lord Jesus Christ — the Son of God and "the carpenter's son" (Mt 13:54) — came to call all men to a holy life on earth and to heaven.[7]

---

[7] Quotations from the writings of Mgr Escrivá could be multiplied to show his teachings on the vocation and mission of the laity. A few works where the reader can find his teaching more extensively studied include: Alvaro del Portillo, *Faithful and Laity in the Church*, Four Courts Press/Ecclesia Press, Shannon, Ireland, 1972, especially pp. 87-145; J.L. Illanes, *On the Theology of Work*, Dublin and Chicago, 1967 (a new edition is in preparation); G.B. Torello, "The Spirituality of Lay People", in *The Furrow*, Maynooth, vol. XVII, 4 (April 1966), pp. 222-235, and also in Booklet no. 97, Sinag-Tala, Manila.

13

Authority and Evangelization

There is more to be got from that pointed comment: "Where is the world?"

We have tried to show that the power struggle mentality is false to the ecclesiology of Vatican II regarding authority, on the one hand, and regarding the distinctive roles of both clergy and laity, on the other. It can be faulted on a third major count. It is apostolicly sterile.

The important issue for the power mentality is, "How do we organize the Church?" The important issue for the service mentality is "How do we evangelize the world?" The parochialism of the first mentality is as evident as the outward thrust of the second.

Nevertheless, it is at times claimed that a Church reorganized and restructured along more "liberal" lines will offer a better image to the outside world and so facilitate evangelization. This claim is no doubt also put forward because it appears to offer a broader justification for trends which in themselves look rather self-concerned and individualistic with no evident evangelizing angle to them: the rejection of celibacy by some priests, the demand for ordination by some women, the campaign by some lay people for a say in running the Church. . . . It is undeniable that a great part of our energies of the past twenty five years has been consumed in these and similar concerns: theological dissenters, Catholics for the Pill or for Abortion, Catholics against the Magisterium, altar girls, sexist liturgical language, undemocratic episcopal appointments . . . these are the "burning" issues that fill so much of our clerical or Catholic writing and debate.

Whether what is behind these concerns is a driving zeal for the salvation of the world or merely a preference for a different type of Church and especially a different personal life-style must remain a matter of opinion. Judging subjective motivations is never an easy thing. What is easier to judge is the effect of such concerns on outsiders. Some rumblings of these concerns reach the outside non-Catholic world. What impression do they make?

One does not have to hazard too much of a guess. They leave the world amused or bemused . . . but in any case, unimpressed, unmoved, indifferent at what it undoubtedly dismisses as so much clerical or ecclesiastical in-fighting. What is there in all of this to impress the world, to reveal to it the spirit of Christ, to attract it to Christ?

Signs of the times

Be that as it may, some still defend the direction marked out by these concerns as one called for by the needs of the times. And they say, a major guideline given by Vatican II was that the Church must be updated, must be reshaped according to the "signs of the times".

This four-word phrase appears in the opening paragraphs of the Constitution on the Church in the Modern World. Probably no other phrase from the Council documents has been so often quoted. "Reading the signs of the times" has become for many people the guiding principle for the interpretation and implementation of Vatican II.

The signs of the times, we are told, are that modern man wants more freedom, more equality, more room for self-expression.... The Church will therefore forfeit its credibility and lose all possibility of appeal for contemporary man unless it appears as a Church where there is true democracy, more individual freedom, more respect for personal rights, less exercise of authority....

One wonders whether those who argue this way have properly understood the sense in which Vatican II invoked the signs of the times. One also wonders whether the new image of the Church they wish to see emerge is in fact likely to carry "credibility" with contemporary man or impress or attract him.

Let us transcribe the passage in *Gaudium et spes* where the key phrase appears: "At all times the Church carries the responsibility of reading the signs of the times and interpreting them in the light of the Gospel, if it is to carry out its task. In language intelligible to every generation, she should be able to answer the ever-recurring questions which men ask about the meaning of this present life and of the life to come, and how one is related to the other" (GS 4).

So, it is not the Gospel which has to be interpreted in the light of the times, but the other way round. The signs of the times are indeed presented by the Council as a starting or reference point, but are suggested as a reference not for a secular re-appraisal of the Gospel but precisely for an evangelical appraisal of modern man.

Vatican II never for one moment thought that modern man is

not ripe for the Gospel. Man is always ripe for the Gospel. The Gospel is Good News for *all* men.

What the signs-of-the-times criterion suggests is that we look at contemporary man and examine his existential situation so as to see which of his aspirations — i.e. his longing for values that he does *not* possess — can be satisifed, at a deeper level, in Christ.

It is true that modern man wants freedom. Men of all times have wanted freedom. Christ's law is the law of freedom. We have to show the world that we have found freedom, precisely within the law of Christ. Meanwhile we have to encourage modern man to ask himself what he wants freedom *from*, and what he wants freedom *for*; and then to see if he will accept freedom on Christ's terms, within Christ's law. Christians know it cannot be found outside.

It is true too that modern man wants equality. That again is to be found in Christ, in the equal dignity of being children of the same Father, enjoying our God-given rights under God-given guidance and authority.

A desire for freedom and equality? Is this all that our analysis of modern man can come up with? A deeper reading of the times is called for if we are to understand the peculiar situation of modern man and how *we* Christians are being challenged to bring him the Gospel.

A bad moment?

The Council itself read the signs of the times of the early 1960s and drew from them a picture of modern man as a deeply dissatisfied being. Modern man "often seems more uncertain than ever of himself" (GS 4); he is in the grip of "spiritual uneasiness" (5); "he feels himself divided" (10); he is "buffeted between hope and anxiety" (4); "every man remains a question to himself, one that is dimly perceived and left unanswered"(21); but he is "forced to look for answers" (4).

In the time that has elapsed since Vatican II modern society has in fact shown signs of accelerated wear and tear: drugs, dropouts, pornography, hooliganism, spiralling crime, international terrorism. . . . Something is happening to modern man. It is happening fast, and he senses that what is happening is not very good.

Beneath these signs of unrest one discovers a deep dissatisfaction, a sense of privation, in contemporary man. Things are missing in his life: vital human values. Among the privations that contemporary man is experiencing, I would suggest that three are outstanding: a lack of certainty, a lack of solidarity, a lack of joy. Man's feelings about life — about himself and about others — are becoming more and more sceptical and negative:

— life is a meaningless trip. There is nowhere to go. And if there were, no one can tell you how to go there.

— life is a rat-race. There is no honesty. There is no loyalty. You can't trust others.

— life is a con-game. it promises happiness, but does not deliver the goods.

It is a bad moment for modern man. It is a good moment for evangelization. The closer man comes to despair, the more prepared he is (perhaps without realizing it) for a message of hope.

Is this uncertain, disunited, joyless situation totally peculiar to twentieth century man? It undoubtedly has had precedents in history, and clearly had a precedent precisely 2,000 years ago.

Here let us develop a reflection which is not a digression. It is commonplace today among secular thinkers and commentators to acknowledge that western civilization is in crisis, in grave crisis. Paradoxically there seems to be in some ecclesiastical quarters a fear of admitting that the Church itself might be in any way affected by this crisis all round it. Some Catholic thinkers rigorously maintain that there are no signs of crisis in the Church. Others allow that there is a crisis in the Church and explain it as simply an overflow of the crisis in secular culture.

It may be that a world in crisis is bound to affect the Church. It is certain and more to the point that the Church is called to evangelize the world and has a particular opportunity to do so when the world itself is in crisis. It was precisely to a world in a similar situation — materially powerful but spiritually empty — that Christ sent his Apostles. And the young Church of those first centuries was strong and vigorous enough not only to protect itself from being paganised from without but to evangelize that surrounding pagan civilization from within.

The pagan world of 2,000 years ago was neither more nor less ready for evangelization than ours. It could at first sight have seemed closed to the message of Christ, with his call to come out of darkness into his wonderful but demanding light (cf. 1 Pet 2:9). Yet the early Christians, all of them apostles, led their pagan fellow-citizens to face up to their darkness and to freely accept the demands of that light.

What was it that gave such convincing — evangelizing — power to the life and leadership of the first Christians? I would suggest that, on the basis of their faith and prayer, it was precisely a combination of certainty, unity and joy. Their certainty in Christ's truth. Their unity under Christ's binding love and authority. And their joy in Christ's mercy and grace.

Certainty, unity, joy: the very qualities that are so lacking in the modern secularised world around us. Here we can get a true reading of the signs of the times and a clue to the challenge it poses to us. If modern Christians can show the same qualities as their brethren of the first centuries, modern pagans will also be drawn to Christ.

Certainty

Christians uncertain of their own faith will not evangelize the world. Christians are meant to be leaders of the world. Uncertain leaders cannot lead. Why should anyone follow a leader who is unsure about the goals, about the road, about which is the right way and which is the wrong, unsure about the very directions that he is receiving and should be following, unsure therefore about his own leaders?

Why should pagans be impressed by the image of a church where nothing is certain, where, they are told, you will be "free" to think and do as you like? They already have that "freedom", and are beginning to discover that thinking and doing what you like easily ends in no longer liking what you think and do. They sense they are in a trap. Christians are meant to lead them out.

It is false to suppose that modern man does not want authority. He, as man of all ages, wants authority *that he can trust*. When he sees that Christians follow the authority of the Church trustingly and lovingly — because they see in it the authority of Christ whom they trust and love — then he may be drawn to wonder if the apparently hard way Christians try to follow may not indeed be Good News.

This is not to say that the image of authority in the Church does not need reshaping. If there has been any hint of dominance or exploitation or irresponsibility in the exercise of church authority, this must go. Authority as service: this is the image to be presented, and the reality to be lived.

But authority itself must remain. In other words, authority must remain authoritative. Only then does it project the image of Christ who leads us in truth and love and whom we follow in all certainty.

Good News must be certain in order to be good; and in order to appeal. Half-certain news — good rumours — is only half-interesting. It must be confirmed as certain before it really stirs interest.

On the basis of "one opinion is as good as another", there can be no evangelization. If my news is as good (or as bad) as yours, what should urge me to spread it, or you to listen to it? It is only the conviction that the Gospel is *the* Good News — the Best News — that spurs people to communicate it.

A Christian who is not convinced he has the truth is not convinced he has Christ. Only conviced Christians have any chance of convincing others. Half-convinced Christians won't even half-convince anybody. They won't convince at all.

Unity

Unity; and love. Disunited Christians will not evangelize the world. Why should anyone want to unite himself to people who themselves are not united, who do not love anyone, or who only love those they like (the pagans themselves do that; cf. Mt 5:47)? Christ said we must love even our enemies. He chose love as his Commandment, and said it must be the distinctive mark of Christians: "I give you a new commandment: love one another; just as I have loved you, you also must love one another. By this love you have for one another, everyone will know that you are my disciples" (Jn 13:34-35).

Something comes to mind that happened some few years ago in London. Jan had come from an Eastern bloc country to do a post-graduate course at the London School of Economics. Accident or God's design brought him to live at a university hall of residence with a strong Christian spirit. Jan, while a non-believer and an active communist, had a good heart and one could see how he became more and more drawn into that atmosphere of warmth and trust and understanding. It so happened that he struck up a close friendship with Frank, a fellow-economics student and a convinced Catholic. At the end of the year as Jan was about to return to his country, Frank told me (I was chaplain to the hall), "I'm going to have a good chat with Jan. He says he does not believe, but he could easily believe. Something has hit him here". Afterwards Frank told me how the conversation had gone. "Look", he told Jan, "you Communists and we Christians both want to change — to revolutionise — the world. But you want to do it through force. And we want to do it through love". Then he explained to him our Lord's New Commandment and some of the anecdotes that have come down to us showing how the early Christians lived that commandment and the effects it produced. The story, for instance, of St John in his old age at Ephesus, repeating time and again to his disciples, "My little children, love one another", and when one finally asked him, "But why do you always repeat the same thing?", his reply; "Because it is the Lord's command, and if it alone is fulfilled it is sufficient". Or the amazed comment of the pagans at *the* difference they saw in the Christians: "See how the Christians love each other!".... Jan listened intently and when Frank finished he remained looking at him in silence. When he finally broke it, it was with the simplest of comments: "Look", he said, "if you people really believe that, *you* can change the world". It is the testimony of a modern pagan impressed by the power and beauty of the commandment of Christ. A testimony which remains a challenge to us. The challenge is clear: "Let's see if you Christians are capable of living up to that. If you are, we are wasting our time. The world will be Christ's, not ours".

In a world where hatred seems to be gaining ground fast, the first Christian concern must be to live and spread love. Love saves and draws to the Saviour. Love is the unanswerable witness to Christ.

When pagans see that we trust one another and others, that we are prepared to help and serve one another and others, that we do not bear grudges, that we know how to forgive, that we are not negative or critical, that we do not gossip or backbite, that we do not speak badly of anyone, neither Catholic nor non-Catholic, neither those "above" nor those "below", neither bishop nor Pope nor layman ... then they may say: here are people with a difference. If they do not find something very special in the way Catholics treat one and treat others, why should they even begin to suspect that Catholics may in fact be following *Someone* very special.

Our love and unity do not mean we cannot have differences. We are bound to have differences: not in essentials — otherwise unity is destroyed — but in accidentals. Our love and unity are shown not in our not having differences but in how we air them: without self-pity, without a tone of grievance, without a sense of victimization, without questioning the good faith of others, without attacks on personalities, without breaking fundamental ecclesial communion and discipline.

The Church is not a debating society. It is not a convention or a parliament. It is not a one-party or a multi-party state. The

Church is a family. And one of the main witnesses it can give to the world is that of how brothers and sisters, despite differences over accidentals, can still find it good and joyful to live together in family unity (cf. Ps 132:1).

Concern for the poor. Yes, that is a particular area where Christians can show the spirit of Christ. That the world is moved when it sees a genuine Christian concern for the sick or the poor is evidenced by people's response to a Mother Teresa or a John Paul II. Whether the world sees a witness to Christ in the work of Christian Marxists is a much more debatable matter. The question is not whether Marxist theologians show a concern for the poor, but whether a Marxist inspired theology can bring about true liberation of the poor. That is the question which the Popes and the Magisterium have answered negatively at the same time as they point out true Christian ways of liberation from social and economic injustices and, more importantly, from sin. It is clear in any case that the witness that some liberation theologians give to the world is unquestionably a witness to Marx, and very questionably a witness to Christ.

Our love for the poor has to bear in mind that all men are poor. Christ's own preferential option is for sinners, and that means all of us. When *no one* is excluded from our love, then we are witnessing to Christ.

Joy

Gloomy and discontented Christians will never evangelize the world. Why should anyone be attracted to a sad Church?

In Christ's followers, the modern non-Christian or post-Christian world must meet Christ, the servant and suffering Christ, who serves and suffers in joy. If the image Christians present to the world is not one of joyful service but one of protest, bad temper and self-pity, there can be no evangelization.

Christian joy has a surprising basis. As Chesterton suggests, it is joy not because we are in the right place, but because we are in the wrong place. We were lost, but Someone has found us and is leading us home. It is joy not because we are alright — we are not — but because Someone can put us right. Christian joy comes from facing up to the one really sad fact of life, which is sin; and countering it with a joyful fact that is even realer and stronger than sin: God's love and mercy.

Some critics of Christianity accuse it of having soured humanity by introducing the sense of sin into what had been an untroubled and happy world. The accusation is absolutely false; the opposite of the truth. The pagan world of 2,000 years ago was deeply troubled and deeply unhappy. As anyone knows who is familiar with the classical literature of the period, the pagan world was dogged by a sense of guilt and sin. Christianity did not bring the sense of sin. It brought the reality of forgiveness. The disease was always there, ravaging man's heart. Christ brought the cure.

What really takes away man's happiness is not poverty or hunger or disease. One meets many poor or sick or even hungry people who are still happy, just as one meets many rich and well-fed people who are miserable. What takes away a man's happiness is not what other people do to him, nor what life or luck do to him. It is what he does to himself. It is his own deliberate choice to be selfish and sinful.

In order to recover happiness he needs to let God do something for him: to forgive him. For his part all he needs is to ask for forgiveness.

"Repent and believe the Good News, the Gospel", is how Jesus began his preaching (Mk 1:15). Until modern man recovers his sense of sin and until he repents, all the "good news" in the world — all the money and power and pleasure that may come his way — will not make him happy, because the roots of his unhappiness remain within himself.

Without repentance, the good news will not be really good. And without faith, the bad news — sickness, pain and above all the inevitability of death — will remain as bad as ever.

Do Catholics today reflect the image of people who find joy in repentance? I wonder. I am afraid that the image projected by some is that of people who would like to have the veto removed from sin so that we Christians can be as pagan as anyone else.

The Church, they say, must keep abreast of the times, and the only way it can retain credibility is by declaring that contraception is not a sin, divorce with remarriage is not a sin, pre-marital sex is not a sin, abortion is not a sin....

Is that a Gospel way? Is that a way of faith? A way of joy? A way of evangelization?

Now — the liberal message goes — look at our new Church. Now if you become a Catholic, you can continue as you are.... "But", the reply might well come, "I would expect a church to show me how *not* to continue as I am. Surely that is what redemption is about?"

Why should our modern pagan be drawn to the Church because

he is told: now in the Catholic Church you will have the freedom to follow your every sexual impulse without any qualms of conscience or anyone telling you that what you are doing is wrong?

Is this the joyful news that is supposed to attract him? Will he not turn away in boredom? Or perhaps reply: "I already have that freedom ... though I do have qualms about many things, and my conscience (when I listen to it) more than half suggests they are wrong. What I want is someone — someone I can trust — to tell my why it is wrong and above all to stop those qualms, that lack of peace inside, by telling me that though it is a sin it can be forgiven, if I repent. I need someone to help me repent. I don't want to be told I'm not a sinner. I want my sins forgiven".

A pagan world does not want to hear that sin no longer exists for Christians, but that forgiveness of sin exists for all men.

For that matter, why should people be attracted to the Church because Christians, like Marxists, say that structures should change? Maybe structures should change. But that is not a saving message. The saving message is not that "society" will be saved if structures change, but that I will be saved if I change. The saving message is to be told how I can change even though I feel that by myself I cannot. The saving message is to be shown that I am not "by myself"; that Christ, who is God, is with me with his divine mercy and strength; and to be led to the sources of that mercy and strength.

It is only on the surface of his being that man wants to hear, "You are OK". Deep inside, in the sincerity of his heart, he knows that the real fact is, "You are not OK".

Christians need to have the elementary psychological insight to realize that this is so. They need to have the more challenging ability to get to people's hearts and stir their inner sincerity and truer self-awareness. And then they need to be able to communicate the full Christian message: "We are not OK. But there is Someone who loves us despite all of that, and forgives and cleanses and strengthens us.... Let's go to him". It is above all by the joy of their own forgiven lives that they will communicate this.

Standard of Life

Joy in repentance. And joy in faith: believing that we are forgiven by a *good* God, by an "incredibly" good God whom we precisely believe to be *that* good.[1]

---

1 The Church does not have to fear "losing credibility". It, like Jesus, has to

The joy of Christians is therefore also the consequence of our having found God who is Goodness Itself and who calls us to him. Faith and hope are the basis of Christian joy. God is good. He loves me. He cleanses me and calls me to share in his infinite happiness.

A desire for a higher standard of living: there perhaps is another sign of the times. If it is what man wants, then Christians can tell him that he is offered God's own Standard of Life. That is the life that Christians already share in and hope to possess in all fullness for always in heaven. The joy that this faith and hope give is a joy which is proof against all vicissitudes. Unlike other joys, no man and no earthly thing can take it from us (cf. Jn 16:22).

Along with this cure of sin, Christ brought the conquest of death — that other great joy-spoiler. The thought of death mars all pagan joys. No philosophy, no ideology, can give man real happiness if it cannot cure the joy-killing character of death. That is the power of the Christian message. Christ has overcome death. If we follow Him, we need not fear death. We will pass through it to eternal life.

Like Jesus Christ Christians have to lead the world with authority (cf. Mt 7:29). Certainty about Christ's truth gives authority to the work of evangelization, while doubts de-authorise it. The unity lived by Christians gives authority to the Christian message, just as dissent and disunity de-authorise it. The joy of Christians gives authority to the message they bear, just as grumblings and discontent de-authorise it.

More certainty, more unity, more joy: that is the formula for evangelization. It is a formula not for structures but for persons. What modern man needs, in order to be drawn to Christ, is not a restructured or remodelled Church — he never meets "the Church" — but remodelled, renewed, Christians; he meets Christians every day, though he is often unaware of it. It is we who have to be renewed, and then we will draw men to Christ.

Self-knowledge — taking stock of our own weaknesses — leads to repentance, and so to the "joy of salvation" (cf. Ps 51:12). Once we have discovered that intensely personal character of the Good News, we are in a position to spread it.

Enough therefore of clamouring about structures or morbidly

---

challenge people to have faith. "Credible" means "capable of being believed in". God, the Church, the sacraments, the christian moral law ... all are credible if we have faith. If we are not prepared to have faith, they remain incredible; their infinite richness remains inaccessible to us and we remain stuck within our own impoverished lives.

highlighting the weak points of the Church. *My* weak points — that is what I have to change, using the strength of the Church to do so.

Then each one of us will be able to help contemporary pagan man in his soul-searching, to help him face up to *his* weak points and to see that precisely the strong points of Christianity have the answer for his weaknesses.

The Gospel is not a social manifesto and still less an organizational programme. It is the Good News of personal salvation and destiny. The Church has been commissioned to carry this message to all men. The ship of the Church — whatever the seas or the times it sails in — is therefore always on a rescue mission. The power-struggle syndrome threatens to obsess the ship's crew with totally secondary issues — "Who will run the boat?" or "What course should we take?" — and blinds them to the fact that the sea all around is full of drowning people.

The early Church also had to survive rifts and rivalries that undermined ecclesial communion and paralysed evangelization. St Paul's letters to the Corinthians show his concern lest the intellectualising tendencies of those as yet immature Christians separate them from the unity of the Body of Christ and prevent them from incarnating the Christian message and spreading it.

Paul makes no bones about defending his own apostolic authority before them. It is no concern for power or personal privilege which moves him to do so but simply his sense of responsibility for the God-given constitution of the Church. Right from the start he speaks to them in the "language of the cross" and reminds them that while the Cross may seem illogical and even mad to a human outlook, it in fact represents the power and the wisdom of God (1 Cor 1:18-25). With deep affection and with forceful reprimands he urges them to overcome their dissensions, their exclusivisms, their tendency to conform to pagan ways....

His apostle's heart seems impatient as well as worried about their self-concern and small-mindedness. He is not happy with them as he was with some of the other Christian communities he had founded. If he urges them "to be united in belief and practice" (1 Cor 1:10), one feels it is also so that the Gospel message can spread out from them as forcefully as it did from, say, the Thessalonians (1 Thess 1:7-8) or the Philippians (Phil 1:4).

If Paul were present with us today I think he would be no less forceful in urging us to unity in the faith and to integrity in the Christian moral code. He would remind us that Christ did not tell us to spend our energies arguing about new church structures or new approaches to church government; He told us flatly to get out and evangelize the world. Paul might well remind us that we will start evangelizing when we stop jostling for a place in the Church and make up our minds to serve — each in his or her own proper way — in the world, fully accepting Christ's authority, Christ's yoke, Christ's Cross, so that our lives, despite all our personal weaknesses, can mirror his spirit and convey his saving message.

14

Authority and Truth

Some of my readers may have taken part in a simple parlour-game which consists in the following: sit ten or twelve people in a row or a semi-circle, whisper a story to the first person, who has then to whisper it to the second and so successively around the row. The last person stands up and speaks out his or her version of the story. The results will be surprising; at times, very amusing. What is certain is that the final version will be different in many important details to the original. If the original story is slightly complex and is sent along a line of twenty or thirty persons, the final version may be almost unrecognizable.

In the case of a game it does not matter if the story is handed on wrongly. That is precisely the point of the game; that is what makes it funny.

But suppose it does matter. Suppose that we are no longer playing a parlour-game, but that the story to be passed on contains an important message and that the lives of many people depend on the faithful reception and understanding of this message which, for whatever reason, has to be transmitted in this person-to-person way. Then mistakes in transmitting the story are not funny. It is essential — if it is possible — to avoid them.

In such a case, if I were the originator of the message, I would (if I could) listen in carefully to each person as he receives the message and passes it on to the next; and now and then I would certainly intervene and say, "No; you did not get that correct. It's not that way; it's this way".

It is obvious that I would not be able to fulfil this corrector-prompter role if the story had to be handed on not to twenty persons living in the same time and place, but handed down to twenty successive generations. Then the problem would be beyond me. I cannot be present in each generation ensuring the validity and integrity of each transmission of the message.

God can. Jesus Christ, God become Man, communicated the message of salvation to his Apostles and told them to go and preach it to the whole world. He was with them, after Pentecost, when they went forth; and he has been with their successors ever since, prompting the true transmission, correcting errors, giving deeper understanding, ensuring that the authentic version of his saving message reaches down through all generations throughout time.

Christ could have said, "Go, teach; and be careful how you do it, because I will not be around. You get on with the job, but don't count on me. I have too many other things to look after". He could have added explicity, "If you run into any difficulties about understanding the message, if there is a difference of opinion among you about its content, then after debating the matter, take a democratic vote and hope for the best".

He of course did not say that at all. He said: "Go, teach ... *I* am *with you* always" (Mt 28:20).

The logic of God's presence

It is what we would expect. Even in human affairs those who found an institution or enterprise with important aims and who expect or want it to last, give it a constitution; and knowing that, however clear the written word may be, men will still differ about its meaning or application, they usually entrust the authentic interpretation of the constitution to some particular body. Then they die; and, from eternity, can watch how their foundation remains faithful to or gradually departs from its original aims.

An example could be the founding fathers of the United States of America. More than 200 years ago, having drawn up a written constitution, they entrusted the task of constitutional interpretation to a Supreme Court. If they have been contemplating events from some vantage point of eternity, one may well wonder whether they can have been happy with all the subsequent constitutional amendments and, especially nowadays, with Supreme Court rulings about what is in accord with the constitution and what is not.

They could do no better than that. God, we repeat, can. God knows that we men, on our own, can mistake even the clearest message, and so He did not leave us on our own. "Go, teach; *I* am with you . . .".

From God's point of view — if we can express it this way — it was a logical thing to do. It is also logical from our point of view. After all, the big question in regard to any major matter of belief or conduct is: *what does Christ have to say on this?* For *He* is the One who knows.

Did Christ just speak once two thousand years ago, and then go silent? Or has his living Voice remained with us, continuing to speak to us today, not saying new things, but prompting and correcting us in the reception and transmission of his saving message, and saying what his Mind is, what the Truth is, if a matter not explicitly dealt with in the Scriptures comes up?

If we have learned to know Christ's Voice in the Gospel, if we have caught something not only of the authority of truth but also of the accent of tenderness, of infinite love, behind his words, then we will constantly ask ourselves, "Where is that Voice today?", and will not rest content until we have found and recognized it and are being led by it.

We can say to Jesus like the Pharisees (but with more faith): "Lord, we know that you are true and that you teach the way of God truthfully" (Mt 22:16). . . . But then, Lord, *You* know the truth about man and about the problems he faces: the problems of the tenth or twentieth or thirtieth centuries. You know whether certain modes of conduct are within the way of God — *Your* way — or outside it. You know what is right or wrong in these matters. Then — tell us! Or is it possible that, although You know the truth, You deliberately choose to leave us in the dark?" . . .

This is not an issue to be lost in abstract philosophizing about the nature of truth; all the less so when, as happens nowadays to many of our secular and religious philosophers, the debate ends up, Pilate-style, in an ultimate questioning: "After all, *is* there such a thing as truth?" (cf. Jn 18:38). The ordinary citizen, who is more versed in commonsense than in higher philosophy, knows that there is such a thing as truth and error in belief, that there is such a thing as right and wrong in conduct. And deep inside, if he reflects at all on life and personal destiny, he wants to know what is true, what is right, and what is not.

Some of our modern philosophers or psychologists may describe the craving for certainty as pathological. It is no such thing; it is a basic tendency of human nature. Philosophers who have got themselves into the fix of not believing in objective truth — i.e. in any truth at all — naturally do not seek truth or certainty. Ordinary people — who are at least as important as the philosophers and far outnumber them — *do*.

No mind likes a half-truth or half the truth, if the full truth is available. Those who want to know the truth in matters of faith or morals, will not be satisfied with being told "anything goes" or "one's man opinion is as good as another's". Christ's "opinion" — his view of the truth — is better than any man's; and if it is available, we want to know it. Is it available? We all have freedom to think "in our own way". Have we the freedom to think in Christ's way? Have we access to the mind of Christ?

If it is not possible for us to think as Christ thinks, if we cannot identify his Thought, if there is no way of knowing with certainty what Christ's Mind is (and what it is not), then we are out of touch with the Mind of Christ; his Voice and the message it conveys are not coming through to us loud and clear, but have got lost somewhere along the line in a babel of human voices and opinions; and we just do not know what is *the* Truth.

But it is not so. Have we concrete and certain access to the Mind of Christ? The answer is Yes. His Mind is available to us in the mind of the Church, in the mind of the Magisterium.

This answer, we repeat, corresponds both to the "logic" of God's design — i.e. to the effective bringing of his saving message to all men — and to the logic of our expectations, that is, to our longing to know the truth.

So powerful is the force of these considerations that they moved Newman, in his *Essay on Development*, to conclude that God, in giving the gift of Revelation, would virtually have given nothing *unless* he also gave a divinely instituted means — an infallible organ — to protect Revelation and to ensure that his true and complete message (and no garbled or adulterated version of it) comes down to each generation.

The important point here of course is not to speculate about what God might logically have done or what we might expect him to have done. The point to see is what God actually did. It is no surprise that he did what was to be expected (the surprising thing would be if he had not done it); but the point in any case is that he did it.

He sent his Apostles to preach, and to teach the saving message: "Go, make disciples of all the nations ... teach them to observe all the commands I gave you" (Mt 28:19-20). And, to guarantee their teaching, He made the promise both of his presence — "know that I am with you always; yes, to the end of time" (ibid.) — and of his warranty and protection: "whatever you bind on earth shall be considered bound in heaven" (Mt 16:19; Mt 18:18); "anyone who listens to you listens to me; anyone who rejects you rejects me" (Lk 10:16).

In other words, he established a Church with a teaching mission and with the guarantee that it would teach with his Truth and his Voice, his living Voice, because he is alive and present in his Church.

When Vatican II in its Constitution on Divine Revelation speaks of the role of the Magisterium, it describes it as *living*: "the task of giving an authentic interpretation of the Word of God, whether in its written form or in the form of Tradition, has been entrusted to the living teaching office (Magisterium) of the Church alone" (DV 10).

It is necessary — so it seems to me — to focus our understanding of the Magisterium in some such way as we have outlined if we are to overcome so many current prejudices: that the Magisterium is a bureaucratic imposition, an asphyxiating force, a devitalising power, a straitjacket for thought, an enemy of theological progress, etc. etc.

The fact of the matter is that the Magisterium is a gift of God. It is not a dead-letter, it is a living thing, for it is the expression of the mind and the voice of the living Christ, it is the presence of the Spirit of Truth (Jn 16:13) guiding the thought of the Church into the fullness of truth (cf. DV 8).

Integrity and authenticity

This matter of the handing on of the faith revolves round two key ideas: integrity and authenticity.

The integral Christian faith — the *whole* of the saving message — has to be handed on. If only part were passed on, while part were lost or discarded, then subsequent generations would gradually be deprived of the full power of the word and grace of Christ.

From apostolic times this concern for integrity has been present. St Paul warns the Galatians not to listen to versions of the Gospel different to the one he had preached to them (Gal 1:6-9). Elsewhere he urges the same thing, particularly in his famous admonition to Timothy, "depositum custodi": guard what has been entrusted to you (2 Tim 6:20). No one has ever made a better commentary on that exhortation than St Vincent of Lerins writing almost 400 years later.

"Keep safe the trust", exhorts the Apostle. "What is this trust? What has been entrusted to you, not what you have invented; what you have received, not what you yourself have formulated, something that comes not by way of original thinking, but by way of teaching; not by private acquisition, but by public tradition; something that has come to you, not that you have created; regarding which you must consider yourself not author but guardian, not founder but disciple, not guide but follower.... What has been entrusted to you, may this remain in you, may this be handed on by you. You have received gold; give gold. I do not want you to put one thing in place of another. I do not want you shamelessly or fraudulently to exchange gold for copper or lead. I do not want the appearances of gold, but real gold".[1]

The task is clear: to pass on the saving faith, pure, whole and unadulterated. But if disputes about the content of the faith arise, how can we know what is genuine or *authentic* and what is not?

By authentic Christian teaching is meant teaching that truly reflects the Mind of Christ, that faithfully communicates the message of Christ to men.

Authentic teaching means in the first place teaching that derives from Revelation in its twofold source of Scripture and Tradition (DV, chap. 2). But it is always possible for disagreement to arise about whether or in what sense a particular belief appears in these sources. That is where the need for authentic teachers arises. Authentic teachers means teachers with the proper credentials. In this matter the credentials are given by God. *Lumen gentium*, having spoken of the authority and infallibility of the Pope (nos. 18-23), goes on to say that bishops too "are authentic teachers, that is, teachers endowed with the authority of Christ" (no. 25).

We are of course not suggesting that others besides the Roman Pontiff and the bishops cannot teach the truth of Christ. We are simply saying that when dispute arises about what is actually the true teaching of Christ, then, in order to authenticate his Voice and to identify his message, it is nothing human that counts: not public image nor personal sincerity nor intellectual brilliance, but a divine mandate. Only the Magisterium possesses that.

Other teachers may be endowed with great authority deriving from their academic positions or degrees, their ability as speakers, their popularity with the media, etc; but it cannot be said of them that they are endowed with the authority of Christ. That hall-mark of authenticity is borne only by the teaching office of the Pope and the College of Bishops.

Under the guidance of the Magisterium, the task of teaching the Faith is shared by many people: priests, religious, catechists, teachers in schools, lecturers in universities, professors in seminaries, etc. Parents especially, as Vatican II strongly emphasizes, are the first and natural educators of their children in the Faith (GE 3).

The theologian, as a teacher of the faith, is basically in the same position as other teachers, the only difference being that, having studied the Faith in greater depth, he should be better qualified

---

1 *Commonitorium*, 22, PL 50, 667.

to teach it. But of course it is the Faith that he is meant to teach.

How about the research aspect of theology — the theologian's search for new insights into Revelation? There are really two points to be considered here: the development of doctrine itself, and the role of the theologian in this development.

Development of doctrine

The revelation of Christ — oral and written — was completed in apostolic times. There can be no new public revelation. Yet down through the ages, the one Voice of Christ continues to speak to us, not in order to teach us new things but to help us understand more and more perfectly what his message is.

This is what is understood by the development of doctrine. Revealed Truth remains the same; new understanding of it can and should be achieved.

So, Vatican II teaches that "the Tradition that comes from the Apostles makes progress in the Church, with the help of the Holy Spirit. There is growth in insight into the realities and words that are being passed on.... The Holy Spirit, through whom the living voice of the Gospel rings out in the Church ... leads believers to the full truth, and makes the Word of Christ dwell in them in all its richness" (DV 8).

If we realize that Christ, with his Spirit, has remained with us in the Church we understand more clearly the unity and harmony and homogeneity of the Christian message. It is one Mind expounding one Truth. There are no additions (though there is development); there are no subtractions; there are no contradictions.

There are no additions. One cannot properly speak of *new* doctrines in the Church. What the Church presents is always the "Same Old Message" of Christ, but seen from new angles and in new depth. More on this in the next chapter.

There are no subtractions. Here a more present and powerful danger exists for men — of taking from the fullness of God's Message, especially when it is demanding. The temptation recurs through the centuries: to want to discover an easier version of Christianity. Easier versions have been invented; but they lack saving authenticity. God does not force us to live up to the fullness of his message; that depends on our individual response. But He does ensure that the message is preserved in his Church and handed on in its entirety.

And there are no contradictions. To think that the Church can change her doctrine in the sense of contradicting or reversing what it taught hitherto in the name of Christ, is either to deny the objective universal nature of truth, or else to deny the living presence of Christ within his Church.

This is not immobilism. It is the truth gathering scope and momentum. The ultimate reason why some things — the essential things — do not change, is that Christ does not change; "beneath all that changes there is much that is unchanging, much that has its ultimate foundation in Christ, who is the same yesterday, and today, and forever" (GS 10).

As time passes, the clarity of the message grows, the power of the voice grows. The Voice of Christ comes over the ages not as something remote. It does not come like a far-off rumour or a gentle murmur. It comes crystal-clear and loud. It makes itself present like a noonday bell or the clap of thunder.

The theologian's role

The deeper understanding of the message of Christ, although necessarily done under the guidance of the Holy Spirit, is not achieved without human effort.

Here particularly enters the research or investigative role of the theologian. The Magisterium — indeed the whole Church — looks to the theologian to fulfil this role; just as, in a slightly different sense, the theologian must look to the Magisterium in fulfilling it. Here, once again, a true ecclesiological perspective sees the point in terms of harmony and complementarity, and not of opposition.

The Church, in endorsing and encouraging theological research, adds the proviso that this research is to observe "due allegiance to the Magisterium" (c. 218). This is the juridical provision. Can we express the basis and reason for this provision in more theological — and more appealing — terms?

The theologian's field of research is in fact the Mind of Christ (cf. Chapter 16). His research task is to see what is there, not to put new things there. Moreover, he is researching a living thing; and he should be prepared to have that Mind speak back at him and even rebuke and contradict him, perhaps abruptly; "you are trying to introduce alien ideas into my Mind.... Those are your thoughts; they are not mine...."

That is why he must keep his own mind finely (and humbly) attuned to the Mind of Christ expressing itself in its authentic sources and through its authentic interpreters.

This should be clear enough if the notion of theology itself is clear. Theology, after all, signifies that reasoned knowledge or study of God and divine things which is based on Revelation and is acquired or developed in the light of the Faith.

The Truth is one; and, truly, the Truth is fixed. But theology (man's investigation into divine Truth) is not fixed. Theology is developing; it is constantly on the move. But it has to remain theology, for which three things are needed: a starting point, a means and a reference point.

The starting point is Revealed Truth (Scripture and Tradition) — which cannot deceive.

The means is human reason — which can deceive.

The reference point is Christ speaking to us in his Church, i.e. the living Magisterium — which again cannot deceive.

There are two elements here — Revelation and the Magisterium[2] — that cannot deceive us or go wrong; God will not permit that. But the third element — man's mind — can go wrong. God does not wish that to happen. But He will not prevent it, above all if man is lacking in humility; human pride has always been a main source of error.

The theologian who reasons from Scripture alone, while ignoring Tradition, is not reasoning from revelation (he is ignoring part of it). The same holds true of the theologian who reasons from Revelation but without due reference to the Mind of Christ speaking in the living Magisterium. In either case he is not reasoning theologically and is likely to go wrong.

The theologian ought not (and of course should not want) to create opposition between his mind and the mind of the Church. But there is only one basis on which he can avoid that danger: by accepting that the mind of the Church is superior. This is the tremendous choice always facing the theologian: either I subordinate my mind to the Church, or I seek to subordinate the Church's mind to my mind.

The theologian's first need, therefore, is for faith. Greater intelligence will not necessarily make him a better theologian (although it should help); greater faith will. And no matter how intelligent a person may be, a lack of faith will radically undermine his theology and eventually disqualify him as a theologian. He can continue to reason and speak about God, the Church, the

---

2 We are speaking of both the solemn and the ordinary and universal Magisterium of the Church. A concise statement of what this is, and of its binding force, is given in c. 749,1.

sacraments, etc. But if he has abandoned the starting point of Revelation or the reference point of the Magisterium, he is no longer doing theology.

"Theologians versus Magisterium"?

There is something deeply unecclesial about the "Theologians versus Magisterium" syndrome currently present in some church quarters. It is not surprising that this syndrome is played up in the secular press; antagonism always makes news. How real is this antagonism? How necessary is it?

I don't think it is real, much less necessary, But before we consider whether there has to be a fight, let us identify the possible opponents more precisely.

"Theologians versus Magisterium" is not a proper description of the line-up for the fight (if fight there be). It is rather "man's mind versus God's gift".

If there is a confrontation it is not between two church blocs, but between a divinely instituted organ for the protection of God's Word and the individual or individualistic interpretations of that Word.

Theology is a human endeavour; and, as such, runs the risks of any human endeavour. Revelation is a gift of God; and as such is divinely protected — through the Magisterium, a further gift of God.

The theologians have the right to do theology; and the duty to do it properly. The Magisterium has the duty — and the charismatic power — to protect the Faith in the service of the People of God.

Theology is a sort of intellectual game — puzzle-solving — which should always be played in God's presence. Properly and humbly played, it can offer intelligible solutions to some puzzles and throw partial light on others.

The exercise of the Magisterium is no game. It is a deeply serious, divinely commissioned task of protecting the Faith for the sake of God's People.

A few further points can help understanding:

a) The rule of the Christian mind is not theology but faith: Revelation. If theology helps understanding of Revelation, fine. But Revelation is the objective supernaturally given datum. Theology is the subjective human analysis.

b) The most firmly grounded, deepest and broadest theology

is that done by the Magisterium, not only because the Magisterium maintains an over-view of theological perspective, but also and essentially because the Magisterium enjoys special divine assistance in theological judgment. That is why it is quite false to give the impression that the theologians are the ones who "do theology" within the Church, while the Magisterium is a sort of inexpert non-theological bureaucracy that does not really know the theological field and has no right to intrude on it. The magisterial function is thoroughly theological. But it is more than theological; it is charismatic. The theologian's function is not charismatic; it is simply speculative and intellectual.

The Magisterium is *in possession* of the Faith. Its main task is not to research it for new insights, but to guard it and expound it faithfully so that each generation can understand it properly and hand it on in its integrity to the next.

The Faith is far superior to any theology or all theologies put together. Doing theology, after all, is a work for amateurs (we all need to realize that we are amateurs in the theological field, like Aquinas who felt that his life work was "straw"). Guarding the Faith is a task that requires superhuman qualifications. God has given them: to definite persons, to a definite organ in the Church.

The Magisterium guides the People of God. The theologians tempt God if they claim to guide the Magisterium. For all their intellectual powers, they lack the charism to do so. It is the Holy Spirit who guides the Magisterium. If there is danger of intrusion, then, it is not the danger of the Magisterium intruding on theology. It is the danger of the theologians intruding on the Faith.

c) The Magisterium does not normally originate theologial speculation; that is not its task. As Guardian of the People's Faith, its role is more properly activated when that faith is in any way endangered by theoretical or practical trends arising outside or inside the Church. It is then that its precise role as adjudicator appears.

It is presumption and intrusion for the theologians to claim authority over the Magisterium. The contrary, however, is not true. The theologians are not judges of the Magisterium. The Magisterium *is* judge of the theologians.

In the theology game, the theologians and the Magisterium do not have similar or equal roles. The theologians are the players; the Magisterium is the referee. Just as a referee can tell a player that a certain move is not according to the rules, so the Magisterium can tell a theologian that he is "off-side" or that a line of speculation he is following is "out of bounds"; i.e. is not within the bounds of the Mind of Christ. The Magisterium has the mission to do this and the assistance of the Holy Spirit in doing it. It alone possesses "the sure charism of truth" (DV 8).

Catholic theology has to be played according to the rules given by the Magisterium. One can play one's own theological game according to different rules. But then it is not catholic theology.

The Magisterium is within the Mind of Christ; the theologians have to enter into it (cf. Chapter 16), and have to ask the key of the Magisterium. The theologian with a Catholic sense rejoices to know who carries the keys.

Some contemporary theologians may find themselves at loggerheads with the Magisterium. Many do not; they realize that for them, exactly as for any other members of Christ's Faithful, the Magisterium is a *service*, a sure touchstone of God's Truth. When, in faith, they accept the service Christ offers them in the Magisterium, then they are enabled to fulfil their own distinctive service mission to divine Truth. Their theological speculation follows sure guidelines. Thus they render service for service; for the charismatic service of the Magisterium they return the intellectual service of theological thought. And so they too help to build up the Church in faith.[3]

Indeed the Church looks expectantly to the theologians for this intellectual service of theirs. Popes, bishops, Councils, have always relied heavily on theologians in maturing their doctrinal statements and decrees. The charism of magisterial teaching cannot dispense with theological reflection although it does not depend on any particular theology for its effect and validity.

Theologians and Magisterium are therefore natural allies, not adversaries. They have always worked hand in hand. Let us cast a glance back along the ages. We see that many great theologians of the past have in fact been bishops, and, as such, part of the Magisterium itself, like Chrysostom or Athanasius or Augustine. But there have been many others who were not bishops, and so were in no way part of the official Magisterium. Nevertheless, these theologians — a Jerome, a John Damascene, a Bonaventure, a Suarez, a Catherine of Siena, or a Teresa of Avila — enriched the mind of the Church in a way which evidences the work of the Holy Spirit. Who could measure the indebtedness of Christian

---

3 The image of *building up* the Church, the community, the Body of Christ, was especially dear to St Paul (cf. 1 Cor 14:5-12; 5:12; 2 Cor 12:19; Eph 4:12, etc.). He insists that individual gifts must be used for building up (1 Cor 14, passim); and warns in particular that while knowledge without love "puffs up", it does not "build up" (1 Cor 8:1).

thought to the theological reflections of men like Thomas Aquinas or John Henry Newman?

Yet though these theologians worked "outside" the Magisterium, they did not work without reference to it. They, as any theologian who understands his task, looked to received Truth and to the Magisterium as their guide and ally and safeguard in their theological investigations. For them a theological reflection out of harmony with Tradition or with the Magisterium meant a thought out of harmony with the Mind of Christ. And that for them was an unthinkable thought, theologically speaking. This remains a norm for sound theology.

Truth and the People

Scepticism about objective truth is the fashion of our age. The fashion will pass because it does not correspond to man's rational nature, to that deep longing for the truth present in every mind and heart. Yet, being the current fashion, it tends to influence even Christians. And Christians should be aware of this influence. If they are not, if they do not discern it and resist it, it can undermine their faith in Christ, the Truth, and in Christ's Church, the guardian of the Truth.

A hankering after democratic processes is also part of the spirit of the age. It corresponds to a fear of tyranny and to a respect for equality. Nevertheless, however much the democratic process may be considered the best means of establishing a government, it clearly is not a trustworthy means of establishing the truth. Few people, if they stop for reflection, will seriously suggest that the truth is to be arrived at by a democratic voting process: "the majority have it". If the majority of directors of a company vote in favour of fraudulent tax returns, does this make the tax returns true? If the majority in a country vote in favour of discrimination against a minority, have they thereby created a new and true norm of conduct?

No. A democratic vote may coincide with the truth, or may not. It does not establish it. Christ was in a minority of One, especially in the critical moments of his life; and yet it is precisely Christ and not "the majority"' who is the source and criterion of truth in the Church and in the world.

However, in a *certain* sense, the majority opinion in the Church does point to the truth of Christ. We are speaking about what is termed the "sensus fidelium" or the "sensus fidei": the sense of the faith possessed by the people. *Lumen gentium* states: "the whole body of the faithful who have an anointing that comes from the holy One cannot err in matters of belief. This characteristic is shown in the supernatural appreciation of the faith (*sensus fidei*) of the whole people when, from the bishops to the last of the faithful, they manifest a universal consent in matters of faith and morals" (LG 12).

Several points would need to be carefully noted here:

a) The whole body of the faithful cannot err when they manifest a "universal consent" in faith and morals, i.e. when they are *united* in belief. If they are not united, if there is no universal consent but rather disagreement, then obviously there must be error on one side or another. That is where the more particular organs of infallibility must be looked to.

b) They cannot err when united in matters of *belief*. It is important to weigh this point well because what people actually *believe* is not always easy to establish — least of all by certain types of opinion poll.

For example, we read in the newspaper that, according to some opinion poll, 60 per cent of Catholics in a given country "disagree with" the Church's teaching on contraception.... One does not have to question the reliability of the poll to ask: and what exactly are we supposed to conclude from that?

Does "disagree with" meant that they *do not observe* the Church's teaching on this matter, or that they would "prefer" if the Church's teaching were different and not so demanding? This may well be. Since all of us are sinners, there will always be some point of the Church's teaching that we do not live up to, and we may well wish that it were less demanding. If the opinion poll is simply meant to show that Catholics are sinners like everyone else, we can have little difficulty in accepting its findings.

But I think that the opinion poll is in an offhand way trying to suggest something else: that the Catholics polled *believe* — i.e. are convinced in faith — that the Church's teaching is *wrong*. This is the underlying suggestion that needs careful consideration.

If we are to know by opinion poll what people actually believe on the subject, then the questions asked should be: "After taking a good look at your faith and a good look into your conscience, do you *believe* that the Catholic Church's teaching on contraception is not only clear and demanding, but also *false*? Do you *believe* that contraception is permitted and approved by Jesus Christ; that it is according to his law and not against it?"

I wonder what percentage of those Catholics who "disagree"

with the Church's teaching on contraception actually believe that the Church's teaching is contrary to the mind of Christ. My experience is that, not to speak of Catholics, many Protestants are not at ease in their heart about the practice of artificial birth control, however much their church or pastors may tell them it is alright. Such unease is quite understandable; contraception after all so evidently *denaturalises* sex.

If it could be verified that 60 per cent of Catholics somewhere "disagree with" the Church's teaching on birth control — in the sense that they do not observe it — one would simply have established a sociological fact. It would be a sad comment on their behaviour, but it would say absolutely nothing about their faith. To show that their practice has deteriorated does not in any way prove that their *faith*, on this precise point, has declined.

c) There is a third point to be noted. When we affirm the infallibilty of the believing Church, when we say that the *whole body* of the faithful cannot err in matters of faith, we have to remember that the Church is not just the Church of this present moment. It is the Church of the centuries. The body of the faithful is not "whole" unless it includes past generations as well as the generation which for the time being is "present". We can therefore truly regard the people in the Church as witnesses to the truth, in their united belief, but not if we exclude past generations. To exclude them would be "undemocratic". The former generations are also members of the People of God. And in listening to their voice we are in fact listening to the people's voice: the whole people's voice. It is the voice of the *whole people* that gives a true echo of the Voice of Christ.

Some further points about the faith of the people:

(i) The faith is the people's. It is theirs not to do what they like with, but to enjoy. It is theirs not to change but to believe and try to live by; and thereby to be saved.

(ii) The faith is the people's. It is their right and heritage. As a heritage it needs protection, so that it can be received from the preceding generation and passed on to the succeeding one, whole and entire. God, through the Magisterium, ensures the protection of this inheritance that He bequeathed to his people.

(iii) Some theologians today claim to be spokesmen for the faith of the people. By what right have they appropriated that role? Even humanly speaking it is not likely that theologians can articulate the people's faith better than the bishops. The bishops are pastorally and physically closer to the people, while the theologians tend to live in a more remote academic world; one sees in practice how the views they advance are often very far removed from the mind of the people. The bishops are not self-appointed. It was God's idea to give them as shepherds and fathers to his people (CG 11-21).

Authority, Truth and Scripture

The seeking of scriptural roots for Catholic doctrine is an endeavour that the Church always encourages. But this endeavour needs to avoid several mistaken approaches:

a) ignoring Tradition altogether, as if Scripture alone were the only and sufficient rule of faith. This is the Protestant position.

b) subordinating Tradition to Scripture, as if Scripture were a higher authority or normative source. The Catholic teaching is that both together "make up a single sacred deposit of the Word of God" (DV 10); they "are bound closely together, and communicate one with the other. For both of them, flowing out from the same divine wellspring, come together in some fashion to form one thing, and move towards the same goal. Sacred Scripture is the speech of God as it is put down in writing under the breath of the Holy Spirit. And Tradition transmits in its entirety the Word of God which has been entrusted to the apostles by Christ the Lord and the Holy Spirit.... Thus it comes about that the Church does not draw her certainty about all revealed truths from the holy Scriptures alone. Hence, both Scripture and Tradition must be accepted and honoured with equal feelings of devotion and reverence" (DV 9).

c) viewing the Magisterium as an artificial and unjustifiable ecclesiastical restraint imposed on the free interpretation of the Christian message.

A few points of reflection can help us avoid these mistaken approaches, and see instead the harmony that reigns between the sources from which we receive Revelation, and the organ by which we are guided in understanding it.

That Scripture alone was never meant to be the exclusive guide to Christian belief is already clear from the fact that for the first fifteen or twenty years after Pentecost there was *no* scripture of the New Testament. During that period, all knowledge of Christ's Revelation came through oral preaching or handing on (Tradition of course simply means "handing on"). It is commonly accepted that the earliest book of the New Testament dates from about 49-50 AD; the last were written some fifty years later. The point is brought out also by the fact that Christ did not tell his disciples to write, but to preach (Mt 28:19-20; Mk 16:16), and it was precisely to their preaching that He referred his promise to be present with them (Mt ibid). A few of them,[4] under the inspiration of the Holy Spirit, consigned essential aspects of the divine message to writing. But the early Christian concern was not to spread these writings, it was to spread the message; and to spread it *orally*. This was a matter of necessity: in part because very few copies of these scriptures existed (books were extremely rare objects then, and in fact remained rare until the invention of printing more than one thousand years later); and above all because the vast majority of those receiving the message simply could not read. The written word could not enlighten them; the spoken word could.

There is a further main point that should be clear. Scripture cannot stand on its own; i.e. it cannot authenticate itself. Many writings have come down to us from the first centuries, claiming to give an account of the life of Christ or his teaching. A long list could be made: the Gospel according to the Hebrews or the Egyptians, the Gospel of Peter, the Acts of Peter or of John, the Letter to the Laodiceans, etc. These books are rejected as non-inspired, by Protestants and Catholics alike. But, by what authority is the Gospel of Luke to be included in the Scriptures and the Gospel of Thomas to be excluded?

What grounds have Christians for believing that the Bible is made up of our present 72 books, precisely those 72 and no others? The Bible cannot vouch for itself. The Bible cannot prove that the Bible is inspired; to maintain that would be to reason in a circle. The only way we can truly know which books are inspired, which books form part of the Bible, and which do not, is through some authority *external to* the Bible which itself possesses a divine guarantee of truth. That is the Church. St Augustine sums up the point when he said, "I would not believe the Gospel except on the authority of the Catholic Church".[5] That is why "internal criteria" for establishing the true sense of Scripture have only a limited value and are not above external criteria such as the *sensus fidei*, Tradition, the Magisterium.

It should be noted that the accusation of arguing in a circle does not apply to the Catholic position. The Catholic does not appeal

---

[4] Seven, to be precise (Matthew, Mark, Luke, John, Paul, James, Peter); or eight, if we take the author of Hebrews to be other than Paul.

[5] *Con. epist. Manichaei, fundam.* no. 6.

to inspired Scripture to prove the Church's claim to divine authority, and at the same time appeal to the Church's authority to prove the divine inspiration of Scripture. No; the Catholic first goes to what actually occurred, i.e. to History; and therefore also to the books of Scripture — but considering them for this purpose simply as part of the historical record. From history he concludes that Jesus Christ existed, that He claimed to be God, and that He proved his claim; that He founded a Church to carry on his work; and that this Church — the Catholic Church — enjoys divine protection in its teaching: also about which books are divinely inspired.

God speaks to us through the Bible. But He must not only tell us what is the Bible — i.e. which books are to be included in it, and which are not — but also what is the meaning He intended in the different passages of the sacred writings. He does so through Tradition and through the living Magisterium.

Scripture gives us God's written word. Tradition conveys the whole message of Christ. And with the help of the Magisterium we learn the true and clear meaning and the application of this divine Revelation. Vatican II emphasizes, "It is clear, therefore, that, in the supremely wise arrangement of God, sacred Tradition, sacred Scripture and the Magisterium of the Church are so connected and associated that one of them cannot stand without the others. Working together, each in its own way under the action of the one Holy Spirit, they all contribute effectively to the salvation of souls" (DV 10).

When we speak of Tradition therefore, we are not referring just to the established beliefs of the first centuries. Tradition is built up and comes down to us over all the centuries. It is an inheritance that is constantly being enriched, not by addition of belief but by increase of understanding. That is the theme of development of doctrine which we took a brief look at earlier. However there are further aspects to this theme that are important enough to merit a chapter apart.

15

Truth and Definition

Nothing can be added to the message of Christ. But more light can be cast on it. Our understanding of it can and ought to grow. Many elements can enter into this process of clearer understanding: prayerful meditation, theological speculation, doctrinal controversy.... But the ultimate responsibility and competence for defining revealed doctrine belongs to the Magisterium.

We have just made use of particular terminology that is pretty certain nowadays to produce a negative reaction among many. "Defining?! Are you actually speaking about *definition* of doctrine? But — surely this is a totally pre-conciliar concept that the Church has by now for all practical purposes abandoned?"

No; I do not think that the Church has abandoned the idea that doctrine needs defining, nor has it abandoned its role in this task. But I agree that the subject of doctrinal definitions is a theological "hot potato". Still, it has to be handled. Maybe some reflection can cool the item and even make it palatable and digestible. To do so our reflection will have to attempt to correct two current mistaken assumptions: a) the idea that a dogmatic definition is something restrictive and negative; b) the idea that if a point of doctrine is not yet dogmatically defined, one is "free" to dissent from it, even to the extent of holding a diametrically opposed position.

Slide-shows

What does the notion of defining doctrine imply? A simple example can help us here. Let us suppose I am attending a projection of slides. A slide appears on the screen — a scene, let us say, of a family group standing in a garden — but it is rather blurred. People generally are not happy with blurred pictures if it is possible to get them clearer, so someone in the audience calls out, "Hey, focus". The operator does his job; he adjusts the lens, and there it is — a clear, well-*defined* picture.

That is what the definition of doctrine does. It makes a picture — an idea, a truth — clearer, easier to look at and see and understand in all its details.

A definition therefore is not something that restricts; it clarifies. It is a service. It does not limit mental freedom or vision or understanding; it facilitates them. What it limits is blurredness; what it reduces is confusion of images and outlines; what it eliminates is over-lapping of borders and edges.... But all of that precisely is necessary in order to have the freedom of seeing a *clear* picture.

Just as a blurred or faded picture restricts our visual freedom, so a blurred or vague idea restricts our mental freedom. Our mind wants to see things clearly; its understanding is hampered, is less free, if it does not.

When that slide was projected at the viewing we have mentioned, the audience was not happy. Objects were poorly outlined, some perhaps were not even easy to identify (is that little child a boy or a girl?), the relationship between bodies and areas and colours was not precise and clear. That is not good viewing.

The same holds good when what we are contemplating is not a slide but a point of Christian belief. If one cannot see its precise meaning, if the relationship between propositions and realities is not clear, that is not good understanding. A hazy mental picture is as unsatisfactory as a hazy visual picture.

Let us take the doctrine of the Incarnation as an example. That Jesus Christ is God and Man has always been the central point of Christian belief. Yet certain projections of this doctrine so blur the real meaning of the terms in which it is expressed, or so distort the relationships between these terms, as to present a vague and scarcely intelligible picture, or one that in fact gives a totally false idea of the Incarnation.

If the doctrine is projected in such a way as to suggest that Jesus is just God and that his Humanity is only an appearance ..., or that he is just Man simply with a special relationship with God ..., or that he has only one nature, or that he has two persons ..., all of that, based on wrong focussing of parts of the picture or of the relationship between the parts, actually gives a false projection of the doctrine.

If this happens — it happened in the first three or four centuries and some of it is happening again today — the Christian audience calls out, "Hey, focus"; and the operator — the Magisterium — obliges. Then, once again we get an intelligible picture of clear definition: Jesus is truly God: he truly possesses the divine nature. He is truly Man; he truly possesses our human nature. And both natures find their union in one Divine Person.

Let us take another example: the Holy Eucharist. To understand the Eucharist simply as the Body of Christ may still be blurred understanding, if one is not clear about the relationship between bread and Body, if the apparent overlapping of the two realities is not clarified, if one is not sure where the bread "ends" and where the Body "begins".

If the projection of the doctrine of the Eucharist suggests that the bread remains bread but simply acquires a new purpose or significance, then the projection falsifies Catholic doctrine; as it does if it suggests that the Body is somehow present along with the bread during the eucharistic celebration but that, after the celebration, the Body "departs" and only bread remains. Such misprojections have occurred in the past, and recur today.

A bit of definition clarifies our picture. The bread "ends" and the Body "begins" at the consecration. What was there before the consecration looked like bread and was bread. What is there after the consecration looks like bread but is not bread. The appearances of bread remain, but the underlying reality — *what* is there — is totally changed; is Jesus Christ. And he remains there, even after the eucharistic celebration, as long as the appearances — the "accidents" — of bread remain. Now, *that* is a clear projection of the mystery of the Eucharist.

The slide comparison can help illustrate further points that are important to our subject.

The operator projecting the slide does not create the picture. The picture is already there; he simply presents it for viewing. When he gives better focus, he is neither inventing nor changing the picture. He is simply facilitating better viewing of an existing picture which was taken perhaps quite some time ago. His job is not to make or vary the picture, but simply to project it in as well-defined and as viewable a way as possible.

So the Magisterium in relation to Revelation. The Magisterium does not originate Revelation. It does not tamper with or vary Revelation. It is at the service of Revelation; and of the viewers of Revelation. It protects Revelation for each generation to see; and defines it, or areas of it, so that it is presented to even the most blurred eyes in all clarity. Safeguarding clarity and definition is the function of the Magisterium. The Magisterium has no power to change the picture of Revelation into another picture. The picture was "taken" — and entrusted to the Church for projection — two thousand years ago. It will remain the same picture for the rest of time.

Feeling "free" about the picture?

This can help us to spot the defective understanding behind the second point mentioned above, i.e. the suggestion that if a point of belief has not yet been definitively or formally defined, then one is not "bound" by it; one is even "free" to hold views that radically contradict it, even if it has been held and taught in the Church for centuries.

Those who feel that this attitude is uncatholic, that it smacks of a minimalistic and therefore a legalistic approach, are right. Yet they might be hard put to show it to be untenable if they limit themselves (as do their opponents) to purely technical or legal arguments. The untenability of this position is only adequately seen on ecclesiological grounds. Then it is seen clearly.

If the Church — the Church of the centuries — has the Mind of Christ, then its teaching reflects that Mind. And Christ does not change his Mind. The Mind of Christ is not an enigmatic mind (though it has depths of mystery). It is not ambiguous or hesitant. It is not a mind that fluctuates over the centuries, denying old truths or introducing new ones. It is not self-contradictory....

That is why we can have *relative but real* certainty in our grasp even of the "non-defined" areas of Christ's Mind. It would of course be preferable to speak of the *"less*-defined" — rather than the "non-defined" — areas, because the projection of even these areas is of sufficient clarity for us to be sure of their substantial content — to be sure of what this content *is*, and of what it is *not* and *cannot* be — even if such areas are open to further definition or clarification. That clarification will necessarily be a confirmation of what is already visible. It will show us what we already see, and show it in greater richness of detail.

The picture we already see will resolve itself into the *same* picture, but seen more clearly. It will not and cannot resolve itself into a totally unexpected (and less still a contradictory) picture.

Just because the picture in our slide-show is not perfectly focussed and every individual detail is not clear in fullest precision, this does not leave me, as viewer of the scene projected, "free" to twist what it represents into anything I choose. I do not (and should not) feel "free" to deny that the picture is one of a group in a garden, affirming instead that it may possibly turn out to be a riot in a city square. I may not see all the details in proper precision, but I see the main outlines with sufficient clarity to be sure of what the details, when properly focussed, may or may not turn out to be. It does not cross my mind to suggest that that ill-defined area of blue in the flower-bed may actually turn out to be a well-defined area of red. Those two figures shaking hands are, it is true, not totally clear; yet I am totally certain that all the focussing in the world will not resolve them into two fencers crossing swords together. I am equally sure that the somewhat blurred figure of a man standing in the centre of the scene will not, on further definition, vanish into thin air.

Yet this is precisely the sort of thing that some theologians in the Church are suggesting today in relation to the picture of Christian teaching. They admit, for instance, that contraception in the Christian view (Protestant as well as Catholic) has been seen until very recent years as seriously sinful. But, they claim, since this has not been *formally* defined, one is "free" to see it the other way round. Since there has been no definition one is free to hold that the message Christ projects for us is precisely the opposite: that the real truth about contraception is that it is acceptable and even pleasing to Him.

"Since there has been *no* definition" ...? This is the essential flaw in the argument. "The Church's teaching on contraception has never been defined" ...? But it has! It has been consistently projected to Christ's Faithful in clearly defined (if not solemnly defined) terms over centuries. Prior to 1960, the Magisterium, the theologians and the faithful were at one in how they understood the message coming to them from Christ on this point. This was a clear black-and-white area of the picture. No one doubted it or saw it otherwise: there can be sexual sins within marriage; contraception is one of them; it is gravely wrong.[1]

The point is that definition is not just a magisterial or juridical act. It is also and even mainly a matter of how a doctrine is projected and seen. That is why, as we have been trying to illustrate with the slide-analogy, there are in fact degrees of definition. A solemn definition is the final possible stage; and it is only possible because the truth in question has been *seen* in clear definition beforehand. A definition, therefore, does not need to be solemn in order to be clear. It does not have to be formulated in the ultimate precision of a solemn infallible document in order to be unmistakeable and unchangeable in its content and meaning.

In short; while a doctrine taught by the ordinary non-solemn Magisterium may not be finally or totally defined, it is not so

1 The agreement on this point of doctrine was ecclesially unanimous. The Magisterium was clear in what it presented. The faithful were clear in what they saw. And the theologians were clear in what they taught; not a single theologian of any repute questioned the teaching before 1960.

blurred or obscure that its main features are unrecognizable. On the contrary, the main features are precisely the ones that cannot be mistaken. Where there is room for adjustment or further appreciation is in relation to the finer details. Even then the process of further definition will always simply emphasize the harmony between these details and the already unmistakeable whole.

Is the Church's teaching on contraception therefore infallible? Since infallible teaching means teaching that is free from error and therefore certainly "true" — because Christ guarantees its truth — I do not see how a Catholic mind can avoid the conclusion that the traditional teaching on contraception enjoys a divine guarantee of truth — in virtue not so much of papal infallibility[2] as of the infallibility of the whole Church: of the ordinary and universal Magisterium, and also of the "sensus fidelium" for centuries right up to the post-conciliar period.

Vatican II itself explicitly lays down that the teaching of the Magisterium on birth control must be followed (GS 51). The post-conciliar dissidence on the matter, by certain theologians, is no witness against Tradition and the Magisterium. It is the dissidents who have to show that they have not departed from the Mind of Christ; or to show how contraception can become "right" today — having been wrong yesterday — without this signifying that Christ, besides having failed to uphold his Church, has practised deceit on his followers and has a confused and self-contradictory Mind.

The Catholic view has never been that defined dogma represents the area of necessary belief, while the ordinary Magisterium represents an area of spontaneous opinion where each one is free

---

2 Although, to my mind, papal infallibility is also involved. All modern Popes, especially from Pius XI on, addressing themselves precisely as teachers of all the faithful on a major matter of morals, have explicitly and repeatedly taught that contraception is a grave sin against God's law and against the meaning and dignity of sex in marriage. The argument that the teaching of Pius XI and Paul VI is contained "only" in an Encyclical (*Casti connubii* and *Humanae vitae*) and that an Encyclical is not normally used for infallible proclamations is no argument. The Pope is infallible not when he chooses to use a particular type of document for his teaching but when, in virtue of his office, he teaches all the faithful a doctrine to be held concerning faith and morals. This is what Pope Paul VI explicitly did in *Humanae vitae*. Consider the force and solemnity of the words with which he introduces his decision that, despite modern arguments urged in favour of contraception, the moral evaluation on this matter remains unchanged: "We, *by virtue of the mandate entrustd to Us by Christ*, intend to give Our reply to this series of grave questions" (HV 7).

to think as he chooses. Both represent the area of truth. Both cover the area of Christ's Mind.³

The ecclesiogically defective approach that claims the right to see what one likes where a teaching, however traditional, has not been formally defined, is of course only one step removed from the approach that claims to see what one likes even when the doctrine has in fact been defined by solemn magisterial act. Quite a number of contemporary theologians have already taken that step. In the name of theological development they suggest that the time has come to resee the whole picture of Christian teaching in such a way that what was seen as black before can now be seen to be white, what was seen as square before can now be taken to be round, what was there before can not be declared to be absent or posited as something to be removed.

The suggestions are made every day. They are made not only in the field of morals, as we have seen: that contraception — or divorce or abortion — though projected before as wrong, can now, to a modern eye, be seen to be right. Parallel suggestions are made in the dogmatic field, in relation to the most basic doctrines of faith: that the Virginal Birth of Jesus Christ, or his Bodily Resurrection, or his Real Presence in the Eucharist, though formerly projected and seen by generation after generation of Catholics to mean what the terms of each doctrine literally express, can now — "given the finer adjustments of understanding that our modern theological research methods permit" — be seen to mean no such thing but to be simply metaphorical figures or symbolic ways of conveying a totally different meaning: a meaning emptied in fact of any objective content or transcendental value.

Close-up viewing

Close examination of the details of a picture always risks losing sight of the picture. Over-concentration on one word or phrase of a message may make one forget the whole message.

For instance, historical-critical methods of biblical investigation are close-examination tools. They are like a magnifying glass; they magnify the text, but in doing so they often blur the context.⁴ A

---

3 *Lumen gentium*, 25 teaches that *both* the ordinary universal Magisterium *and* the solemn Magisterium are infallible.

4 The context here is historical — in the most precise sense. It is the *fact* of the Incarnation, and all that flows from it (Revelation, sacraments, Church...).

magnifying glass in any case is not the best instrument for viewing an entire picture.

It is not criticism of the theologian to say that the reason why he must use close-examination tools is that he is short-sighted. All of us are short-sighted in relation to Revelation. Magnified examination of the details should be a help to us not in order to view those details in isolation but so that, seeing them better, our over-view of the whole picture is magnified. Tradition is the main over-all magnifier.

Some contemporary theologians deserve criticism, however, not for being short-sighted but for being *narrow*-sighted. Narrow-sightedness, in relation to Revelation, is something no Christian can afford. Our perspective must be broad enough to cover the whole picture.

In taking a close-up view, we cannot afford to lose our over-all view. That is what is happening to some of our theologians. They have been caught in the trap of the specialist: "knowing more and more about less and less". They have brought their minds to concentrated focus on a particular research area — some aspect of Christian belief — and as a result they have totally lost perspective. Further, their narrowed view becomes normative for them. What lies outside its scope — Tradition, the Magisterium, the *sensus fidei* — becomes irrelevant. They judge the picture by the part — their view of the part. And what they then see is in fact no longer the Picture.

The close examiner may find himself so engrossed in his work that he feels he has neither time nor room to stand back, to recover that broader view. Then especially he needs the humility to make constant reference to the over-view given by the vantage point of the centuries (Tradition, the *sensus fidei*), or given, right now, by the Holy Spirit through a particular organ (the Magisterium).

The human tools of the theologian — philosophical systems, critical exegesis, etc. — are useful provided they are used simply as *tools* and in order to do *theology*. Theology is not theology if its reference or verification point is the tool used. Its reference point is the Faith, Revelation (the whole picture, already there

If a scholar does not work within this historical context, he is not working as a Christian. Other historical or literary reference points are completely subordinate to the fact of the God-Man and his Revelation. For the exegete, as for any theologian, the first and fundamental questions are: Do I believe Jesus Christ to be God and Saviour of all men? Do I accept his Divinity — and his Revelation — as my starting and reference point? Do I accept that his Mind and Will come to me through the Church's Magisterium?

and already clear), the Magisterium. If the tool becomes the self-verifying reference point, then the whole picture is lost. It becomes a picture in the mind of the viewer, variable according to the variations of his mind or imagination, but with no objective content in itself.

The broad-viewed ordinary believer who sees the *whole* picture of Revelation, even if not in great analytical depth, theologizes better than the narrow-viewed theologian who views one aspect of the Christian message but not in the context of the whole of Revelation.[5] The picture of Revelation is clear, but only to the eyes of faith. Eyes of human intelligence alone are blurred, and blur the picture.

Pluralism

The slide-projection image remains suggestive in further ways. For instance, we could say that the picture of Revelation is "three-dimensional". It stands out like the real thing full of life and movement that it is. Therefore it can be viewed by different viewers from a variety of angles. A man is a man whether seen from behind or in front. Depending on the angle, he looks slightly different; but he is still seen as a man. If he is not seen as a man but as something else, then it is not the angle of view that is at fault. It is the viewer's eye; his vision is faulty.

This could serve to illustrate the reality and the limits of theological pluralism, i.e. the fact that different theological explanations can be advanced for the same doctrines of faith. Pluralism in theology corresponds to this "three-dimensionality" of the truth. Changing ways of viewing a doctrine are legitimate provided it is the angle of vision that changes, while the object seen — the actual doctrine — remains the same.

---

5 Already in the second century, St Irenaeus rejoiced to contemplate the unity of the Church in believing the truths of faith handed down from the apostles. "The Church believes these truths, as if it had but one soul and one heart, it preaches them and hands them on as though it had but one mouth. For although there are many different languages in the world, even so the strength of tradition is one and the same. The Church founded in Germany believes exactly the same and hands on exactly the same as do the Spanish and Celtic churches, and the ones in the East, those in Egypt and Libya and Jerusalem, the centre of the world. As the sun, which is God's creation, is the same throughout the whole world, so the preaching of the truth shines in all places and enlightens all men who wish to come to the knowledge of the truth"(*Adv. Haer.* I, 10).

The Eucharist — seen in a Catholic sense, as the true Body of Christ — can be viewed from a variety of angles: the viewpoint of Sacrifice, the viewpoint of Banquet, the viewpoint of Presence; the further viewpoints of its effects on the individual or on the community, etc. But it is still the same Eucharist that is being seen from all these angles.

Now if someone's angle of view on the Eucharist is such that he says, "I don't see the Body of Christ there, not his true Body" ..., then that is not one more view within a pluralism of views. It is not seeing the same Object from a different angle, it is seeing a different object. That is no longer the pluralism of reasoning *differently* within the *same* Faith. It is reasoning outside the Faith.

In theological pluralism one sees Revelation as it *is* — from different angles. If one starts seeing Revelation as it *is not*, that is not pluralism. That is to interfere with the Mind of Christ, attempting to take things out that should be there or to put things in that should not. And then Christ speaks his Mind through the Magisterium: "Those are not my thoughts. You are not seeing my Revelation clearly. Clarify your sight or your angle of vision. Let me clarify it for you. This is what I mean. This is *my* Revelation. Take it or leave it. Do not twist it or tamper with it".

Pluralism means contrast, but not contradiction, between angles of belief. Pluralism means diversity of approaches within the one Faith, complementarity of views of the same Truth, different but interconnected understandings. We can and ought to revel in such pluralism. It is a cause of joy because it is a sign of Catholic richness and variety (cf. Chapter 17).

Pursuing our analogy we could describe the *sensus fidelium* as the "audience-response" of those countless publics who have contemplated the picture of Revelation down the centuries. Audience after audience has shown its appreciation in a way that becomes normative for the true interpretation of Christ's Performance. Their breathless response to Christ in his Mysteries — to Christ in the Manger, Christ on the Cross, Christ Risen, Christ in the Eucharist — has never been a mere poetic reaction to "suggestive myths" or "moral stories", but a heart and soul response to *real events* which really took place, which centuries later really affected their lives and in which they could take part with deepest effect. It was that response which led to so many popular expressions of faith and piety: family and public devotions, Passion plays, images. . . .

To ignore or not to attempt to appreciate the depth and power of such audience responses is to narrow one's own understanding.

It is in a certain sense to fail to learn from Christ viewing himself. For only Christ can understand his own Mind in full depth, and view Himself from all possible angles. The development of doctrine could be described as that process by which Christ, in his members, reflects on himself. This process will continue until the Body of Christ attains the total understanding communicated by the Head to his members.

Each audience of each age (and each individual viewer), while seeing the whole picture, has perhaps responded with more marked enthusiasm to some particular detail or other. It is possible that an audience of a later generation (or you or I as individual viewers) may not be so attracted by that particular detail. This, if it refers to incidental details, is our freedom. It could also be our impoverishment. The more one sees and appreciates not only the overall picture of Revelation but each and every one of its details, and the more one appreciates the flames or flickers of faith or of simple devotion that each detail enkindles or reflects, the richer one's response to the universality of the Mind and Heart of Christ.

There is in fact *nothing* in the history of genuine development of doctrine that is irrelevant to the *full* grasp of the message handed down from the Apostles.

The ordinary Christian viewer of Revelation, and especially the theologian, needs this constant reference to the past if he is to clarify his viewing and not risk changing the object viewed. The viewing angles of the Fathers, of the Saints, of the centuries, will help him focus his eyes in depth, give keenness to his gaze, to look more deeply in the right direction — i.e. towards the same Object — whatever his stance and angle of view.

Some contemporary theologians seem to have lost this ability to see with the eyes of the ages, or this sense that their own views need to keep within that developing harmony of all-round vision.

A fundamental question of the Christian thinker is: do my views, do these new insights entering my perspective, square with the audience view of the past? If they do not, then there should be a fundamental readiness to change them.

The more the audience of the past saw what I fail to see, or the more I see something radically different to what they saw, the more likely it is that *I* am the one whose vision needs correcting.

One gets the impression that many modern theologians do not think or act this way. Rather — if they think of the audience reactions of the past at all — they simply dismiss them as the narrow and credulous views of backward people who would never have been able to appreciate the picture of Revelation scientifically corrected and redrawn according to twentieth century standards.

Revelation is God's Work and the people's patrimony. Yet some modern experts have taken it into their own hands, to cut and patch and repaint, as if they had authorship rights over it, as if its worth depended on their authentication. There would seem to be as much presumption in their efforts as there is a lack of psychological perception of the effects of these efforts on the people.

What has been the response evoked by modern theologies of secularisation and demythification of the Gospel? Plaudits from specialist groups or clerical coteries; boredom from the great audience of normal Christians. Why should a Christ who is not God, who is not Risen, who is not present in the Eucharist, interest me?

Experts are always faced with the temptation of reducing the worth of a masterpiece to the level of their own appreciation of it; or of thinking that its fame is due in fact to them and not to its intrinsic value.

Rembrandt or Raphael or Velazquez came to be considered geniuses not first (not even mainly) because some experts judged them so, but because they evoked a deep response in the common man. That popular and spontaneous judgment of the beauty of their paintings is in fact a greater pointer to artistic worth than the detailed analyses of the experts.

Modern art experts wax enthusiastic about the work of some contemporary painters whose paintings nevertheless cause laughter or boredom among the ordinary people. Who is to say which judgment is sounder?

The true expert can deepen the popular understanding of the beauty of a masterpiece; but its beauty ante-dates him. Time points more surely to its worth than does individual judgment. Philistines have traditionally gone against the judgment of time; and time, in the end, has reasserted its judgment against them.

It is true that there is another function which certainly calls for expertise: deciding whether a newly presented painting claimed to be, say, an authentic Rembrandt, is in fact authentic or not. If we apply the analogy to our subject, the required expertise is in ultimate possession of the Magisterium.

How far does infallibility go?

Certain recent writers have criticised the Church's claim to infallibility as if it were a sort of "thought-throttler"; as if, by saying that the truth goes "thus far and no farther", it seeks to limit progress in theological knowledge. Some critics add a more explicit accusation of pride, as if an infallible Magisterium were claiming to be in *exclusive* possession of knowledge, or even to be in possession of *all* knowledge, thus attributing to itself a God-like quality.

The confusion here is elementary, but noteworthy. Infallibility does not refer to extent of knowledge or understanding, but simply to *freedom from error* in knowing. It refers to certainty about the truth and to correctness in what is taught and believed.

Infallibility implies no claim that the doctrine in question cannot be further understood or better expressed; such a claim would exclude any possibility of development of doctrine. The claim implied in infallibility is not that the doctrine taught is exhaustively expressed, but that it is *truly* expressed. So infallibility leaves the way wide open for the development of doctrine. What is evidently excluded is any "development" which contradicts what has already been infallibly taught. It pertains to elementary theological sense to be able, as Newman put it, to distinguish a development from a "corruption".

An even deeper ignorance of the nature of infallibility is shown in the suggestion that the Church in its pretensions to infallibility is guilty of "hubris": the colossal pride of claiming to possess the *fullness* of divine knowledge. God alone evidently has the fullness of divine knowledge. It is true that the Church *shares* in divine knowledge, insofar as God has revealed this knowledge; but this is the gift of Revelation which should not be confused with that of infallibilty. Revelation communicates divine knowledge — a divine message — to the Church. Infallibility enables the Church to hold and teach that knowledge without error: not to get the Message wrong. So, what has been given to the Church in the divine gift of infallibility is not knowledge but certainty: certainty that what the Church believes is *true*, because Christ is present guaranteeing that truth.[6]

A separate point, under this same heading, is the thesis put forward by certain theologians that the infallibility of the Church is limited to dogmas of *faith*: what we must believe. In their

---

6 The doctrine of the Blessed Trinity could illustrate our point. The Church claims to teach this doctrine infallibly. In other words, it claims that the doctrine that there are Three Persons in One God, is certainly true. The Church has never claimed to understand or explain this doctrine *fully*; who can comprehend that Truth adequately except God Himself?

opinion, the Church has no mandate to hand down infallible teaching in the field of *morals*: what we must do.

This thesis could be sustained only on one of two suppositions: either a) that the message of Salvation has nothing to do with practice; only with theory (sola fides!); or else b) that even if practice is important, we have no way of knowing with certainty how we should try to behave on concrete issues (contraception, abortion, etc.); we have no access to Christ's Mind on such issues. Both suppositions are incorrect.

Christ never preached salvation by faith alone. He gives moral norms (Mt 5:21-22; 27-28; 7:1; Mk 7:21-23; Lk 12:15; Jn 13:34, etc., etc.), insists that keeping his commandments is the proof of love for Him (Jn 14:21; cf. Mt 7:21), and sent his Apostles to all nations with the mandate to "teach them to observe all the *commands* I gave you" (Mt 28:19-20).

Christ's contemporaries came to Him and asked his opinion about moral issues: is it lawful to divorce or not? (Mt 19:3); is it lawful to pay taxes to Caesar or not? (Mk 12:14). And Christ gave his opinion. Are we to believe that He has no opinion — nothing to tell us — about contraception or abortion or homosexual conduct? The proposition of a "no-comment" Christ or a Christ who has "gone silent" makes no sense to anyone who recalls those promises: I am with you always.... Whoever listens to you listens to Me....

But — it is sometimes objected — the Church has never in fact defined moral matters. This is simply untrue. Definitions on moral matters have been given both through the solemn Magisterium[7] and, particularly, through the ordinary and universal Magisterium (which we repeat, is also infallible). Over the centuries the ordinary Magisterium of the Church has defined a whole moral programme of Christian living, in such crystalline clarity that no one can have any doubt about Christ's Mind on matters such as swindling, blackmail, slander, extramarital sex, contraception, homosexual conduct.... The Church, in line with the strong words of Scripture (I Cor 6:9-10; Gal 5:19-21), has always taught that such conduct breaks communion with Christ and, for as long as deliberately held to, excludes from the kingdom of God.

---

[7] For instance, the Council of Trent taught solemnly that polygamy is forbidden by divine law (DS 1802/972), and that sacramental and consummated marriage is indissoluble (DS 1807/977).

16

Truth and Communion

Fantastic Journey, a science-fiction movie of years ago, told how a team of scientists in a submarine were reduced to infra-microscopic size, and then injected into the bloodstream of a genius with the mission of passing through his heart and exploring his brain.

With apologies, if necessary, to the reverential sense of some readers, I would suggest that we could see here a certain analogy with the role of the theologian.

The theologian's mission is to explore the Mind of Jesus Christ. For that it is important that he swims in his bloodstream — soaks himself in Christ's Life pulsating down the centuries — passes through his Heart, and so comes to his Mind.

It is especially important for his task that the theologian become small; or rather, since all of us are already so small compared to Christ, that he retain the sense of his own diminutive stature for the size of his task. Alice, said Chesterton, has to become small if she is to be Alice in Wonderland. The theologian is Alice, and the Revelation of the Mind and Heart of Christ is Wonderland. A theologian incapable of wondering at the marvels he is seeking to contemplate, lacks the humility essential to theology. Even the most brilliant theologian ever is working in a field that infinitely surpasses his mental capacity. If his talents — however great they may be — are to bear fruit, he needs to hear a divine invitation echoing continuously in his ears: "Enter into the Mind of your Master" (cf. Mt 25:21). It should echo there not yet as a reward merited, but as an urgent call to humble responsibility.

Thinking with Christ

In Chapter Fourteen we recalled the infallible reference-points of theological science (Revelation and Magisterium), and the fallible means with which it must be developed: human reason, man's mind.

The theologian who sees Revelation and the Magisterium as external restraints placed on his own mind, can fight many battles of dissent, kicking continually against the goad, but he will render little service to true Christian theology.

He will achieve a unity of theological vision and a sense of theological freedom only if, seeing Revelation and Magisterium as being within the Mind of Christ, *he situates his own mind there also*.

Theological thinking is not thinking on one's own. It is thinking with Christ. The Catholic vision of theology is of many minds thinking *within* one Mind. One can understand how the truly great theologians have been saints. For sanctity is necessary if a person is to think the thoughts of Christ. In the measure of his union with Christ, the theologian can say, "I think. Now it is not I who think, it is Christ who thinks in and through me, and I who think in and through Christ" (cf. Gal 2:20).

The theologian's task then is not to shape Christ's Mind to his, but to shape his mind to Christ's. The Mind of Christ, our Master and Teacher, is after all *the* theological mind of all time. Christ is necessarily the Church's Number One Theologian. Catholic thought flows from Catholic tradition, from Christ. There is no new — never previously tapped — source of Christian thought to be discovered; the source of all Christian thought is Christ; and, through Him, the Father. No theologian therefore teaches "original" doctrine, in the sense of producing something that is new, underived and totally his. He, much more than Christ, must say, "My teaching is not mine ..." (Jn 7:16).

As the theologian sets out on his Fantastic Journey, he realizes that the Mind he is investigating — infinitely broader and deeper than his own — is ablaze with light. Its main areas are brilliantly lit up — crystal clear in shape, content and definition — although, in the nature of things, each viewer's mind can always reflect this beauty and truth in a new way.

There are no doubt certain corners or recesses of that Mind which must contain further riches, although we have not yet managed to see into them with full clarity. They therefore invite particular exploration. The theologian's job, with the help of grace, is to *project the Light of Christ* into those deeper recesses.

This point merits dwelling on. Only in a relative and secondary sense is Christian theology the work of the Christian theologian. It is primarily the work of Christ himself.

Theology is indeed an attempt to illustrate God's Revelation, to throw further light on it. But that light comes less from the theologian's mind than from Christ's mind. The light of theology is truly the *Lumen Christi*: the Light comes from him. "By your light we see the light" (Ps 36:9). This shows us the theologian's humble but glorious task: to gather the Light of Christ from all its sources, to wrap himself in it, and to reflect it on to further areas of the Mind of Christ, for the enlightenment of God's People.[1]

Theology calls for communion

Images like these — which express profound truths — can make it clearer why so many contemporary theological approaches — "freelance" theology, theology that spurns Tradition or Magisterium, theology of "doing one's own thing" or "going it alone" — are just not theology. Theology is a united endeavour, a common search, a joyful sharing. Theology can only be done *in communion*; in the communion of the Faith, in communion with the Church, in communion with the Mind of Christ, with the light of that Mind as reflected and refracted in the minds of all those who have shared that faith down the ages.

Some writers today prefer to speak of "theologies" rather than theology. The plural can be admitted provided it signifies that, while there is just one Faith (Eph 4:5) and one Revelation, there can be many human attempts to achieve understanding of that faith. But all true theologies are linked to a common centre and therefore to one another. All sound theological approaches are like guy-ropes, strengthening the edifice of truth from different directions. But the central pillar around which the edifice is built — the towering structure of Revelation — has its own inherent support and steadying force: the presence of Christ in the Magisterium.

In the last chapter we attempted a critical evaluation of the attitude, "After all, one is not bound by any teaching that is not formally defined". This reserved attitude is frequent enough today. The many attempts to present it as a noble claim made in the name of rightful self-respect cannot cover its defensive and negative character and its essential individualism. The ultimate criticism of this attitude in any case is to be made from an ecclesiological viewpoint: while it can (perhaps) be defended in terms of strict legal rights or obligations, it is utterly indefensible in terms of *communio*, that central theme of Vatican II.

Communio means sharing in the life of Christ. Not just me alone

---

[1] This reminds us once more that the Mind of Christ is not a thing of the past that needs to have new ideas added to it. It is the present Truth that simply calls for new light to be shone onto its recesses.

with Christ; that is still individualistic sharing. Me, with others, in Christ, through his Church; that is true Catholic sharing. Communion in the sacraments, the discipline and the Faith of the one Church: the Church of the centuries. Lack of communion with the ages is lack of communion with Christ, "who is the same today as he was yesterday as he will be forever" (Heb 13:8). If I cannot share the Faith of yesterday, then my faith of today may be different tomorrow, and is certainly not the faith of always, the faith handed down from the Apostles.

In our opening chapters we saw how the spirit of *communio* and the spirit of individualism are opposed and mutually exclude one another. If this is true in the sociological field, it is even truer in the field of theological thought.

Theological development and wholeness are found in community, not in isolation. Theological research in the spirit of *communio* is a search for the *common* truths and insights that bind me to others in Christ. The solitary thinker who follows no guidelines but his own mind, thinks himself into further isolation and loneliness. The thinker who is attuned to the Mind of Christ in the Church, is never alone. He is in communion with Christ and with the whole community of Christ's faithful who have lived and thought and believed in fellowship since apostolic times.

What a lack of desire for fellowship and communion is revealed in that attitude, "I am not bound to *share* in the views of others"! Perhaps I am not; but it is a pity if I cannot do so, if I cannot at least establish a vital and mutually supporting link between their views and mine. If their views and mine are Christian, the link is already there in Christ. Let us seek it and strengthen it. That way we think in communion and think ourselves *into* communion. The contrary is to think ourselves *out of* communion. It is to choose that process of "self-excommunication" to which we referred earlier.[2]

It follows that a serious criticism to be levelled against those contemporary theologians who "wage war" on the Magisterium, on Pope and Bishops, is that of superficiality. They are not reasoning their case in depth. They are not weighing, or certainly are not presenting, its real issues. Consciously or unconsciously, they are not at grips with their true problem.

Their cries of intellectual or academic "freedom" and their protests about "inquisitorial" proceedings only serve as a smokescreen that hides from the public, and perhaps from

---

2 Cf. pp. 68ff.

themselves, what is really at stake in the battle going on in their minds and hearts; a battle that threatens to turn their Catholic faith and that of others into a wasteland.

If they think that they are just battling against an outdated centralist mentality, against a Roman or episcopal authoritarianism, they do not see their own warfare clearly. What they have to contend with is not a bureaucracy, it is the Faith of always. What they are struggling against is not a mentality but a Mind: Christ's Mind.

We are all tempted to wrestle with that Mind, as Jacob did with the Angel (Gen 32:26); and yet our Opponent — who is in fact striving to be our Ally, if we let him — is greater and stronger than Jacob's Angel.

We are all tempted to want to overpower that Mind and draw It to our side and our opinions; and we have to be drawn to It. We are all tempted to want to share in that Mind on our own terms — in other words, to subordinate that Mind to our mind — and we can only share in It on Christ's terms.

What we have just said, while referred to the theologian in particular, applies of course to all Christians. All of us have to meet and try to counter the worst temptation which is that of pride. Pride itself has perhaps no worse expression than the refusal to open one's own mind to the Mind of the Church, the Mind of Christ. The Christian who is not too proud to think with the Mind of Christ enters into the vast wonderland of creeds and symbols and dogmas with their infinite perspectives (a dogma, it has been said, is not a wall that stops us seeing but a window that opens out our view onto infinity) where Truths are certain and Truths are great.

Those who prefer, in their humility, to be ever uncertain about the truth or the worth of any point of Christian belief can have their humility. In my pride, I believe that Christ has offered me his Mind, through his Church. I am certain ths offer is worthwhile, and I want to accept it. I prefer my pride and my certainty.

I realize that some people, through no fault of their own, never achieve certainty. They deserve sympathy. But a preference for uncertainty is pathological. It needs not just sympathy but a cure. Like Newman I hold that "certitude is a natural and normal state of mind, and not (as is sometimes objected) one of its extravangances".[3]

---

3 *Grammar of Assent*, Chapter 6.

New York and theology

I have always maintained that a visit to New York can be a great theological experience. It is best had at the World Trade Center, with its twin towers each 1300 feet high. They make you dizzy. No need to go to the top and look down. You just stand at the bottom, close to one of the corners, and look up. 1300 feet rising in one straight line makes the head reel.

Well, that is a very tiny way of illustrating the effect that the mere idea of God should produce on us. It should make us dizzy; and until it does we do not have even the rudiments of a theological outlook.

God is much "higher" than 1300 feet — or 1300 million. Yet at times we think we have him measured: I've figured God out, I've got him cut and dried. And then of course it is not God we are dealing with at all. "I believe in God — up to a point", someone said to me once. You can't do that. Or if you do it, it is not God you believe in. If you believe in God then you are in the realm of the infinite and totally out of your depth. If you think you have your theology all figured out, then you are thinking in finite terms and you are not taking a theological stance at all.

Some theologians seem to regard theology as a field to be mastered. There they go wrong. None of us can ever master theology. We are simply not tall enough to reach the heights of God's Mind. By his side we are all midgets. In theology it is not enough to look at one's subject. One must look *up* at it, and look up high (if the effort pains our necks, so much the better. It's a probable sign that they were a bit stiff and the effort was needed). Some theologians nowadays seem badly in need of a Theology Refresher Course made up essentially of mind-raising exercises: "Don't start writing or even thinking about God or the Faith or the Church until you have looked up. Yes, that way but — higher! *Higher still*!! . . . You are beginning to feel dizzy? Ah, that's better. Now go off and do theology".

The theologian must never get used to his task. He needs to keep exercising himself in vertigo so that he does not lose sight of the heights and depths he is seeking to explore.

All theological matters partake in some way of the infinity of God: Revelation, the Church, the papacy, the sacraments . . . all participate in a sacredness that should overawe our mind. When we venture into the theological field we are always treading on holy ground and we need to bare our head and feet for we are in the divine presence (cf. Exod 3:5).

We can explore Christ's Mind; we cannot measure it. And we can never figure it out.

The Mind of Christ is there in full scope and splendour and power. Our finite mind must enter his infinite Mind in amazement and wonder. The more we wonder and open our mind to Christ's Mind, the more Christ may deign to let our mind glimpse something of the secrets of his.

We cannot force entry into Christ's Mind. We must enter by the gate of humility. And we must go and get the key that lets us in: the key of this kingdom has been entrusted to the Magisterium.

Communion and power

Communion with Christ's Mind is the condition for receiving, and passing on to others, Christ's Truth in all its power.

The Apostles felt the power with which Christ sent them to preach his saving message (cf. Mt 28:18). Our evangelizing mission today can have the same power only if we sense that we are sent by the same Christ and to preach the Christian message.

"The same message? A message that is *always the same*? ..." To some modern ears this sounds deadening. Something that remains the same suggests, to them, something stunted and static.

How communion with Christ's Truth can be stunted, how communion with his Mind and Heart can be static, is anything but clear. Nevertheless, the prejudices here are so deeply rooted that it is best to reason the matter out.

It is certainly true that the whole idea of established or defined truth irritates some people. The reason, they say, is that it implies narrowness or a stagnant quality that cramps the mind and deadens the dynamism of the Christian message.

There is notable confusion here. That a truth is well-defined means that it is clear in content and extent. It in no way suggests that it is narrow. It has its limits, but these can be very broad limits. The defined, identifiable, nature of Christian truth has everything to do with content, clarity and power. It has nothing to do with narrowness. On the contrary, the Christian message is immensely broad. It is precisely the combination of staggering breadth and staggering clarity that gives it such power. It challenges the theologian's mind as it challenges the world.

But surely, even if the idea of established truth is not narrow, is it static? ... Here we need to clear the air of ambiguities. To what is the term "static" referred here: to the contents of the message, or to the reaction of those who receive the message?

It is obvious that the contents of a message must remain fixed if it is to have any value as a message. But the fixed clarity of an important message — tapped out time and again on one wavelength — can galvanise the listener into action. There is nothing static about that message's effect.

An ill-defined, garbled message, with no beginning or end and with only confusion in between, moves no one. Nor does a constantly changing message. If a message is to move me — to think or to speak — it must say something definite. If it can be taken to mean anything or nothing, why should I bother about it: to listen to it or to echo it?

This is worth bearing in mind in evaluating contemporary calls for an "open-ended" approach in theology, an approach untrammelled by definitions and a priori concepts. So much of our modern open-ended theology turns out, on examination, to be an empty package. You look down both ends, and find that the *contents* have fallen out; there is nothing inside.

So if I am told that the concept of defined or settled belief is "static" — paralysing theological thought and evangelizing action — whereas an open-ended theology is the dynamic instrument we need because it will move people to more effective thought and evangelization, I flatly contradict the assertion. Just the opposite is true.

Take the Catholic belief of always: that the bread-like object on the altar or in the tabernacle is actually God. That, if it is really true, is a dynamic truth if ever there was one. It is bursting with God's vitality: the over-flowing power of his Love. It makes me want to get up and go out and tell people about it. That is a truth worth sharing.

But if the fact of the matter is not really so, if God does not actually come, if the bread remains bread with a passing spiritual significance, then what is there in all that to get excited about or to move me from my pew or my inertia? People may if they wish call that a more dynamic concept. I don't see it; it leaves me unmoved: static, stuck.

But no — someone may object — it is the idea of a God "stuck" in the tabernacle that is static...! I draw the opposite conclusion: that *abiding* all-loving Presence becomes dynamism for me.

Similarly, if Christ truly rose from the dead, then death has been defeated, the way to another Life has been opened to us, and I understand and want to share the Apostles' dynamism about the matter. There you have a world-revolutionising belief.

However, if Christ did not truly rise, then let others, if they wish, preach whatever they might then still find in Christianity. For me personally, as for Paul, it would have lost all interest (cf. 1 Cor 15:14).

Some theologians complain of the cramping effect of the intervention of the Magisterium. In practice, however, it is so often *their* theories that reduce and narrow the scope of the Christian message, stripping it of its riches and of the strength and comfort it offers to the individual Christian. The Magisterium is fighting on the side of the Faith, but also on the side of the faithful: to defend Christ's message against all narrowing or impoverishing interpretations; and to defend the people's patrimony — their right of access to the broad scope and rich content of Christ's gifts to men.

Restoration of communion

The rupture of communion of the sixteenth century was a colossal wound in the Body of Christ. It still lies open and unhealed. All Christians feel the hurt of this rupture, the scandal of the deep divisions so clearly contrary to Christ's will and purpose (cf. Jn 11:52).

It is idle to seek to attribute blame for the happenings of four centuries ago. What matters now — what God clearly wants — is that we heal them (UR 1). The aim must be to restore what Christ prayed for: that all be one (Jn 17:21); that there be just one flock and one shepherd (Jn 10:16). How can this be brought about?

Ecumenism is understood superficially if it is thought that unity will be achieved by a give-and-take process that results in some form of human consensus. If it were to come about that way, it could (and would) also be subsequently broken by human disagreement and dissent.

The search for Christian unity is a search not for a consensus but for a centre. The centre is Christ. It is not just a reunion among one another that has to be sought. It is a re-union with Christ, a renewed comm-union with Christ, having rediscovered Him — how He is, how He speaks, what He wants — having relocated where He is, and having gone to Him there.

Christian reunion means to be re-united not just in the Heart of Christ — his Love — but also in his Mind: his Truth. To be one in the charity of Christ is a great thing, but it is not enough.

We have also to be one in his Mind. "One heart *and* one mind", like the Early Christians (Acts 4:32). Communion in charity and communion in faith: within the richness of charity and within the richness of faith; but *within* — not outside.

The scandal of Christian disunity is not so much divided hearts as divided minds. Hearts can be united more easily than minds, because men feel together more easily than they think or agree together. But feelings do not last. What is needed is a common faith: the *will* to believe together. A common faith means a shared belief in the same things: in God and his Revelation. It means a common tribute to the authority of Christ, as and how He chooses to speak to us.

That is why the question of Christian unity always comes back to the question of whether or not Christ, in choosing to reveal his saving Truth and entrusting it to the Church, also chose to institute — within that Church — a divinely protected organ for faithfully interpreting that truth.

Christian unity was disrupted basically through a collapse of faith; a failure to believe in Christ present and speaking to men in and through the institutional Church, and a choice instead of subject the Truth of Christ to the will of the individual believer — to make what he liked of it.

The democratic approach to ecumenism is, ultimately, to turn the Truth of Christ into whatever we want or vote it to be. The approach of *faith* is to accept it as it is; i.e. as it comes to us through the teaching authority of the Church. One has to choose between one or other of these approaches, for *there is in fact no middle way*.

Renewed Christian communion depends on our renewing our communion with Christ's way of thinking and planning: also with the particular point of divine logic which underpins his plan to save us through Revelation. Faith in Christ and love for Christ can and should lead us to see that if Divine Truth is to be protected from men's errors, a principle, an organ to guarantee and define that Truth is required. It was required from the start. It was divinely instituted from the start. It has (despite men's defects) always been there. It simply needs to be acknowledged and accepted. Christian unity can be built around no other centre.

Clarity in dialogue

The ultimate goal of ecumenism is that "little by little, as the obstacles to perfect ecclesiastical communion are overcome, all

Christians will be gathered ... into the unity of the one and only Church, which Christ bestowed on his Church from the beginning" (UR 4).

Some of the obstacles to be overcome were no doubt created in the past by Catholics themselves, through their authoritarian approach, through their tendency to judge persons, forgetting that ultimate judgment is reserved to God (cf 1 Cor 4:4), and to condemn intentions without allowing for subjective sincerity, and particularly through the scandal of their own personal sins. Ecumenical reflection and dialogue can lead Catholics to a greater knowledge of their grievous failings in these respects.

For there to be real ecumenical progress, however, Protestants for their part must face up to the formidable obstacles to unity that are present on their side; above all the radically anti-incarnational, anti-sacramental and anti-scriptural principle of private judgment[4] with its rejection of the external objective authority for preserving and interpreting Revelation that Christ willed to bequeath to his Church.

If ecumenism is to be a serious endeavour to bring Christian denominations together into *one* Church, then both Catholics and Protestants should make ecclesiology, and not just history or faith or scripture, the main field of discussion and study.

But — it may be objected — all of this seems to imply that the ultimate ecumenical hope from the Catholic standpoint is that Protestants will reunite themselves to the Catholic Church.

Of course it is! We would be absolutely false not only to our own beliefs but also to the sincerity that should characterize ecumenical dialogue if we were to suggest differently. Not only must we Catholics not be afraid to state this but we should realize that any averagely intelligent Protestant will *simply not respect* the Catholic who maintains otherwise. He will conclude: this person is not sincere, or else he just does not know his own Catholic faith.

The spirit of ecumenism is a mutual charity. The aim of ecumenism is a common faith. The spirit of ecumenism is to treat each other well, despite differences of belief. We do not treat each other well if we pretend there are no differences or that the differences are unimportant. We would then lack respect for each

---

4 The rule of private judgment in interpreting Christ's Message is on a par with moral subjectivism or legal positivism. There is no objective truth, or none is attainable. The individual creates his subjective norm in everything. Truth becomes a matter of opinion. Opinion becomes the standard of Truth. And then there are as many "truths" as there are opinions.

other — and for the truth — because we would not be taking each other's beliefs seriously. That way it would become totally impossible to overcome differences of belief.

Private judgment and communio

Time alone will tell whether or not the cause of Christian unity has progressed in inter-denominational relations in the past twenty years. But it is already obvious that, within the Catholic Church itself, Christian unity has suffered in this period. We are referring not to the desirable growth of diversity within Catholic unity, but to the relativization of the very concept of a *common* Catholic Faith, to the point where one finds writers, theologians, publications, groups, holding contradictory views on basic matters — infallibility, contraception, abortion, etc. — yet each claiming that his views are valid expressions of Catholicism.

It is muddle-minded to call this pluralism. Pluralism means legitimate variety within true communion. What we are faced with today in certain sectors of the Church is not desirable pluralism. It is stark disunity; a rupture of ecclesial communion as serious as that of the sixteenth century. Deformation, not reformation, is always involved in splitting the fundamental unity willed by Christ for his followers.

The loss of the sense of Catholic identity is no help to ecumenical dialogue. How can we Catholics work for Christian unity if we ourselves are not living — with diverse but complementary positions — within the broad unity of one clearly definable Catholic Faith?

Persons with unidentified positions cannot achieve a rapprochement. Self-definition or definition of terms and positions is a first requirement for rational debate or meaningful dialogue. One engages in dialogue to see if it is possible for two parties to approximate to one another's position, or to find new intermediate common ground. But how can I possibly think about approximating to someone else's position if I do not know my own — if I am not even sure where I stand or what I stand for?

This has always been a Protestant problem. Protestants have been relatively united in standing *against* (protesting) certain things: church authority, papal primacy, Tradition, defined doctrine, Real Presence.... But they have never been united in what they stand *for*; except in the principle of private judgment which as a principle is divisive of its essence and utterly opposed to *communio*. The progressive fragmentation of Protestantism is simply the logical consequence of this principle.

What Catholics stand for has, until recently, been clear to everyone: a communion with Christ, in the faith, sacraments and discipline of the Church that he founded and protects and lives and speaks in. Some Catholics today can no longer identify with that clear idea of catholic communion. They say they are Catholics; yet at the same time they cannot say what being a Catholic means. They profess an unidentifiable Catholicism. Their position however can be identified — but not within Catholicism.

In this matter of ecumenism two points could be made about those Catholics who have assimilated a non-Catholic approach to apostolic faith, to the sacraments, to scriptural interpretation, etc.:

a) They are not really doing an ecumenical work. *They* no doubt have been drawn closer to Protestantism. But they have been drawn farther from Catholicism. They have not narrowed the ecumenical gap; they have simply passed over to the other side. But the gap remains as wide as ever.

To them the ecumenical problems seems easy of solution. But the solution they see consists not in a *communio* of one Faith, but in a sort of *pax ecumenica*, a broad tolerance grouping mutually contradictory views of Christ's message under one Christian banner. Such a solution may be acceptable to them. Is it acceptable to Christ? It may be what they want. Is it what He wants?

Christ never spoke of a federation of sheep or a coalition of folds, but of *one* flock. That is the objective. And it must be held non-negotiable if ecumenism is to remain a serious endeavour.

Their ecumenical solution simply imports all the centuries-long problems of Protestant disunity into the Church. It is a step not towards Christian unity but in the opposite direction. It baulks at the acceptance of objective authority which provides the only focal point and basis for unity. It rests instead on the principle of private judgment which does not and cannot unite.

b) They are not facing up to their own ecumenical problem, their own problem of communion: they themselves are not seeking a centre; they are not seeking oneness. They do not want to share the faith that has come down from the Apostles, the faith of always. They stand apart from the views of the centuries. They do not hear the voice of Christ in Tradition, in the Fathers, in the Councils, in the Popes. They do not find his love in the lives of the saints or the popular piety of the ages. They do not find his will in the discipline of the Church. For them Christ lived his life 2,000 years ago. He has not continued to live it over these twenty centuries, and does not continue to live it today. What communion can one have with a man who died and is no longer with us?

It is an unhappy situation, a voluntary severing of links with Christ, with the risen living Christ who promised to be with us always. It is a sad process which can be summed up in one word: "*ex-communio*", understood not as a juridical act or a canonical declaration, but as a self-imposed situation of fact. The evident isolation of some Catholics today — theologians, priests, ordinary faithful — is the bleak consequences of their inability to find Christ, on Christ's terms, in the Church and in the Faith in which he has seen good to reveal and communicate himself.

If they choose to re-define Catholicism in protestant terms, Christ will once again react saying: that — the image you present — is not my Church. They cannot force a different image on the Mind of Christ. Either they correct their image, or else their distorted vision must necessarily lead them outside the limits of communion with Him.

Ecclesiology — the crisis area

In the early stages of the projection of the Christian message, in the very first centuries after Christ, it must have been a relatively easy matter for sincere people, with good will, to misread the picture, i.e. to stray from the Faith and fall into heresy. Some did so; and, precisely because they had good will, they came out again. Others stuck to their particular views, and so lost the communion of the Faith. The christological controversies of the fourth and fifth centuries offer abundant examples.

This should not be so easy today, after twenty centuries during which the message of Revelation has been taught and re-taught, projected and re-projected, while particular sectors or details of it have been focussed and re-focussed, defined and re-defined, in such a way that the Picture stands out today in the crystal clarity of its whole, and the harmonious inter-relationship of its parts.

Nevertheless, there are contemporary viewers of Revelation who still manage to blur the picture. Right now, in this latter part of the twentieth century some Catholics, who are otherwise pious and zealous, are giving way to questionings and doubts about truths that lie at the very heart of catholic belief: the factual-historical character of the Gospel narratives, the unique powers of the ministerial priesthood, etc., etc. They are no longer sure if they believe in doctrines that have been part of the common patrimony of the Faith, shared in and passed on by their brothers and sisters down the centuries. They no longer possess the certainty of sharing in the fellowship of the Apostles. There is a growing rupture of communion in their lives that threatens to leave them permanently adrift in a heaving sea of doubts, dilemmas and dissent.

Ecclesiology is the crisis area today. Faith in Christ's message grows weak if there is not faith also in *how* his message comes to us, in the *means* He uses to transmit it to us. Christ — his Word, his Grace, his Love — comes to us through the Church. A weakening or a collapse of communion is bound to follow from a failure to grasp and accept the mystery of the Church: concretely that aspect of the mystery which sees the Church as the faithful guardian and interpreter of Christ's Message, as the "Church of the living God, which upholds the truth and keeps it safe" (1 Tim 3:15).

The vast majority of both Protestants and Catholics will agree that a Christian is someone who believes Christ to be God. If one allows oneself christological doubts — maybe Christ is not God ... — then one is ceasing to be a Christian.

But if the first question is christological — is Christ God? — the second question is ecclesiological: did Christ found a Church to carry on his word and his work? Did he found a Church — and then depart? Or does *he* remain in his Church in such a way that in listening to the Church we are listening to him, in communing with the Church we are in communion with him, in breaking that communion we break with him? These are the essential questions we have been attempting to examine and answer.

If Christ is not God, then his claim to *be* the Truth (Jn 14:6) is monstrous in its arrogance. If the Church is not founded and protected by Christ, then its claim to *possess* and *teach* the Truth is equally arrogant and intolerable. Yet if Christ *is* God and if he *did* found the Church, neither claim is arrogant. Both claims are rather the warrant for our joyful certainty and for our sense of freedom. "You will know the truth and the truth will make you free" (Jn 8:32).

When a well-known English theologian who was a Vatican II peritus left the Church shortly after the close of the Council, some of his former theological associates reproached him for having done so, and for not having stayed with them so as to work for the reform of the Church, from within.

He replied that he had left the Church simply because he no longer believed in the infallibility of the Catholic Church; and that he felt it was not he who had to justify his position but those who share his view yet remain in the Church.

The prayer one utters is that they will try not to justify their position but to change it.

Consciously or unconsciously, the approach of many Catholics today represents a progressive rejection of *communion*. "I will go my own way, I will not share the way of others. I have my own mind, I will not share the Mind of Christ".

The mental attitudes that lead to this sort of self-excommunication are cast in deep moulds. Sincere reflection, humility and above all prayer are the only means that can bring a person to stand apart from his attitudes, to review them and see where they are wanting, and to set about the difficult process of remoulding and changing them. If they are not changed, the loss of communion is bound to become complete.

17

Communion, Unity, Diversity

Communion is the central theme of Vatican II. All the reaching out for community of the post-conciliar years has its roots in this great theme.

A disunited community is a contradiction in terms. It is legitimate therefore and necessary to ask if the Catholic Church appears as a more united community than twenty-five or thirty years ago.

Perhaps not — some people might reply, immediately adding — but we are more varied; and that also is a good thing desired by Vatican II with the clear conciliar emphasis not only on community but also on personal rights, on individuality, on local differences, as evidenced by the importance the Council gives to matters like particular churches, liturgical variations or inculturation.

It may be true — they might add — that variety is being stressed today more than unity; but that is simply a necessary swing of the pendulum, to correct the excessive centralisation of pre-conciliar times.

This, it seems to me, is not a very satisfactory analysis. It rests on the supposition that Vatican II stressed seemingly opposed things; it allows, without resolving it, the apparent antinomy between unity and variety; and it just possibly rejoices in the "triumph" of variety over unity.

A proper relationship between unity and diversity is essential to the life, dynamism and growth of the Church. How do these two values in fact relate? Can they be practically or honestly combined? Which of the two is more attractive? Which impresses the world most? Which is more important? Must one value triumph over the other? Must one necessarily be sacrificed to the other? Questions that are truly worth considering.

Is it possible to harmonise these two values while giving full validity to each? Or is it inevitable either that unity suffocates variety, reducing its expressions to a merely fictional level, or else that variety results in fragmentation and the loss of *communio*? If one sees the two values as mutually opposed, the easy answer is No to the first question and Yes to the second.

Which value is the more attractive? Which surprises people most? It depends.

Diversity as such is not very surprising; unless precisely it is diversity within order. Diversity without order or without harmony is chaos. A garbage heap is diverse, but it is not interesting. It attracts no one except scavengers.

Unity is more surprising; one meets it less often. Men have never found it difficult to be at variance, to disagree, to separate, to stand at a distance, each one defending his particular rights and claims and character. Men have aspired after unity; but it remains a difficult goal that always seems to elude them. The twentieth century history of international organisms like the League of Nations, the United Nations, or UNESCO points up these lessons.

As against this, unity without diversity is not surprising. It is boring; or perhaps even terrifying. For it can be imposed; consider the relentless political unity of a totalitarian state. The surprise comes when in a voluntary body one finds non-imposed unity presiding over rich variety. That combination is both surprising and attractive.

Pagans are not surprised to find that we Christians are different among ourselves; that is to be like them. They are surprised if they find that we are at the same time united. That is to be unlike them. That is the difference that attracts. Jesus said that men should be able to recognize his followers by the fact that they love one another (Jn 13:24); his special prayer was that they should be one (Jn 17:21). It was his first concern; it should be ours.

So, if we ask which of these two values is more important, which is the more fragile and in need of more care, the answer should be unhesitating: unity. But we need immediately to add an important clarification.

Does the priority of unity mean that diversity has to be sacrificed? Does strengthening and building up unity mean that we have to weaken and repress diversity? No. Here we meet the first of the great Catholic paradoxes in this matter: *both* must grow.

Unity and variety are complementary and essential features of the beauty of the Bride of Christ. They are powerful characteristics of the Church that — both together — make us rejoice.

We rejoice in Catholic variety. We do not want that variety to be lessened, we want it to grow. We rejoice at the same time in Catholic unity. We do not want that unity to be broken, we want it too to grow. In a Catholic vision both diversity and unity are seen *growing together* as expressions of the infinite vitality and dynamism of Christ living in his Church.

Unity, diversity, Trinity

Oneness does not mean sameness. There is no greater Unity than that of the Godhead, of Divine Nature Itself. And yet that Divine Nature consists in Three Persons who are really distinct. Those Three Persons are One; but They are not the same. Each, within that indivisible unity of Truth and Love, maintains his own unique distinctiveness. The Trinity itself is the ultimate source and the greatest expression of the principle of unity in variety and variety in unity (cf. UR 2).

It is tempting — but risky — to indulge in speculation here. Let us risk it, knowing that we are peering into depths that man's mind is hopelessly inadequate to plumb.

How different are the Persons of the Blessed Trinity? The full answer to that is, please God, something reserved for us to see in Heaven. But am I mistaken if I suggest that our present inclination is to think that the differences between the Persons are only "marginal"? Do we not tend to feel that the Divine Persons are more alike than They are different? Probably the question itself is misleading (are men more alike than they are different?). However that may be, it seems to me that the Three Divine Persons, being consubstantial, are *intensely* different — beyond any possibility of ours of appreciating differences. Each has a most unique and distinct Personality: so much so that only the infinity of God's Life can comprehend their individual distinctiveness. And yet the unity between these Three Persons is such that They are not merely intimately united, but *are* One. Further they are not One "despite" their distinctiveness. The Divine Unity rests — if one can express it so — on the knowledge and love generated and inspired by the very distinctiveness of Personality.

Thus, if there is no unity as great as that of the Godhead, so there is no diversity as striking as that of the Trinity of Persons.

The trinitarian principle of unity in variety and variety within unity is to be seen in God's work of Creation, just as it characterizes the Redemption He worked and, concretely too, the Church He founded.

God made a varied world. God rejoices in variety. The variety of creation is itself a revelation of the infinite richness of God's own life. The higher one rises in the order of creation, the more richly varied individuals within each species become. Man is the masterpiece of visible creation. There again, within a common human nature, God made men different. He rejoices in human variety. He does not want us all to be the same. Yet He wants us to be united. The Redemption of mankind is a great drawing together of men into one. "God desired that all men should form one family" (GS 24). "It pleased God to call men to share in his life and not merely singly, without any bond between them, but He formed them into a people, in which his children who had been scattered were gathered together" (AG 2). On Pentecost, says *Ad gentes*, "was foreshadowed the union of all peoples in the catholicity of the faith by means of the Church" (AG 4). And *Lumen gentium* teaches that God has established the Church so that it may be "the visible sacrament of this saving unity" (LG 9).

Within the one Church of Christ the principle of variety operates. The very catholicity of the Church means that it is not just for one age or clime or class or nation. It is for all.

The history of Christianity is the history of variety in unity. The Holy Spirit has continued over the centuries to incarnate the Gospel in different persons and movements and cultures. The acceptance of the Gospel, with its demands and challenges, has always led to many incarnations: diversifying and unifying. Diversifying mankind, without scattering. Uniting mankind, without uniforming. Growing variety, growing unity: that is God's plan.

We have in fact been given a model of the unity-variety relationship that is more accessible to us than the Blessed Trinity. We find it in the Incarnation. It is not only that the extremes united in the Person of Jesus — divine nature and human nature — are totally diverse, but that in the infinitely rich Humanity of Jesus the individual humanity of each man can and should find its reference point both for personal growth and growth in relation to others.

God became Man — for all men. Christ reaches out to everyone with his saving grace, to save each soul, to save each individual humanity; and to draw all together into a varied unity.

In the measure in which each one responds to the call of Christ, in which he "puts on Christ" (Gal 3:27), his humanity is not only redeemed; it unfolds, develops, becomes more distinctive. He becomes more truly human, more truly himself. He becomes more different from others, and at the same time more at one with them.

Unity, diversity, sanctity

The saints are of course the great examples of this incarnational principle and process, this unifying and diversifying identification with Christ.

Knowledge of the saints helps us understand the richness and operation of Christ. The saints are so varied, so different; and yet so united. Each of the saints incarnates the spirit of Christ in a different way. Each represents a distinct high-road leading to, and out from, the same centre.

The closer they come to Christ, the more truly they become "themselves". The distinct personality of each one is deepened and intensified, and at the same time acquires an element of universality. They became more truly at one with others.

In an earlier chapter we used the idea of three-dimensionality to illustrate how true theological pluralism is built up of harmonious contrasts; how it is the simple and natural result of viewing the living Truth of Christ from different angles. Here we can perhaps say that there is a "multi-dimensional" aspect to the Life of Christ, as He lives it in his saints. Each saint incarnates a special aspect or aspects of Christ's Spirit, and so helps to illustrate its overall richness.

The life of Christ is recorded not only in the pages of the Gospels, but also in the lives of the holy men and women of the ages. The more we understand the particular way in which each saint imitates Christ, the better we will understand Christ. The more we love with the heart of each saint, the more we will love Christ.

The variegated work of the diversifying Spirit is to be seen not only in the concrete and contrasting lives of the saints, but also in the foundations many of them undertook. In this way they opened up new spiritualities and apostolic movements destined to change and enrich the lives of countless souls. It would be an impoverishment if this broad variety of charisms were to be lost, or if they were merged into a vague, standardised spiritual or pastoral approach lacking in distinctive character. The danger of such a process taking place is not absent today.

Christ came to save man and all that is human: also to save civilizations and cultures — because they too stand in need of redemption.

In opening itself to the demands of incarnation, a culture unfolds and develops. It flourishes and becomes more truly distinct from other cultures.

At the same time any culture that represents a true Christian incarnation acquires an element of universality, of communion, of inter-communicability with others. Its particularity is not impermeable to other cultures. On the contrary its distinctiveness always carries with it an element of universal appeal. Understanding comes easily between incarnated and truly Christian cultures. There is mutual appreciation, mutual attraction, mutual enrichment.

Lumen gentium says, "In virtue of this catholicity each part contributes its own gifts to other parts and to the whole Church, so that the whole and each of the parts are strengthened by the common sharings of all things and by the common effort to attain to fullness in unity" (LG 13).

So it is important already to note that diversity does not mean *non*-connection. It means inter-dependent variety. Non-connected diversity (diversity without *communio*) is what we must avoid.

The law of variety and unity

Let us see to what extent we can formulate the Christian law of variety and unity, of personality and universality, looking first at the inner dynamics of this law, and then considering the external means through which it operates.

The law of Jesus our Saviour is contained in the whole of Revelation. In its saving application it always remains the law of the Cross. Close to its heart lies that paradoxical principle, "whoever seeks his life will lose it". Startling works which warn us that the process of self-realization can easily become a dead end. All one has to do is to take a wrong turning; and the wrong turn here is to seek one's self. In order to find oneself, one must forget oneself and seek Christ. It is not one's own identity one must seek. It is identification with Christ. The Gospel is absolutely explicit on this point. You will find — you will become — yourself when you forget yourself. There is no other way. Do not seek your own identity. Seek Me.[1]

Excessive concern for one's self, over-protectiveness of one's own identity or one's own independence, stand between the individual and full communion with Christ.

The person who rejects the law of Christ or who subordinates it to the "law" of his personal circumstances or preferences, is seeking self (in the bad sense intended in the Gospel phrase), and will not find true self-fulfilment. All he will find is an ever-tightening self-centredness, less and less fulfilled within itself, less

---

[1] "No one is freed from sin by himself or by his own efforts, no one is raised above himself or completely delivered from his own weakness, solitude or slavery; all have need of Christ who is the model, master, liberator, saviour, and giver of life" (AG 8).

and less open to the true grace of the Gospel and to the good values of others, less and less capable of being enriched from outside.

The effect of excessive concern with self is to separate one from Christ and from others. It is to leave one's self in isolation, "incommunicado": in withering "un-communion"; and, as a consequence, in apostolic fruitlessness. The man who does not maintain his vital links with Christ is doomed to ultimate sterility, however great his personal activity; "separated from me you can do nothing" (Jn 15:5).

"Doing one's own thing" scarcely sounds like a Spirit-given norm for Catholic diversity. What should be said about the idea of "being Catholic *in one's own way*"? It is a formula with individualistic overtones, but it can pass provided it is intended to stress each one's right to be *Catholic* in a unique way, i.e. in the particular way that *Christ wants for him or her*. That way one has the right (and will find the power) to be Catholic. If one ends up as something else than Catholic, one has not followed the way Christ wanted.

There are many ways of being Catholic. There are also many ways of not being Catholic. One has to remember that "being Catholic" has an objective content, as we saw in Chapter Six. Protestants are not Catholics in any way. Protestants and Catholics are Christians, but in differing ways. The difference of the Protestant way is so great that it denotes a fundamental rupture of the communion willed by Christ for his Church.

Particular churches

Particular churches too find their identity — their principle of life and health and growth — by seeking Christ. They find Christ by maintaining full and active communion with him present in the life and faith of the universal Church. This point is emphasized strongly by Vatican II in describing a particular church as one "in which the one, holy, catholic and apostolic Church of Christ is truly present and active" (CD 11).

If a local church were to become so "particular" as not to be vivified by the active presence of the universal Church, if the channels of life linking it with the faith and worship of the whole Church were to become blocked, then it would be in danger of ceasing to be "church" in the conciliar sense. It would cease to receive and communicate the full flow of the dynamism of Christ. That is why the Council insists that "the local Church must represent the universal Church as perfectly as possible" (AG 20).

Excessive particularism means lack of universal vitality, receiving little, giving little; with the danger of the branch finally separating from the vine. History speaks all too clearly of this; and underlines how those who let individuality or diversity become their overriding concern have gradually come to regard unity as a major and eventually intolerable irritant.

The current emphasis on diversity will avoid such dangers if it is a *local* emphasis on *Christ*, not if it is merely a local emphasis on "self". If it is a local emphasis on Christ, it will at the same time be a local seeking after communion, and all will be well. In words of *Ad gentes*, speaking of particular churches: "Bishops and priests must feel and live with the universal Church, becoming more and more imbued with a sense of Christ and the Church. The communion of the young churches with the whole Church must remain intimate, they must graft elements of its tradition on to their own culture and thus, by a mutual outpouring of energy, increase the life of the mystical Body" (AG 19).

De-centralization, in ecclesial thinking, is a legitimate and indeed a positive concept if it is understood in strictly *administrative* terms, if it is seen as an exercise of the principle of subsidiarity. But it gets unhinged from a true ecclesial framework once it is understood in terms of (or leads to) de-universalisation. Universality or catholicity is an ecclesial note, not an administrative concept or a bureaucratic form that can be discarded. It is essential.

So, localisation does not mean de-universalization. After all, if a Catholic culture in a particular area were to be so "local" as to be completely unrecognizable to Catholics from other areas, where would be the experience of oneness? People are deprived of the sense of sharing in the richness of the universal faith if they do not feel one with the People of God in other countries, in other cultures, in other ages.

Inculturation through seeking Christ

Self-seeking instead of "Christ-seeking" is a deadend for mankind. This can happen to individuals and communities. It can also happen to whole civilizations or cultures.

As long as western society puts its hopes solely in pleasure and material comforts, it will remain closed to Christ; and, seeking such impoverished "self-realizations", it will lose its soul.

The same holds good for communist societies, with their explicit materialism and formal rejection of God. To seek one's life in the service of material progress and the worship of a godless State is a sure way of losing it.

The position of the Third World societies — richer in natural values than the developed countries — is not yet clearly defined. Their main danger would seem to be that their values and spiritual reserves be engulfed in "developed" materialism. In God's providence this may yet not happen; but they need to be alert to the danger.

The Gospel, still recently planted, may let down firm roots into their native soil and inheritance, taking what is best there, redeeming and preserving it, purifying and uplifting it: the authentic process of inculturation as outlined in the Decree on the Church's Missionary Activity (AG 9) and the Pastoral Constitution on the Church in the Modern World (GS 58).

Such inculturation is the natural and gradual result of true evangelization, of facing up to the full challenge of the Gospel, forgetting self in the service of Christ and therefore finding oneself.

Here the reference to sanctity continues to mark out the main guidelines. The saints became so rich in personality precisely because they were totally unconcerned about their own personality. Their goal was not "self-development". Their goal was Christ and bringing other to Christ.

So with cultures. If Christ (and evangelization) is their centre and goal, they develop: in all richness. But there is the danger of putting culture — one's own patrimony, one's own personality — first. The Gospel comes first. The Gospel gives the key to culture, and to its deeper values. It is not the other way round.

The deeper values of a native culture are going to be "fortified, completed and restored in Christ" (GS 58) only by persons who have steeped themselves in Gospel values and in the whole inheritance of the Church's tradition. Only those who are formed in a Catholic outlook and have assimilated a Catholic mind can carry out true inculturation according to the mind of Christ. Peering into one's local present and past will not of itself suffice for inculturation. One must also have the background and capacity to be able to look out to the Catholic cultures of other places and times. Only universal minds will particularise in a genuinely Catholic way.

The saints, so different one from another, were so interlinked because they were all linked to Christ. Interlinked inculturation proves catholicity. Isolated inculturation can end, at best, in sterility; also from the apostolic viewpoint.

An excessively self-concerned inculturation develops an inward-looking frame of mind. This could have serious consequences for the whole Church and its mission in the world. *Ad gentes* says that as indigenous churches grow through "the living of a full Christian life, they should contribute to the good of the whole Church" (AG 6). This has particular importance for the task of evangelization. The world today, above all the West, needs new evangelizers. The pointers are that they should come from the peoples of the Third World, especially Africa, because they have the natural resources of the spirit which, put at the service of the Gospel, can bring mankind back to Christ. But the evangelizing potential of the Third World countries could be frustrated if inculturation in these countries were to become too introspective. Self-concerned Christians do not convert their non-Christian neighbours or contemporaries. Inward-looking Christian communities do not evangelize the pagan societies they may meet.

Unity needs to be loved more

Looking at the dynamics of the interplay between unity and diversity, two points stand out:

a) It is easier to create diversity than unity. Men tend more easily to separate — into single individuals or into disconnected groups — than to come together in a rich and harmonious whole.

History shows many more examples of variety destroying unity than of unity stifling variety. Only the Catholic Church has managed to overcome the opposition between unity and variety, to harmonise both, and to make them grow together.

Both unity and diversity are to be loved. But unity, we repeat, needs to be loved more, because it is more fragile; more easily broken, more easily lost, and harder to restore. Christian unity, ecclesial unity, is moral and voluntary. It cannot be imposed. And it cannot and will not be maintained unless it is loved.

Christ did not tell his apostles to be different. He knew that that would take care of itself. He told them to be united. He knew that this would have to be an over-riding concern among them and those that came after them.

Diversity tends to come of itself (and if it comes without direction or control, it tends to turn into divergence and division). Unity does not come without an effort.

If we are obliged to make a choice, then, we should put unity before diversity, just as we should put *communio* before pluralism.

If we first seek the unity of our Father's kingdom, all other things — family variety included — will be given to us as well. Richness of personal identity, harmonious pluralism, strength of local culture, evangelizing force: all follow from the search for communion in Christ.

The world is not impressed to see us different (we *are*; and they *will* see it). The world is impressed to see us united; that is *the* difference that can draw them. The Church, local and universal, is always called to be the sign and promise of unity for men: that great and hard goal that men seek and do not find and will not find except in Christ.

b) Unity and variety are inestimable values, and also difficult values to combine. Without special graces and docility to grace, the dangers we mentioned at the start of the chapter can develop: unity stifling legitimate variety and imposing uniformity; variety becoming centrifugal and ending in fragmentation. Both extremes need to be guarded against. But the latter is clearly the more dangerous.

The interplay between unity and diversity is bound at times to involve some tensions. But it would not be right to exaggerate these tensions or to regard them necessarily in a negative light. Some tensions are a sign of life and are life-giving. This applies to structures too. There are structural tensions that destroy; and there are structural tensions that maintain the structure.

If love for Christ is paramount, unity in Christ and diversity in Christ are expressions of the same love, forces that pull in the same direction. To love unity without loving variety, or to love variety without loving unity, would be to love Christ defectively.

The same applies (though more emphatically) to the views of those who see this whole theme in terms of a "power-struggle" between a centralised unity party and localised diversity parties. This is to divide and dismember Christ (and one's love for Christ). It is to see head and hands and heart struggling against one another. It is to fail to understand the divinely-given trinitarian-modelled constitution of the Church. The Catholic Church is not a federation of semi-autonomous churches. The Catholic Church is the unity of particular churches. Each particular church is the Catholic Church, always provided it maintain its vital and loving links of unity with the Head and the other members.

A charism at the service of both unity and variety

Christ wanted his Church to be both richly diverse and at the same time fully united. What did He do to ensure that this would be so, and growingly so, through the ages? He gave his followers an evangelizing command — go teach all nations — that was to bring about the universal expansion of his message. This of itself favours diversity. The tongues of the day of Pentecost already expressed that catholic variety which is the work of the Spirit. What did Christ do to ensure unity?

One guideline we have already mentioned: the law of seeking Him and forgetting self. This is a fundamental law meant to operate from within each individual, from within each local community. It cannot be imposed. It can be understood: with reflection. And it can, with an effort, be put into practice. The proper understanding and voluntary embracing of this law at the grassroots level is a first condition for the dynamic growth of variegated unity.

With did He do on the institutional level? He gave us the hierarchy: the Pope and the Bishops. Their *diakonia* is a charismatic service to both unity and variety.

Some people are suggesting today that a main role of the local bishops (and of national Episcopal Conferences) is to defend local or regional diversity as against the uniforming centralist tendency of Rome.

This is not so; it is doubly misleading. It ignores the fact that while Rome must indeed be concerned with unity, it does not have to seek (and currently is clearly not seeking) uniformity. It also ignores the fact that *the* main responsibility of each local bishop is to defend and maintain the integrity of the faith and the bonds of universal ecclesial communion. This has been the essence of the bishop's role since apostolic times.[2] Vatican II teaches: "all the bishops have an obligation of fostering and safeguarding the unity of the faith and of upholding the discipline which is common to the whole Church (and) of schooling the faithful in a love of

---

2 In the ceremony of his ordination, when a bishop-elect receives the episcopal ring, the consecrating bishop says to him: "Take this ring, the seal of your fidelity. With faith and love protect the Bride of Christ, his holy Church". In the same ceremony he makes a public declaration before his people of his resolve "to maintain the deposit of faith, entire and incorrupt, as handed down by the apostles and professed by the Church everywhere and at all times"; and also "to build up the Church as the Body of Christ and to remain united to it within the order of bishops under the authority of the apostle Peter" (cf. *The Rites of the Catholic Church*, Vol II, pp 92ff).

the whole Mystical Body of Christ" (LG 23); "Let bishops so sanctify the churches entrusted to them that the mind of the universal Church of Christ may be fully reflected in them" (CD 15).

Within each particular church there are already many factors at work stressing diversity. Some of these factors are good; some are not so good. It is the bishop's duty to defend his people's rights in this matter. This undoubtedly means he must respect the due freedom of those who seek legitimate variety; and, if the case were to arise, he should protect them (using proper ecclesiastical channels) against abuse from above. But it also means that he must defend the rights of the rest of the faithful entrusted to him against abuses of "lateral" authority (cf. Appendix III), and against the abusive activity of those who promote a diversity that damages or ruptures *communio*.

The bishops then have a hierarchical mission to protect the catholic communion of the Faith. At the summit of the hierarchical level Christ gave another gift to foster and protect the united and varied growth of his Church: the See of Peter.

The Vatican II Decree on Ecumenism says that Christ "chose Peter ... (and) entrusted all his sheep to him to be confirmed in faith and shepherded in perfect unity" (UR 2). The Dogmatic Constitution on the Church, speaking of the relationship of the Holy See to the whole episcopate, says: "In order that the episcopate itself might be one and undivided Christ put Peter at the head of the other apostles, and in him he set up a lasting and visible source and foundation of the unity both of faith and of communion" (LG 18). The same Dogmatic Constitution, speaking of the relationship of the Chair of Peter to particular churches, says that it "protects their legitimate variety while at the same time taking care that these differences do not hinder unity, but rather contribute to it" (LG 13).

To think that the Holy See's only concern is unity and hence to regard it as a force opposed to variety, is to mistake its charism and function. Its role is to foster both Catholic unity and Catholic variety.

It is certainly true that if a conflict situation arises between the two, it is clearly to unity — as to the more delicate value and the one most expressly willed by Christ — that the Apostolic See must give its first responsibility.

In such a case a positive response to the directives of the Holy See will be facilitated by one's love for the Church, one's faith in Christ's gift to Peter, and one's awareness that any initiative, in order to be a true incarnation of the Gospel, must be Catholic as well as local or particular. The charism to make a sound judgment on this point has been entrusted to the Roman Pontiff.

Love for the Church

The Church, one and varied, is composed of members who are in it because they choose to be. The Church of its nature remains a voluntary body. God gives us the grace to live together within that Body. But it is always the free choice of each member that keeps it united with the Head and the Heart. Each member needs to rejoice in the guidance it receives from the Head (unity guiding variety), as it rejoices in its own distinctive action contemplated both in itself and in the contribution it makes to the well-being and life of the whole Body (variety expressing unity).

Unity marshalling the dynamism of variety; variety manifesting the dynamism of unity. These complementary facets of the Church's life bring out its power and beauty. They make it more unique, more truly a Church to be loved.

This should be the summary and conclusion of all ecclesiology. The Church today badly needs to be loved. Or rather it is we who badly need to renew our love for the Church.

Catholics who love the Church, who are passionately in love with the Church — there is one of the great needs of the present day, the absolutely necessary condition for true renewal.

Love for the Church. Love for the institutional Church. The dominant thought running throughout the pages of this book has been that the institutional, visible, hierarchical Church is a gift of God through which the Truth and the Grace and the loving but demanding Will of Jesus Christ come to us in divine challenge and saving force.

The Church, seen so, is seen to be truly lovable, despite the defects of us men who are its members. While we should not love those defects, we should love to trust in Christ present and working (with the logic of the Incarnation and the law of the Cross) also in and through those very defects.

Love for the Church. Love for the Holy Church. Because the Church (again despite and over and above men's defects) is holy. The Church is holy not because we are holy but because Christ makes it holy. If we can become holy, it is because Christ through his Church sanctifies us.

Love for the Church. Love for the Church our Mother. Christ

wants us to become like children. Otherwise we will not enter the kingdom of heaven (Mt 18:3). He wants us to learn to be children within the same family. He wants us to be saved in a family way, with family ties and loyalty and responsibility, and under family authority.

For that we need a mother. In fact we have two: the Virgin Mary and the Church. Mary herself "model of that motherly love" that animates the Church's mission (LG 65), draws us to our Mother the Church. It is God's design that, within family warmth and family unity, our good and holy Mother the Church should teach us to be truly brothers and sisters to one another, truly children of our Father in Heaven; remembering what St Cyprian says: "No one can have God for his Father if he does not have the Church for his Mother". Not to love the Church would be a clear sign of loss of catholic identity. After all, only denaturalised children do not love their mother.

Our holy Mother the Church is currently faced with the task of trying to bring up a brood of particularly turbulent and unruly children. We individual members of the faithful need to think less of doing our "own thing" and more of the *family concerns*. We need to live more in family communion, to renew our family sense: the joy of belonging to one home filled with mutual loyalty and service and affection. A home where there are many children and as a result there are bound to be many differences of mood and character and opinions. Yet these differences never become a threat to family unity; the children have come to love the family too much to allow that, and when necessary they go to their Mother to settle the matter.

She has the knowledge, the experience, the love and the firmness — and in particular the divine guidance — to protect the family inheritance of warmth and wisdom for her children of today, as she did for those of yesterday and will do for those of tomorrow: for her children of the whole world, for Christ's purpose is that the whole world enter into this family.

May our Mother Mary teach us to love our Mother the Church.

APPENDIX I

Legal Positivism

Human laws are bound to show imperfections, as all human works do. This will happen even if a society has a *sound* concept of law, i.e. even if it accepts that law should respect and reflect the Divine and the Natural Law.

However, if a society or its law-givers have a *wrong* concept of law, its laws can be very bad indeed. And a society suffers immensely from bad laws.

The root error is the thesis that man-made law is the source and test of all justice; in other words, that there is no law higher than man-made or positive law. This error is termed Positivism.

Positivism means that the will of the law-giver is supreme;[1] he enacts what he likes. As a result it leaves those who may not agree with the law-giver without any court of appeal against what they consider unjust laws.

Positivism can be a useful instrument to non-democratic regimes; cf. the racial laws of Hitler or of South Africa. The law-giver in this case may be in a minority; but he has the power to impose his will. And there is no redress for those who suffer injustice.

But positivism can also be present in the legal system of democratic countries. One of the greatest exponents of legal positivism, the American jurist, Oliver Wendell Holmes, summed up the democratic positivist philosophy when he said he knew of no other criterion of what is right and wrong in law except *the will of the majority*.

Now that sort of positivism may, at first sight, carry a certain appeal to the modern mind. But democratic positivism can equally lead to injustice, and is in fact doing so more and more in today's world. If the majority will is absolute, then there is no defence for a minority group if a majority decides to penalise it. There is no defense for the unborn if the majority legalise abortion. There is none for the new-born if the majority legislate infanticide (e.g. for the defective). There is no protection for the aged if the majority legislate compulsory euthansia. Here we are facing a great contemporary danger.

Holmes, a practical agnostic and a man opposed to any concept

---

1 That is why it is sometimes also called Voluntarism.

of stable and fixed truth, opened his most important work with the words: "The life of the law has not been logic; it has been experience". The maxim may be a useful reminder that law is not to be applied according to a narrow logic, i.e. in a legalistic way, taking more account of the law's letter than of its spirit. But it can destroy a main function of the law — the protection of the rights of the weak — if it is taken to mean that law should adapt itself to man's experience, i.e. should adapt itself to what men happen to think or tend to in any moment, and not that men's experience or way of living should be modelled according to the law of his nature as given by God and discovered by reason.

"Logic" can easily be used as a term of contempt. But logic really means sound reasoning at work. If reason is not at the basis of law, then law quickly becomes an instrument of tyranny and exploitation.

Positivism; subjectivism

The prevailing atmosphere of our modern world is positivism in law, just as it is subjectivism in morality. Neither public order nor private morality will survive on such a basis.

What is right or wrong has become, for many people, a matter of opinion or of votes; a matter of preference, of what people want. In politics or in law, the only criterion of right or wrong is the *majority* will. In personal conduct, the only criterion is *my* will.

What the majority wants is best for the country.... What I want is best for me (I am my own majority).... The two approaches are connected; but are also in potential opposition. If the majority wants something I do not want, why should I have to accept the majority's preference?

Is the majority's opinion always right? Must the minority always surrender its opinion? If one man's opinion is as good as another's, why should one opinion not be as good as two others? Or am I bound to surrender my opinion just because I am faced with two contrary opinions? Are two persons always "righter" than one? . . .[2]

If I am a black citizen of a country and a majority of my fellow-citizens approve a law that all blacks are to be deprived of their civil rights, am I supposed to accept that law as binding?

---

2 Either one man's opinion is as good as another's (and then you get potential chaos), or there is One Opinion that is better than anyone's: i.e. God's. That is why if, as Christians believe, God has revealed his "Opinion" — about man and men's affairs — there, in God's Revelation, is the true basis for life.

On the other hand, we can also ask: is a minority opinion always entitled to hold out against a majority? Have I the right to toss bombs into all the butchers shops I see just because I feel deeply that animals should not be slaughtered?

In any society of men there are bound to be many differences of opinion about the management of human affairs (level of taxes, educational curricula, foreign policy, etc., etc.). These differences of opinion about social, economic, political affairs, etc. do create some tensions. But society can survive the tensions as long as they are simply about the *management* of human affairs. However, if the differences of opinion are about the very roots of social and human life, if people do not agree about the very nature of human society or the very nature of man himself, then the tensions become explosive, man will not get along with others (he no longer sees "*fellow*-men" in them), and society itself will split apart.

If society is to hold together, a norm of behaviour, a criterion of right and wrong must be found that is objective, i.e. that is not a product of each individual's subjective emotions or whims but stands outside each individual (that is what we mean by objectivity), and so is easily understandable by all (because it appeals not to feelings or whims but to reason), and, given a minimum of good will, is acceptable by them.

This objective character of the norms of social conduct offers the only hope of making these norms acceptable to men in general, and so represents the only basis for holding society peaceably together. By contrast, a purely subjective and individualistic approach to law or to morality removes the one basis on which stable and just society can be built — i.e. a *common* acceptance of rules of behaviour.

A man holding a subjective social morality cannot get others to follow him, or will not follow others. He cannot find grounds for buiding a society. He is an island; and he is arguing that all others are islands too, and that there is no shared ground — not even deep beneath the surface — on which to build bridges to link them together.

If our only basis for building society is men's opinions, everything is fluid, and everything can fall apart. In opinions is where men so easily differ. In *nature* is where men meet and are at one. So at least we believe. We see no other way for men to learn to live together, unless they can be convinced that despite their varying opinions, they all have one thing in common: their very human nature. And here we connect with Appendix II.

APPENDIX II

Natural Law

By natural law we mean the norms of human conduct, of right and wrong for man, that are derived not from any positive law but directly from *what man is*, i.e. from his *nature*. For men share the same human nature; and the natural law is simply the law of that nature governing the development and fulfilment of its human potential. The concept of natural law is in fact basic to any treatment of man's life, whether he is considered as an individual or in society. It is vital to see that there is such a thing as human nature, that it has its law, and that human life degenerates and human society tends to collapse when this law of man's nature — the natural law — is denied in practice.[1]

Different in personality; like in nature

Men differ from one another. No two men are the same. Each one is a distinct individual, a unique person. Personality or personhood is the root of each man's distinctive being and dignity.

Yet these different men share a great likeness. There is clearly a bigger difference between man and mouse or man and mountain than between man and man. Men are not zebras nor are they cows. They are not trees or flowers. When we speak of men therefore — e.g. as distinguished from animals or plants — we are speaking of a group of beings that have something distinctive in common. They share something basic which is in fact what makes them *human* beings and not just animal beings; and that shared basic something, which enables us to call them men, is human nature.

It is because all share in same human nature that we can speak about "humanity" or "mankind", knowing that when we do so we are speaking about *all* men.

---

1 It is also vital to see that Catholic morality in major areas, especially that of sexual conduct, is simply an expression of the natural law. If one does not see this, there is a danger of thinking that the moral teaching of the Church, in areas such as marriage and sexuality, is out of touch with human reality and is contrary to man's true interests and development; whereas precisely the opposite is true.

It is because all share in the same nature that all these distinct persons have the same radical equality and share the same basic rights and obligations (cf. GS 29).

Some men are richer and others poorer, some are stronger and others weaker, some are wiser and other stupider. Yet we all share the same human nature and share it equally. We are all equally men. The richer and the poorer, the stronger and the weaker, all are equally human. No man is more — or less — human than any other man. All men are equally human because, sharing in the same nature, they share in the same basic human dignity and rights of man.

All men are equal before the law. They share the same rights and obligations before the law. Before which law? The law of the State? No; not primarily. Primarily before the law of their nature; i.e. before the Natural Law.

The Ten Commandments

It is true that the notion of natural law is not very popular today.[2] Popularity of course is no criterion of validity or truth, and should not worry us very much. After all, the Ten Commandments have never been popular either, and the Ten Commandments are basically an expression of the natural law.

To steal and lie and kill are actions that are wrong today, will be wrong tomorrow and were wrong yesterday as far back as time goes. There is nothing "artificial" about their wrongness; it is natural. They are wrong not because someone one day declared them wrong,[3] but because such actions are in themselves contrary to how man should behave, to what man should be. They are wrong because in stealing, lying, killing, one does violence to what one owes to onself or to others, i.e. one does violence to human nature.

Despite all theoretical doubts about the natural law, people of all times and places have recognized and recognize that certain actions are right and wrong in themselves, independently of any

---

2 It is significant that the *Encyclopaedia Britannica* has no entry on natural law in the sense in which we are discussing it, although the *Encylopaedia Americana* has.

3 They did not begin to be wrong about the thirteenth century B.C. when God gave the Commandments to Moses. They were wrong "before" that. They were wrong from the start: always. Four hundred years before Moses, Joseph knew that it was wrong to commit adultery (Gen 39:9). It was no positive law, but his own sense of the natural law, that told him.

human lawgiver. But this is to recognize the existence of a natural law. That a natural law exists is all the more clearly shown by the fact that this universal awareness of basic right and wrong is not something that men have assimilated from "outside". It springs up within each one. Within each man, from his earliest days, there is a voice speaking the same basic message: "Good is to be done. Evil is to be avoided. This is good; do it. That is bad; avoid it". It is the voice of conscience (GS 16). And of course the existence of conscience is itself one of the great proofs of the existence of a natural law.

It is good that children are *reminded* that e.g. stealing or lying is wrong .[4] But they don't have to be taught it. They know it already. Their conscience told them.

Human rights mean natural rights

Perhaps some people deny or at least ignore the concept of the natural law because they think it is necessarily connected with belief in God, and they are or profess to be atheists. Yet it is possible to show that many people today who deny the existence of the natural law and perhaps also of God, in fact make constant appeal to the natural law. For instance, all those who advocate and defend human rights.

It may be possible to believe in the natural law without believing in God. What is not possible is to believe in human rights without believing in the natural law. This point can be shown quite simply.

Suppose I am a human rights campaigner. I say, for instance, that racial discrimination is evil; I have no doubt that it is a clear violation of human rights. . . . But what if someone objects: why should it be so bad if it is in fact the *law* of a particular country?

Because — I would answer — that law is unjust. Exactly; which means I am judging that law by a *higher* law. I am judging it by a *law of man*, not created by positive law. That is natural law: a law for man, but not made by man, and not to be violated or changed by man.

Human rights means rights that men have essentially as men, not primarily as citizens. They derive these rights not from the

---

[4] Such reminders and explanations of the content of the natural law precepts are part of moral education, i.e. of the process of forming the conscience. But it is not moral education that gives rise to conscience. Conscience is already there. Moral education forms the conscience if the principles taught are sound and true, and deforms it if the principles are unsound or false.

State, nor from other men, but *from their own nature*. They are natural rights.

Man can always appeal to what is his by nature. Other men may perhaps take away what *they* have given you. But they may not take away what *God* has given you. That is why there is no security in a Godless state.

Men may take away your *power* to exercise a right. They cannot really take away your right. It is yours by nature. A man unjustly imprisoned has the exercise of his freedom taken away. His right to freedom remains.

This would not be so if human rights derived from positive law or from the State; the State which gives could take away what it has given. But the State does not give us our human rights. It can and should recognize them and defend them. It does not give them or originate them. A sound Constitution should express basic human rights, and provide a process for their defence. It does not create or confer those rights.

If there is no natural law, if there is no such thing as a shared human nature making us equal, then we have nothing in common, no duties towards one another, no mutual rights.

If there is no natural law, then we have really nothing to appeal to, no defence against those stronger, against tyranny.

The understanding and defence of the natural law is vital if society is to be human and just. Without natural law human rights have no basis; they do not survive. Society becomes inhuman and man becomes a tool of the State or a mere object of exploitation by the more powerful.

Laws of Life

The natural law is designed to put order into life. It tells us that life has its laws, and that they must be respected if life itself is to be human and liveable.

In reflecting on this it can help if we distinguish the laws of life into physical laws and moral laws:

— physical laws, that state what *necessarily* happens given what is fixed in the nature of things. Physical laws govern the world of necessity;

— moral laws, that state what *should* be done if man, in his freedom, wishes to attain his end. Moral laws govern the world of freedom.

One needs to know the physical laws of life, and there is clear danger in ignoring them. A person would be regarded as very ignorant of life if he did not know not just that one must breathe or eat in order to live, but other things that are not quite so obvious; things that experience — or, better still, teachers — must teach: e.g. that a live electric wire can kill, that exhaust fumes are poisonous, that certain diseases are specially contagious, that too much milk and butter can cause hardening of the arteries....

Knowledge of these physical laws enables a man to ensure the well-being of the body. These laws govern man. He can ignore them or break them — but not without consequences. "I'm Superman; I'm going to stand on the railway track and stop this express train"; well....

But there are moral laws as well to ensure the well-being of the spirit. A man also needs to know and observe these moral laws, e.g. that his relations with others should be governed by the law of justice and truth. If a man does not obey this law, he may be a successful cheat, but his spirit has suffered, he is less of a man.

A particular point is worth noting. In the physical world the consequences of breaking a law are quickly observed; e.g. when you run into a brick wall. In the moral world, the consequences are not always noticed so quickly; but they are there. "I lied, and nothing has gone wrong". *You* have gone wrong. And that damage — to your spirit — eventually catches up: always. The liar, as we have just said, is less of a man. He is also less of a friend. People come to suspect that he is a liar, and eventually won't trust him. He becomes isolated. He suffers.

Two worlds

The fact is that man moves in the two worlds that we have mentioned: the world of necessity and the world of freedom. In the world of necessity, the subject can *not* disobey the law: the stone falls, the plant grows.... In the world of freedom, the subject *can* disobey, but suffering the consequences: the consequences, for instance, of refusing to eat or of taking drugs....

Non-rational beings live in the world of necessity. Man alone lives in both worlds. He cannot disobey the physical laws; he cannot *stop* that train. He can disobey the moral law — but with consequences. He can *try* to stop that train — and suffer the physical consequence of death, and the moral consequence of suicide; both consequences of doing something that is too much for him as a man, something that his nature cannot and is not meant to stand. He can abuse his nature; but abused nature always makes man pay the price of the abuse.

If people think, they will admit that man must pay the consequences of untruthfulness, drugs, selfishness.... Some may comment: "But if he wants to go that way, that is his right. He is under no obligation to be truthful; these are not laws that "bind". He has the right to act against them". The right? No; he has the power, but not the right.

Rights derive from nature, as do obligations. A right or an obligation is something due to one's nature. We have the power of speech, and the right to free speech. We do not have the right to deceitful or abusive speech. To use the power of speech for true communication is something due to one's own nature and to that of others. There *is* an obligation to be truthful. You have the power to use your freedom in a wrong way, but not the right. That is why you do a *wrong* thing. No one has the *right to do wrong*! One may have all the power in the world to do wrong, but never the right. Might does not make right.

Binding, universal, unchanging

Natural law marks out the order human life should have if it is to be and remain human. Natural Law is rooted in what we might call "essential" man; hence derive the distinctive characteristics of its precepts, which are *binding, universal* and *unchangeable*.

a) These precepts are binding. Man cannot be man without observing them; and man is meant to be man. Man does not really know the exact way of his own fulfilment. God does; and has spelled out his directives for man in the natural law. If we look for the ultimate reason why the precepts of the natural law bind man, why he is under an obligation to respect them, it is because man does not possess a full and free title to his own life. He has no right to dispose of his life just as he wishes. He has received his life, with its conditions, from God. In other words, the authority of the precepts of the natural law derives from man's rational nature as given by God. Their authority therefore ultimately comes from God.

b) The precepts of the natural law are universal: for all times and for all people. For the tenth century, the twentieth and the thirtieth. For you, for me.

c) The precepts of the natural law are unchangeable. The natural law does not change because it derives not from some perfectable human reasoning but from God's perfect wisdom. The natural law was not given by human authority and is therefore independent of all human authority. It is not the end result of human experience, or the changeable trial-and-error finding of human experimentation. It is God's plan for man.[5] God has not had to experiment with man, probing or groping around to see if He can find laws that suit man's condition best. From the start, in creating man, He gave him the laws that enable man to be human, i.e. to fulfil and not to frustrate his potential. It is we men who tend to experiment, trying to substitute other "laws" for the natural law. The result of our experiments is to make individual life and social life less and less natural and less and less human.

An evolving nature?

Objections are raised nowadays to this idea of a natural law with universal and unchangeable precepts. Some writers reject the whole concept of a human nature that is objective and "given", and propose instead a human nature that is fluid and evolving. Man's life, they say, evolves; surely the laws of his life should evolve too? Their position can be shown to be untenable; it is largely due to a failure to make proper distinctions. One has to distinguish above all between man and his circumstances. The circumstances of man's life change, but not his nature or its laws.

If man's nature were changing, then we could not really speak of man at all; not as a continuum throughout history. "Man" of X centuries ago would be a different species of being to "man" of today or of X centuries from now.

If man is changing in his nature, then we cannot speak about what is "human" as something of universal application. What is "human" becomes no more than a relative concept; a concept therefore that is valueless as a guide or as a standard of judgment for the life of individuals or societies. If what was inhuman and wrong yesterday can be human and right today, then humanity is a meaningless term. We cannot speak abou the history of mankind because there is no mankind.[6] All there is, is an

---

5 Here we are of course prescinding from the economy of grace.

6 If man's nature is changing, then the human nature Christ took solidarises him only with those who share that same nature, i.e. those of twenty centuries ago; not those of today or those of 4000 A.D. If man of 4000 A.D. will have a changed nature, then he will not be man, not as Christ was; and Christ, then, would not have died for him — whoever or whatever he will be. The thesis of an evolving human nature utterly destroys the universality of the Redemption worked by Christ.

evolving species — that is not even a species because there is no essential link of nature between its apparent members. If what was inhuman and wrong yesterday can be human and right today, then why should what is inhuman and wrong in Africa not be human and right in Europe? Why should what is human to me be human to you? ... I don't have to respect your humanity or human standards, and you don't have to respect mine. Each man is a law and a world to himself.

Man's nature does not change. His circumstances at times do change drastically. The twentieth century man's mode of housing or dress or transport, for instance, are very different to those of the man of ten centuries ago. Does this mean that his nature and its laws have changed? No. He is necessarily bound by the same basic laws governing the essential *human* quality of his conduct. Despite changed circumstances, the same basic standards of right and wrong apply to his conduct.

Let us take just two concrete examples: speech and trade. Twentieth century man uses a different mode of speech — probably a totally different language — to tenth century man. Yet the law of truthfulness in speech binds the former as much as it did the latter. It was as wrong for tenth century man to tell a lie or to use his power of communication to deceive others as it is for his modern counterpart, as it will be for thirtieth or fortieth century man.

Tenth century man traded largely by barter. He knew nothing about cheques, had no banknotes, and probably seldom saw a coin. Yet he was as bound — no more, no less — by the law of honesty and justice in business dealings as is twentieth century man.

The law of truthfulness in speech and honesty in business are laws that will bind as long as man remains man. If man were ever to "evolve" into some other — non-human — being, then these laws might cease. A different sort of being would have a different nature, with its own proper laws. Such "evolutions" exist in the imaginations of some scientists and in fantasy story-books; not outside.

Circumstances change; but they do not change man's nature, nor the law of man's nature. Can changed circumstances modify the *application* of the natural law? Yes; this can happen. But that very modified application simply underlines the justice of the natural law in judging varying human circumstances.

Usury, as understood and practised in the twelfth century, was wrong and naturally immoral for men. Usury, as we understand it today — interest paid on a monetary loan —, is not necessarily wrong for modern man. Has man's nature or its law changed? No; the nature of usury or money-interest has changed. The norm of justice, which is constant, is applied in a different way to different situations.

Static? Dynamic?

Some people would say that the idea we have given of the natural law is too "static", and that the times demand a more *dynamic* concept. Otherwise, they say, natural law conceived as something fixed becomes a dead weight holding men down, an obstacle blocking their progress.

This is a false appreciation. It is the opposite of the truth. The natural law such as we have described it, is indeed dynamic. Its "dynamic quality" does not mean that *it* is changing, for then it would be valueless as a norm for human conduct. (If the moral laws were changing, then "Do not commit adultery" could gradually come to mean, "Do not commit *much* adultery", or "too much" adultery...!) The dynamic quality of the natural law simply means that it has the dynamism, that is, the *power to change individuals and societies* into what they are meant to be, so that men live as men and societies are truly human.

It is also true that the natural law is in a dynamic situation in that it is in constant tension with fallen human nature. It is calling man from within to keep his balance and to rise, whereas man so often tends to decline and fall.

The natural law is bound to be in tension with cultures too, insofar as their customs, laws and institutions embody a way of life that is contrary to human rights and dignity. The natural law is constantly calling them to reform, to remodel their society along patterns of true humanity.

There is a growing realization that today's society is in danger of being dehumanized; not only human rights but all the truly human aspects of life seem endangered. Without a return to a proper understanding of the natural law there is no hope of rehumanizing our contemporary world.

★ ★ ★

A last point to be made is the relation of the natural law to the teaching of the Church.

It is true that the natural law is knowable by human reason and is written in the hearts of man (cf. Rom 2:15). It is also true that knowledge of the principles of the natural law does not as such require revelation. It does however require clear thinking; and clear thinking depends in turn on uprightness of heart.

If it is easy for man to come to false conclusions in his mind, it is so often because his heart — his will — inclines his mind to accept ideas that accord with what suits his convenience more than with sound reasoning.

That is why a full and adequate knowledge of the natural law is hard to acquire without some form of divine guidance. So it was that God gave us the Ten Commandments (basically just natural law precepts). And so it is that part of the mission and competence of his Church is the protection and explanation of the natural law.

APPENDIX III

Abuse of Authority

Physical force can easily be abused. Power can become coercion. A police force or an army can use their strength wrongly, to blackmail, to terrorize, or to plunder.

Can moral authority be abused? Most certainly; and in a variety of ways. It can be over-exercised, i.e. in ways that do not respect the personal dignity or legitimate freedom of those subject to it, thereby placing an excessive strain on their moral duty to respond. It can even be abused, as we have seen elsewhere, to such an extent that a person is bound in conscience to resist it.

Moral authority can of course also be *under*-exercised, not fulfilling its function of speaking out in defence of people's rights, or not giving sufficient guidance to those whom it is meant to serve. This too is a misuse of authority.

Both extremes can be an abuse. Permissive parents can do as much harm to their children as parents who happen to be dictatorial.

Authority can be abused if it is not exercised with due regard for truth, or justice, or also for prudence or even charity. It can be abused if it does not respect or protect individual rights, and especially if it does not serve the common good. In fact the most frequent abuse of authority is probably that of its being exercised for the sake of some personal advantage to the detriment of the broader good of the community.

It is important to note that when we speak here of authority we are not speaking just about authority that comes from "above" or from "the top", i.e. from some established and recognised organ of government or management of a society or community.

In any group or society, besides the authority coming from above, many other types of authority are present and active. It helps to recall one of the definitions of the term "authority" given by the Oxford Dictionary: "personal influence, especially over opinion"; a definition that not only stresses the moral quality of authority but also brings out its breadth and its scope.

This sort of moral authority is all around us today. It does not come only or even mainly from the top. It is a sort of "lateral" authority that, so to speak, comes at us sideways, at times with great force. TV commentators, newspaper editors and columnists, experts, pundits, palmreaders, psychologists, counsellors, psychiatrists ... all exercise colossal authority or influence over people's daily lives. The less a person is aware of this authority or the less he questions its credentials, the more it is likely to influence him — for good or for bad. Because of course this sort of authority can be used well and responsibly, with due regard for others and for the common good; or it can be used for selfish purposes and so misused.

Think for instance of the authority that attaches to a newspaper article written by some well-known columnist that contains what seem to be important statements of fact. The statements — so *author*ised — spread quickly and have an effect, even though they later turn out to be untrue.

There is a clear abuse of moral authority in such a case, as there would be in the case, say, of a pop-star who uses his popularity to promote drug-taking or hatred among his teenage fans.

Authority from above can certainly be abused. However in a truly free society this sort of abuse is rendered less likely, at least nowadays, by the fact that it will immediately be exposed to public criticism especially through the media.

Yet, just as we tend today to be very sensitive to possibilities of abuse coming from above, so we tend to be rather unaware of lateral authority or influence. The danger of abuse from this type of moral authority is therefore made all the greater in that its operation is so often unfelt; moreover it is, in so many cases, influence that derives from the media themselves.

Abuse of authority can come at us "sideways", and not just from above. It can even come from "below". A referee can abuse his authority if he unjustly sends a player off the field. But a well-known player, with a lot of prestige, can also abuse *his* moral authority — e.g. the influence that his popularity gives him among his team-mates — by encouraging them to back him when he protests a *just* sanction that the referee has imposed on him.

Legitimation of moral authority

Is there any way in which we can measure the legitimacy of moral authority? A political party elected in fair elections acquires not only governing power but also a certain measure of moral authority clearly based on a mandate to govern which has been legitimately and openly obtained.

The legitimation of the lateral authority of many modern

commentators, writers, publicists and pundits, is not quite so clear. They may allege their "popularity" as a warrant for their infuence and authority. But as anyone minimally acquainted with the operation of the media and the laws of modern publicity knows, popularity itself (and therefore the influence or authority that accompanies it) is often a deliberate and largely artificial creation.

Some people still seem to think that the popular media speak for the people, i.e. represent the views of the people. This more often than not is a delusion (fostered, naturally enough, by the media themselves). The media do not so much speak for the people as speak to the people. Above all they tend to *think for* the people and try to get the people to accept *their way of thinking*. Newspapers, magazines, etc. plus the other media, are almost always controlled by a small group with well-defined business or ideological interests; and the media under their control publicise what the group wants the public to hear and accept. That is why it is frequently a matter of conjecture whether a book is publicised because it is popular, or is popular because it has been publicised. In any case, from the fact that a well-publicised writer is dubbed popular, it does not follow that his ideas represent what people think. There is always a real possibility that his popularity may be due less to any intrinsic merit of what he says (though he says it very well) than to the fact that his way of thinking has been to the liking of a particular group in the media who therefore deliberately set about using the resources they dispose of to make him "popular".

Given a certain attractiveness of personality and a minimum acting ability, it is Hollywood that creates its stars. Nowadays, in fact, acting ability and personality may not be enough; a potential actor may not make it unless his or her ideological position is acceptable to the star-makers.

Abuse within the Church

Let us now turn from these general (but pertinent) reflections to consider the question of possible abuse of authority within the Church, remembering always that the Church is not a police state or a concentration camp. It is a free system; a voluntary society. Within it physical force or coercion has no place as an expression of authority. Authority in the Church is moral of its nature.

It should be stating the obvious to affirm that the hierarchy are not the only ones exercising moral authority in the Church. On the contrary, there are many levels, and especially many kinds, of "lateral" authority within the Church. Religious publishing houses, pastoral committees, missionary movements, religious institutes, theological faculties or societies, all possess moral authority in greater or less degree, as do individual preachers, writers, teachers or counsellors, whether cleric or lay. Think for instance of the immense moral authority possessed by a Mother Teresa of Calcutta. How well she deserves it and how well she exercises it!

Moral authority of this lateral type can be used well; or of course it can be misused or abused. It is important to bear this in mind since, in the current debate about authority, it seems to be taken for granted that abuse of authority can only come from the "top", i.e. from the Pope, the Roman Curia, the bishops. . . .

No one will deny the possibility of such abuse coming from above. Popes and bishops can misuse their moral authority, seeking personal advantage from their position or over-taxing, with unreasonable demands, the free response of those subject to them.

This can happen although, as is pointed out elsewhere,[1] the subject may well choose to see the Will of Christ and the Cross of Christ in those taxing demands and then summon up a greater — and therefore a freer — personal response to Christ in them.

The superior will then have to answer to God for having governed badly; for having asked too much, unreasonably. But the subject will gain more merit for having obeyed well, even when he or she found obedience difficult.

In any event, the possibility of abuse of authority coming from above, within the Church, cannot be denied. The new Code of Canon Law has specific provisions designed to avoid or remedy such abuse.[2] Nonetheless, abuse of authority from above is today probably a lesser danger in the Church than it has been for many centuries. The very sensitivity of people to the issue largely precludes it; as indeed do the presence and power of the public media, plus the fact that they are generally hostile to church authority.

But in this matter, should we not also take a good look at the many types of lateral authority that we have just mentioned? Is this authority necessarily used well in every case? Is it always used in the true interest of the common good? Is it too not subject to the danger of abuse?

Let us take some cases of exercise of authority, and consider

1 pp. 83-84.
2 Cf., for instance, cc. 57; 270; 698; 1505; 1649; 1732-1739; 1747.

whether, and from what quarters, abuse can enter into the matter.

A theologian is asked by Rome to clarify some point in one of his works, or to rectify some passages, or to spend a period of time in specific research; or perhaps he has the title of "Catholic" theologian officially withdrawn from him on the grounds that he no longer accepts some fundamental aspects of the Church's teaching. These are exercises from "above". Are they abusive? abusive?

Many people might instinctively say Yes, inasmuch as — they feel — such measures violate the theologian's right to think as he sees best.

But is this an adequate analysis of the issue? The issue is surely not a theologian's right to think what he likes; no one after all can stop a person thinking as he chooses. The issue is not even the theologian's right to publish his ideas. The issue is his claiming the *authority of the term "Catholic"* for his ideas, and claiming the right to publish them precisely as *expressions of Catholic theology.*

This is the substantial issue. It could be expressed somewhat differently but even more importantly by saying that the issue is the right of the *people* to know what theological authority — i.e. what authority in terms of the faith — attaches to the theologian's views: whether they are just his views or whether they are a legitimate reflection or interpretation of the mind of Christ.

A man may be entitled to whatever influence or authority he has as a result of his facility as a writer, his skill as a speaker, his possession of academic titles, his popularity with the media, etc. This authority gives him the *power* to influence others as he thinks fit; but it gives him no *right* to do so precisely *in the name of the Catholic faith.*

The fact is that *extra* authority accrues from the status of being a spokesman for Catholicism. His claim that his views are Catholic needs to be substantiated; if it cannot, the claim is groundless. If he nevertheless continues to buttress the authority of his position or his views with the added qualification of "Catholic theologian" or "Catholic views", then at that stage he is certainly guilty of a misuse or abuse of his authority.

One is free to think, as a Catholic, within the broad limits of the faith. One is free to think outside those limits; but then one cannot rightfully claim that one's thinking is Catholic.

It is of course the particular competence of the Magisterium to judge whether theological opinions are within the scope of the Faith, or outside it (cf. DV 8; LG 20). But if certain views of a theologian are not Catholic, then he has no right to claim that they are; and he is being deprived of no right when the public are informed that they are not.

Who seeks what?

What is behind the actions of the Magisterium in reviewing or censuring the views of this or that theologian? What is the Magisterium seeking? What is it defending?

Do the Pope and bishops wish to browbeat the theologian in question? Are they seeking to stifle theological research? Are they afraid for their own power, or afraid of an "open"church? Are they defending triumphalism, immobilism, entrenched positions, personal viewpoints (personal viewpoints are after all what the theologian is certainly defending)?

Each one can reflect on and answer these questions as he wishes. But it might be worth considering, on its merits, the possible answer that the Pope and bishops — who clearly gain no personal advantage in pursuing what is inevitably an unpopular course — are basically concerned for the People of God whom they have been appointed to serve.

Their concern is precisely that the people can know the Catholic faith, can live in a church where there is open and clear access to the Truth of Christ, which it is the hierarchy's mission, with the special assistance of the Holy Spirit, to teach and protect.

Lumen gentium (no. 25), describing the hierarchy as "authentic teachers, that is, teachers endowed with the authority of Christ", adds that they "preach the faith to the people assigned to them, the faith which is destined to inform their thinking and direct their conduct"; insisting that they must "watchfully ward off whatever errors threaten their flock", the Council refers to the passage in Scripture where Paul tells Timothy to "proclaim the message, welcome or unwelcome, insist on it. Refute falsehood, correct error, call to obedience" ... (2 Tim 4:1-4).

Nowadays if the hierarchy raises the least question concerning theological opinion, this invariably causes a hue and cry about violation of freedom and abuse of authority. Nevertheless, to expect that the hierarchy should never censure an opinion could only be justified either by supposing that men (theologians included) are incapable of error, or else by claiming that the hierarchy do not possess authority; or that, if they do, they are morally bound never to exercise it. The fact of the matter is just the opposite: the hierarchy do possess God-given authority, and are morally bound to exercise it. Non-use of authority, where its exercise is called for, is misuse. It is an abuse. Under-exercise of authority is as bad as over-exercise; perhaps it is worse.

If authority is service, as we have had occasion to repeat, one can ask; who serves the community — the common good — better: the theologian who wants his own ideas, however contrary to Scripture or Tradition, to be sanctioned (i.e. "authorised") by the Church, or the Magisterium which fulfils its duty (generally an unpleasant duty) of telling the People of God: these ideas are not in harmony with the mind of Christ; these are not Catholic ideas. The theologian remains free to hold and preach his ideas as before; but the people are no longer in danger of being led into thinking such ideas are Catholic.

Authority and popularity

The twentieth century has probably seen no more popular figure than Pope John Paul II. The media generally reflect this, with a tendency perhaps to present him simply as an outgoing warm-hearted man who loves people. It is an image which already gives him immense personal moral authority.

However, Pope John Paul's unambiguous views on divorce, contraception, abortion, etc., though well known, are not so well reflected and are in fact habitually described by the media as being "unpopular".

No one seems to have considered whether his moral authority is lessened or whether it is in fact possibly increased by these clear but "unpopular" views of his. An interesting question that I leave the reader to ponder.

In any case, the media seem to find a contradiction between the Pope's liberal heart and his conservative mind — without apparently considering that his opposition to abortion or contraception may proceed not only from his faith and his love for God's law, but also precisely from his love for people, because he is convinced that these practices do grave harm to those who follow them.

The Pope's ideas are not popular (in the sense at least in which the media use the word), although he apparently cares immensely for people. The ideas of some contemporary theologians are popular, or at least they are widely publicised; and they no doubt feel that they too care for people.

The point of these remarks is this: popularity confers authority in the sense that it confers an ability to sway or influence others. But how should we analyse the *worth* of this authority? Popularity confers authority; but does it do so as truth does? In what way can popularity be regarded as a measure of or a pointer to the truth? What reference in fact does popularity have to truth, or to rightness or wrongness? What for that matter has it to do with love and charity?

If the history of Jesus Christ teaches us anything it is that the truth — about man's life and destiny — is not very popular; or at least that it has to go through many ups and downs before it becomes popular; that if it is popular to begin with, such popularity does not tend to last.

The truth preached by Jesus by no means got a good hearing from everyone. The simple and the sincere people — basically those who realised they were sinners — were drawn to him and his message. The powers that were — the opinion-makers of the time: the Pharisees, the Scribes, the politicians, the zealots — with very few exceptions, were not. And of course it was those same powers who in the end manoeuvred and produced a "popular" rejection of Jesus and a demand for his crucifixion.

No; the truth is not always popular and popularity is no necessary measure of truth. Nevertheless the truth holds a powerful attraction for men's minds and hearts. The truth of Christ, preached by his first followers in all its demanding impact, gradually spread and won men; and this despite calumny, organised opposition, and even bloody persecution. But it took time; and though it gradually won many, it only won those who freely opened their minds to its power.

If the truth of Christ could be preached openly today in Soviet Russia or Communist China, it would undoubtedly draw an immense response. That of course is why it is forbidden. And yet, if it were freely preached there, some no doubt would still refuse to accept it, not necessarily because it did not sound true to them but because it sounded difficult; it demands too much. That was so in Christ's time; and it remains so today. Truth is not always popular; but that does not prove that it is not true. Have the Ten Commandments ever been popular?

Indeed the very fact that the truth is so likely to prove unpopular underlines the need for some divinely instituted organ competent to teach the truth — popular or unpopular, welcome or unwelcome — in God's name and with his backing.

Popularity is a statement of fact, not a criterion of value. It speaks of how people respond to someone or his views. It gives no clue as to the real worth of the person or the truth of those views. Popularity is a surface phenomenon; it does not go to the heart of things. It appeals to something in men, but that something is much more likely to be feelings or preferences rather than mind or conscience.

Popularity speaks of an emotional attraction based on factors such as personality, appearance, coincidence of interests, and such like, rather than of inner values, or any deeper awareness of right and wrong.

The authority conferred by popularity is clearly of a much lower order than the authority that derives from natural truth, or that which derives from supernatural mission.

Index

authority 13, 19, 30, 62ff, 82, 109-120, 136-148, 149-166, 190, 211; exercise of 22, 209, 228-230; response to 63, 106, 119, 225; abuse of 140, 191, 209, 225-233
bishops 93-94, 154, 163, 204, 208-209, 230
Body of Christ 10, 97, 147, 160, 177, 189, 204, 208, 209
certainty 76, 139-141, 151, 164, 170, 179, 185, 195
charisms 90, 94, 158-160, 208, 209
Church, the *passim*; as an institution 29, 39, 96-108, 190, 195, 210; love for 95, 198, 206, 209, 210-211; as sacrament 98ff, 200; particular churches 197, 203-204, 207-209
Code of Canon Law 34-38, 228
common good 16ff, 117, 119, 225, 228
communio 9ff, 32, 61, 104, 183ff, 197, 202, 204, 206, 209
community 22, 32, 38, 116-119, 197, 214
compassion 73, 119
conscience 51-66, 92, 116-118, 217; "follow your conscience" 71ff
contraception 60, 64, 71, 73, 171ff, 180, 192, 231
creativity 93-94
Cross, the 82ff, 108, 147, 202, 210, 228
democracy 13, 20, 29ff, 118, 161-162, 190, 212
diakonia 25, 113, 134, 208; see also under "Service"
dissent 59-77, 167, 172, 181, 189, 195
diversity 94, 142, 176, 192, 197-211
doctrine: definition of 167ff, 187; development of 155ff, 179
ecclesiology 9-12, 39, 107, 112, 121, 130, 156, 170, 173, 182, 191, 194-196, 207, 210
ecumenism 134, 189ff, 209
evangelization 85, 109, 121-123, 132, 134, 136-148, 187, 205-206

faith 50, 63-64, 82, 100-101, 104-105, 129, 151, 157, 162, 175, 184, 190, 195
freedom 11, 31, 40-50, 61, 78, 92, 96, 127, 177, 182, 184, 196, 218-220, 228, 230-231
guidance 68ff, 115, 126
hierarchy 29, 100ff, 109ff, 124, 127, 130-131, 208, 227ff, 230
Holy Spirit 87-95, 98, 103, 106-107, 153, 155, 159-160, 166, 174, 200-201, 208, 230
humility 44, 57, 66, 75, 115, 156, 157-158, 174, 181-182, 185, 187, 196
identity 202; of a Catholic 61ff, 192-193, 211
inculturation 197, 200, 201, 204-206
individualism 13-39, 66, 117, 183-184, 203, 214
infallibility 56, 107, 162-163, 172, 178-180, 192, 195
laity 109-148
lay ministries 110, 122, 131-132
law 9-108 *passim* 212-224
lawlessness 9-22
liberation theology 11, 111, 143
liturgy 26, 94, 104, 132
love 50, 188, 189; for God 45, 50, 84, 207; for others 142, 191, 231; for the Church 104, 210-211
Magisterium 57, 66, 88, 93, 105, 107, 152-153, 156ff, 167-168, 178, 187, 189-190, 229
Mind of Christ, the 66, 151-152, 154, 156, 160, 170, 172-173, 176-177, 180, 181ff, 194, 196, 205, 229
morality 11, 55-56, 92, 144, 147, 151, 162, 171, 180, 213
natural law 15, 21, 78-79, 85, 215-224
obedience 48, 54, 83-84, 91-92, 228, 230; and maturity 19-22, 49
obligations 14ff, 25ff, 67, 220
people of God 9-39, 88, 200, 204, 230

Pope, the 88, 91, 108, 114, 116, 154, 209-210, 230
positivism 19, 212-214
power 19, 94, 109-120, 187, 207, 212, 225, 230
priests 25ff, 34-35, 67ff
Reformation, the 88, 94, 203
renewal 9, 12, 24, 35ff, 121
Revelation 93, 169, 174ff, 179, 181
rights 11, 12, 14ff, 25ff, 60ff, 67, 119, 217-218, 229; defence of 33-35, 228
roles in the Church 109, 121-135
sanctity 81-82, 88, 104, 126, 132, 134, 200-201, 205, 210
Scripture 57, 93, 154, 164ff
service 109-120, 160, 168, 211, 231; by the clergy 25, 88
signs of the times 137-139, 146
society 13-22
subjectivism 11, 214
theologians 28, 89-90, 117, 154ff, 172, 177, 181, 184-186, 195, 229-231
theological pluralism 175ff, 183, 192, 201, 206
theology 156ff, 181ff, 186, 188
tradition 57, 93, 154, 164, 166, 174
truth 57, 62, 75, 81, 232; and authority 149-166; and definition of doctrine 167-180; and communion 181-196
unity 94, 142, 147, 175, 192, 197-211
world 122ff, 136ff